P9-DCQ-255

Perennials

The TIME LIFE Complete Gardener

Perennials

By the Editors of Time-Life Books
ALEXANDRIA, VIRGINIA

The Consultants

Steven Still is professor of landscape horticulture at Ohio State University, where he teaches courses in woody and herbaceous plant materials. His book *Herbaceous Ornamental Plants* (1993, 4th edition) is used as a standard teaching text at approximately 100 universities and junior colleges. A contributing editor of *Taylor's Guide to Perennials* (1986) and *Taylor's Guide to Shrubs* (1987), Still has also published articles in numerous professional journals. He serves as executive secretary of the Perennial Plant Association and is a member of the American Society for Horticultural Science, the Professional Plant Growers Association, and the Garden Writers' Association of America.

André Viette is a horticulturist, author, and lecturer, and owner of the André Viette Farm Nursery in Fishersville, Virginia, where he grows more than 3,000 varieties of herbaceous perennials. He is an instructor in horticulture at Blue Ridge Community College and hosts a gardening program for WSVA radio in Harrisonburg, Virginia. A graduate of the State University of New York, Farmingdale, and Cornell University's School of Floriculture, Viette serves on the boards of directors of the American Horticultural Society and the Lewis Ginter Botanical Garden in Richmond, Virginia. He is also a board member and past president of the Perennial Plant Association.

Library of Congress Cataloging in Publication Data
Perennials / by the editors of Time-Life Books.
p. cm.—(The Time-Life complete gardener)
Includes bibliographical references (p.) and index.
ISBN 0-7835-4100-7
1. Perennials. 2. Perennials—Pictorial works. I. Time-Life Books. II. Series
SB434.P47515 1995 635.9'32—dc20 94-30269 CIP

Second printing. Printed in U.S.A.
Published simultaneously in Canada.
School and library distribution by Time-Life Education, P.O. Box 85026, Richmond, Virginia 23285-5026.

This volume is one of a series of comprehensive gardening books that cover garden design, choosing plants for the garden, planting and propagating, and planting diagrams.

Cover: *Yellow Corydalis lutea, pink Chrysanthemum coccineum, and deep pink Dianthus deltoides cheerfully combine in an Oregon border.* ***End papers:*** *A California garden's limited color scheme emphasizes the spiky forms of violet-blue Salvia x superba 'May Night', blue oat grass, and lavender Nepeta x faassenii.* ***Title page:*** *Achillea 'Coronation Gold' and Delphinium make a bold pairing in a South Carolina garden.*

CONTENTS

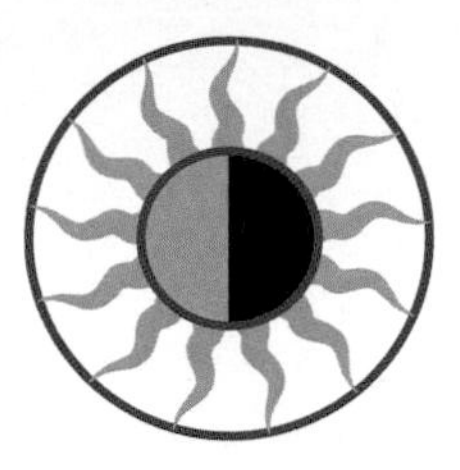

Chapter One

PLANNING YOUR GARDEN 7

Choosing the Site 8

The Many Garden Styles 12

Choosing the Right Plants 18

Selecting Plants for a Long Season of Bloom 25

Chapter Two

ESTABLISHING THE GARDEN 35

Readying the Ground 36

Choosing Your Perennials 44

Putting Plants into the Ground 45

Gallery

A GARDEN SAMPLER 51

A Guide to the Gardens 62

Chapter Three

MAINTAINING YOUR GARDEN 67

Routine Care for Perennials 68

Staking Perennials to Add Support 72

Enhancing the Bloom 75

Chapter Four

PROPAGATING PERENNIALS 79

Plant Multiplication the Fast and Easy Way 80

Propagation through Stem Cuttings 86

Propagation through Root Cuttings 88

Growing Perennials from Seed 90

Reference

Answers to Common Questions 92

Troubleshooting Guide 96

Plant Selection Guide 104

Zone Map/Guide to Plant Names 110

Encyclopedia of Perennials 112

Acknowledgments 162

Picture Credits 162

Bibliography 163

Index 164

CHAPTER ONE

Planning Your Perennial Garden

Perennials have become the favorite flowers of American gardeners. Valued for their beauty, variety, and robustness, these herbaceous plants live at least 3 years and usually much longer, and in an age when leisure time seems ever scarcer, home gardeners are increasingly turning to perennials to create gardens that provide lovely views year round and require little maintenance.

Like all gardens, the successful perennial garden is the product of a well-conceived plan that takes into account climate, site, the gardener's personal tastes, and basic design principles. Such planning is evident in the Santa Monica, California, garden at left, where spikes of foxglove and delphinium look down on no fewer than 10 other types of perennials. The splendid island bed is supplemented with bulbs and annuals to produce 10 months of bloom each year.

Many perennial-garden design possibilities, along with guidance in how to develop and implement a garden plan, are detailed on the following pages. With an understanding of the principles and a little imagination, you can create a unique garden plan of your own.

A. *Buddleia davidii (3)* **B.** *Lavandula dentata var. candicans (15)* **C.** *Borago officinalis (2)* **D.** *Digitalis purpurea (15)* **E.** *Delphinium elatum 'Pacific Giants' (15)* **F.** *Pelargonium crispum (2)* **G.** *Verbena rigida (1)* **H.** *Campanula rapunculoides (1)* **I.** *Iris 'Beverly Sills' (1)* **J.** *Nepeta x faassenii (2)* **K.** *Rosa 'Reine de Violettes' (1)* **L.** *Salvia officinalis 'Icterina' (1)* **M.** *Rosa 'Graham Thomas' (1)* **N.** *Solanum sp. (1)*

Note: The key lists each plant type and the total quantity needed to replicate the garden shown. The diagram's letters and numbers refer to the type of plant and the number sited in an area.

Choosing the Site for Your Garden

Whether they are placed in a winding bed or a formal border, located by themselves or with other plant types, perennials play an integral part in today's dynamic, easy-care gardens and should be seen as just one component of a larger scheme for your property. Devising a master plan for this larger scheme begins with an assessment of the site.

The climate in your region of the country will be the fundamental shaper of your garden. This includes but is not limited to the average low winter temperature, as designated on the United States Department of Agriculture Plant Hardiness Zone Map *(page 110)*. But even given general climatic elements such as winter cold, summer heat, rainfall, and elevation, growing conditions can vary greatly from site to site right on your property. Two key factors in the selection and success of plants are the amount and intensity of sunlight or shade your garden will receive.

Determining Areas of Sun and Shade

Strictly speaking, an area receiving full sun lies in direct sunlight literally all day—a condition unlikely to be encountered on a property containing a house, fences, trees, shrubs, and other fixtures of urban and suburban living. For the perennial gardener, an area that receives at least 6 hours of direct sunlight daily during the growing season—including 4 hours in the afternoon—is considered full sun and should be planted with varieties that specify that condition.

Full shade, in the same manner, refers to a spot that receives no direct sun from dawn to dusk. But from the standpoint of cultivating perennials, an area exposed to direct sun for fewer than 4 hours a day is considered to be in full shade, and the range of perennials suitable for growing there will be limited, though no less beautiful—evoking, perhaps, the feel of a woodland garden.

At many sites, the light conditions will fall between full sun and full shade, with structures, trees, and shrubs filtering or blocking the sun's rays at some points during the day and not at others. The amount and intensity of the light that strikes your garden will also change with the seasons, especially with the emergence of leaves on deciduous trees and shrubs in the spring, and their loss in the fall.

The majority of perennials flower from midspring to midsummer, so it is best to assess sun and shade conditions during that period, and then make adjustments for specific plant varieties and for conditions that occur earlier and later in the growing season. For example, a piece of ground cast into all-day shade after August would not be the best location for fall-blooming plants that need full sun, such as chrysanthemums or asters.

But don't rule out a plant you love because your light conditions are marginal for its requirements. Only by experimenting will you learn, for example, which full-sun perennials do well in afternoon shade and which will grow leggy and flower less.

Getting to Know the Property

Many expert gardeners who are new to a property like to wait a full year before implementing a garden plan. If you take this approach, the wait will not only allow you to assess climate and light conditions but will also give you time to learn such critical information as the nature of your soil, the location of wet spots in winter, and the condition of existing plants, shrubs, and trees. You can also use this fallow period for making large quantities of compost to use later in amending your soil *(page 38)* and, most important, for ruminating on your proposed garden as design decisions begin to gel.

Sometimes a property has soil that is naturally rich in plant nutrients and possessed of that slightly moist, crumbly structure described as friable. You may, however, encounter heavy clay soil, which may be flooded for days after a steady rain and be rock hard and dry in drought; or sandy soil, which will not hold moisture or nutrients. Some soils will be too acid, others too alkaline.

Many perennials can grow in soil conditions normally deemed poor and a few even thrive, but almost all plants will benefit if the soil is amended with organic matter. As or-

PROJECTING BEAUTY ON ALL SIDES
From the white Helianthemum 'The Bride', growing to a modest height directly in front of the window, to the purple geraniums and brilliant vermilion double blooms of the Papaver orientale 'Fireball' farther back, this perennial bed achieves the gardener's goal of making the view as enjoyable from within the house as from the yard.

ganic additives break down into humus, plant roots find the room and oxygen they need to grow deep and strong, and the soil retains moisture while still permitting drainage. If conditions prove intractable, however, you can build raised beds *(page 42)* and fill them with soil created to your own specifications.

During your property review also examine the health, size, and ornamental qualities of mature trees and shrubs. While a handsome specimen of Japanese maple might be the perfect anchor for a new perennial bed, you may well find it best to remove an overgrown and sickly weeping willow to open up an area for a new border. Use the site analysis to figure out ways to correct other problems as well. You might want to plant a screen for privacy or as a windbreak, for example, or build a new patio away from trash-storage areas, or rework walkways for enjoyable strolls through the garden.

Selecting Vantage Points

Consider how the garden will look from a deck or a patio—places where most of your time enjoying the garden will be spent. Then go inside. Views from strategic points within the house can greatly affect a decision to locate a perennial bed in one place or another, or to include particularly showy perennials such as giant onion or bear's-breech. From a kitchen window, a garden of perennials can

VIEWS FROM INSIDE AND OUTSIDE THE GARDEN
A bench set amid colorful spring-blooming tulips, pansies, wild blue phlox, iris, azalea, and delphinium provides a quiet spot from which to enjoy this Atlanta shade garden. Slightly elevated, with its perimeter edged by curving brick steps, the garden can also be enjoyed from a terrace at the back of the house.

offer a picture of the changing seasons: columbine and candytuft in the spring, daylilies and Russian sage in the summer, Japanese anemone and asters in the fall, ornamental grasses and sedum in the winter.

Creating a Base Plan

Once you've thoroughly analyzed your site, it's time to put your observations on paper and create a base plan—a map of your grounds. The first step is to take a walk around the property and make a rough sketch that includes all structures and features. Then draw a more precise version of the plan to scale *(opposite)*. The base plan will let you see both the desirable features of your site and those that need improvement, and will help you create a garden that will play to the strengths of your property and minimize its flaws.

The sample base plan on page 31 shows a home on a site that was once rural but has since been absorbed into suburbia. The L-shaped house consists of an original log cabin with a new clapboard wing on the north side. The log cabin and stone chimneys still convey a rustic feel, as do a few old trees and shrubs. Situated on a quarter acre, the home is bordered by other similarly sized lots and faces a subdivision street. The house is set back pleasantly within the site, but the presence of neighboring homes is felt.

The fundamental design issue on the sample property is that of coping with a site that wants to look out over farmland but finds a modern subdivision instead. On a more practical level, the site analysis reveals a need to provide privacy for the patio, to enliven views from inside the house, to better anchor the house to its site, to remove an ailing tree, and to fix drainage problems on the southern side of the property.

As you study your own base plan and take stock of existing conditions, you will instinctively begin to think about important fundamental design features and where they can or, more important at this stage, cannot go. By developing a sensitivity to the character of the property, its contours, and its areas of sun and shade, you will produce a plan that works with your site's ecology and is true to the spirit of the place.

Preparing the plan will also put your imagination to work. Old ideas will be either confirmed or discarded, and successful new ones will come to you. Then you will be ready to move to the next step—considering your new garden's style.

Creating a Base Plan

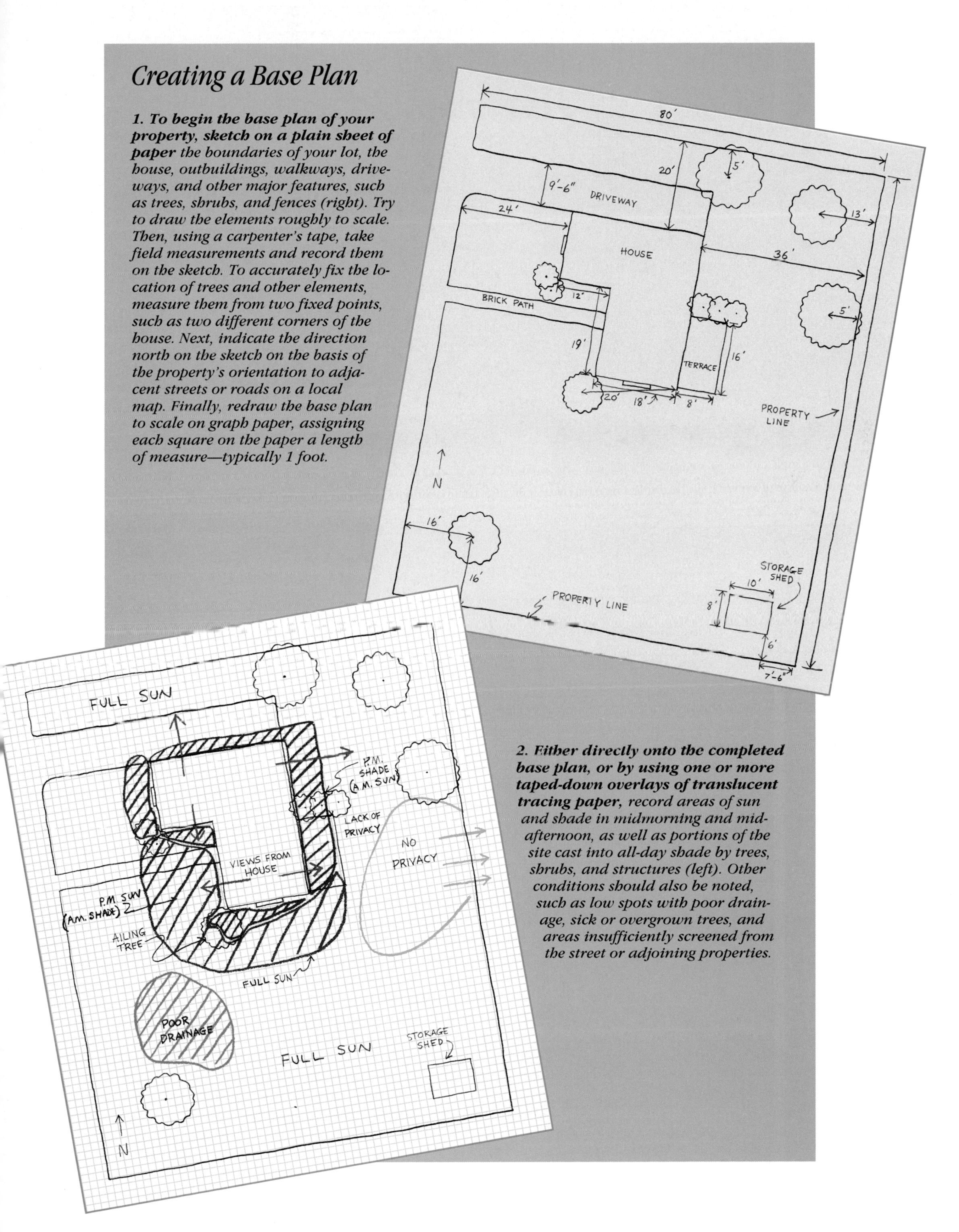

***1. To begin the base plan of your property, sketch on a plain sheet of paper** the boundaries of your lot, the house, outbuildings, walkways, driveways, and other major features, such as trees, shrubs, and fences (right). Try to draw the elements roughly to scale. Then, using a carpenter's tape, take field measurements and record them on the sketch. To accurately fix the location of trees and other elements, measure them from two fixed points, such as two different corners of the house. Next, indicate the direction north on the sketch on the basis of the property's orientation to adjacent streets or roads on a local map. Finally, redraw the base plan to scale on graph paper, assigning each square on the paper a length of measure—typically 1 foot.*

***2. Either directly onto the completed base plan, or by using one or more taped-down overlays of translucent tracing paper,** record areas of sun and shade in midmorning and midafternoon, as well as portions of the site cast into all-day shade by trees, shrubs, and structures (left). Other conditions should also be noted, such as low spots with poor drainage, sick or overgrown trees, and areas insufficiently screened from the street or adjoining properties.*

The Many Styles of Perennial Gardens

SYMMETRY—THE HALLMARK OF THE FORMAL GARDEN
This Pennsylvania garden uses an arbor to impose formality on its plantings of dark violet Salvia x superba, pale violet Nepeta, pink Dianthus deltoides, and blue oatgrass.

As you search for an appropriate style for your garden, the possibilities will be almost endless. You might wish to evoke a garden known in childhood, or one seen on a vacation abroad. Your inspiration might come from the fictional garden in a novel, or from historical precedents: perhaps the plantation gardens of the South, the wildflower meadows of Texas, the mission gardens of California, or the prairie landscapes of the Midwest. Your models might be as much horticultural as regional—a rock garden, a cutting garden, and a shade garden are examples.

Be careful not to design a garden that is beyond your ability to construct, plant, and maintain. A 200-foot double border—one that flanks both sides of a walkway or driveway—on an English country estate is wonderful to see, but takes hundreds of hours, great professional expertise, and large sums of money to install and sustain. Similarly, a serene Japanese garden you may once have admired likely began with major earth working, backbreaking stone placement, and endless pruning of trees and shrubs.

Garden Ideas to Borrow

Countless gardeners before you have wrestled with making gardens, and the fruits of their labor—and imagination—are evident in

the pages of gardening books and magazines. Additional ideas abound in public gardens, which are also useful to study because they give a true measure of how well specific plants will grow in your area.

Use these gardens for inspiration—to borrow an idea or two or mix and match a few plant combinations—but resist the urge to copy them plant for plant. Tempting as it might be to take this course, even if you were to succeed at duplicating one of these elaborate productions, you would rob your garden of its own character and yourself of the satisfaction of creating something unique.

Nor is it necessary to re-create a whole landscape to capture its essence. Some plantings of columbine and Solomon's-seal in your own shady corner might be sufficient to rekindle fond memories of a hike through a favorite upland forest. Likewise, a single mature lavender plant in a terra-cotta pot might be all that is necessary to recall a stay in a French country inn.

The Design Framework

One thing you will want to decide on from looking at other gardens is your design framework—whether you prefer your garden to be formal or informal, or a mixture of both. These are loose concepts; what is formal to you might seem quite relaxed to a neighbor. Clearly, however, some gardens are more architectural and ordered than others.

Formal Gardens

Generally, the mark of a formal garden is the straight line—in its paths, pools, borders, hedges, and even in the way a view is directed along an axis. In the most formal gardens, spaces are crafted into open-air boxes by the use of walls or hedgerows. Often, columns of marble, stone, wood, or even living trees are used to suggest walls and linearity. In classical

MIMICKING THE INFORMALITY OF NATURE
The mossy path curving through this informal shade garden evokes a woodland scene, framed by a blanket of mondo grass, a backdrop of white foamflower, and, in the foreground, purple phlox and a variegated variety of Solomon's-seal.

PLANNED CHAOS OF COLOR IN THE COTTAGE GARDEN
The daisies, delphiniums, poppies, and snapdragons of this garden are grouped tightly in a color plan of blues, pinks, and whites, with yellow added as an accent—answering to the mandate of the cottage garden for color and lots of it.

Perennials for a Cutting Garden

Achillea (yarrow)
Allium (flowering onion)
Aster (aster)
Campanula (bellflower)
Chrysanthemum (chrysanthemum)
Coreopsis (tickseed)
Delphinium (delphinium)
Digitalis (foxglove)
Echinacea (purple coneflower)
Echinops (globe thistle)
Eryngium (sea holly)
Gaillardia (blanket-flower)
Gypsophila (baby's-breath)
Heliopsis (false sunflower)
Iris (iris)
Lavandula (lavender)
Liatris (gay-feather)
Paeonia (peony)
Phlox (phlox)
Rudbeckia (coneflower)
Solidago (goldenrod)
Thalictrum (meadow rue)
Veronica (speedwell)

models, the power of formal geometry is reinforced through symmetry, with one side of the garden mirroring the other.

Most such elements would overpower the typical domestic garden, of course, but it is possible to have formality on a more intimate scale. You might create a small knot garden—so called for its knotlike shape—where you arrange the beds in a geometrically balanced pattern with, perhaps, brick walks in between. The beds in a knot garden are usually edged in miniature boxwood, but some gardeners in warmer climates do the job with perennials and herbs instead, using lavender, germander, and rosemary.

You might elect an even more subdued level of formality, using a patio's straight edge as the boundary of your garden, for example, or choosing to plant perennials in borders instead of in freer-form beds. A simple curve with a fixed radius can lend a formal air to a border in a way that a winding curve will not.

Without changing the contours of a rectilinear garden plot, you can either sharpen or moderate its air of formality by your choice of plantings. If you prefer the less formal, plant the garden's straight borders with perennials of different colors and relaxed form. On the other hand, if order and regularity are to your liking, you could lay out a neat pathway through the plot with a mass planting on both sides of a graceful perennial like *Nepeta* (catmint) or a showy one like peony.

THE REFINEMENT OF THE BORDER
The same general color scheme and some of the same plants as in the cottage garden appear in this perennial border in Atlanta, but its neat edging and the layers of plants rising to a vertical element—the clipped hedge—give it a more elegant and formal aspect.

Informal Gardens

Curving lines and asymmetry are the key characteristics of the informal garden. The landscape is no less crafted than in a formal garden, but the borders, if there are borders, might take a rambling course alongside a lawn. Often, the plantings are in beds rather than borders, the walkways are curved rather than straight, and trees and shrubs are located randomly and pruned only for their health, not for shape.

Choosing a Garden Style

Within both formal and informal design frameworks, you can choose from a series of specific garden styles. Perennials will have a major role regardless of the style you select. They form such a rich and diverse family of plants that they can be molded to fit into virtually any scheme.

Cottage Gardens

One of the most popular styles is the cottage garden, whose air of rustic domesticity may better suit a suburban property than would grand classical allusions. The cottage garden's origins lie in the old-fashioned villages of England, where the occupants of small thatched- or tile-roofed cottages filled their gardens with annuals and perennials. These were species plants—not today's highly developed cultivars and hybrids, which usually cannot reproduce themselves faithfully from seed. The old plants set seed freely and perpetuated themselves, yielding a riot of color amid an undisciplined growth of vegetation requiring little care from the owner.

In the late 19th and early 20th centuries, leading gardeners in England developed a style based on the cottage garden but refined to a high level of sophistication. They took

LEAVING ROOM FOR WORK AMONG THE PLANTINGS
The rocket larkspurs, irises, and daisies in this wide flower bed remain accessible to the gardener from a maintenance path paved in woodchips.

GIVING THE BORDER A CERTAIN EDGE
The deep pink hardy geranium and the catmint at the front of this perennial border (opposite) spill forward but, thanks to an edging of paving stones, remain well clear of the lawn. The line of stones also sharpens the formality of the border with its geometric preciseness.

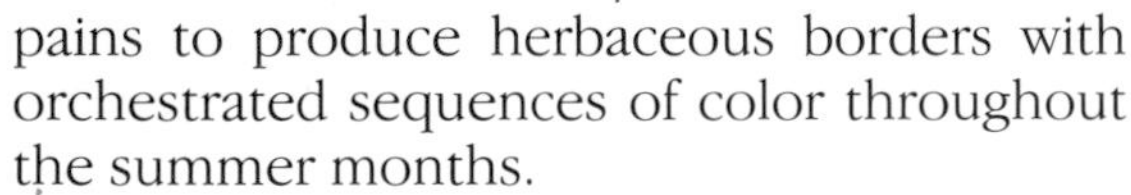

pains to produce herbaceous borders with orchestrated sequences of color throughout the summer months.

Today's American cottage garden lies somewhere between the two, in a part of the continuum where color schemes and plant selection are important but not as rigid or demanding as those of the English border. The plant palette is different, too, with a greater reliance on hardy perennials that are distinctly American, such as daylilies and rudbeckias.

Cutting Gardens

Nothing announces serious gardeners or their love of flowers more than a cutting garden, where plants are grown expressly to produce blooms for indoor arrangements. Although the cutting garden is less ingrained in the American landscape than other styles, it deserves consideration.

Again, perennials are an ideal ingredient, especially long-stemmed plants like delphinium, solidago, and iris. Most will not rebloom, as cut annuals do, but they will present an array of flowers across the season if enough different kinds are planted.

Traditionally, the cutting garden occupies its own beds; even a small area, about 10 by 10 feet, will yield hundreds of blooms in a season. But if space is at a premium, you can grow flowers for cutting in between plants in the vegetable plot or within display beds and borders.

Perennial Borders and Beds

The two commonest ways to display perennials are in a border or a bed. The border typically forms the edge of a garden space and lies next to a vertical element—a wall of the house, a fence, or a hedge, for example.

The width of the border can vary, but it is an important factor in choosing plants. In a conventional border, the rule of thumb is that no plant should be taller than one-half the width of the space. If your border is a thin strip of ground between a wall and a sidewalk, the scale of the perennials you place there must be modest—perhaps a row of pe-

tite plants such as candytuft, threadleaf coreopsis, or ajuga.

One advantage of the border garden is that its vertical element offers a handsome backdrop for the flowers. Be careful, though, of color clashes, particularly against red brick walls, where strident red or orange blooms might be jarring.

A bed doesn't have the visual anchor that is inherent in a border; it often takes the form of a free-floating island. But the bed does valuable service: It can channel views across a lawn and supply a visual framework for important features such as decks, patios, and swimming pools, a function that might otherwise call for a full-blown stand of shrubbery. Also, a bed might be the only place on your property where you can grow perennials in full sun.

There are pitfalls to watch out for, however, in deciding on island beds. Islands must be made large enough to hold their own in an overall design. Even at that they might need the added visual weight of some shrubs or small trees in order not to be overshadowed by imposing elements nearby.

Both borders and beds, if they are broad enough, will need maintenance paths—narrow, hidden trails that give you access to plants without the risk of your stepping on them or compacting their soil. In a bed, you might create a path from woodchips or river stones that, from a distance, is hidden by plant foliage. In a border, your path might run between the back of the plantings and the wall or hedge. Apart from the access it affords you, the path will also improve air circulation among the plants and prevent lingering dampness that might put them at risk of fungal infections.

Borders and beds also benefit from edging, especially if the adjacent ground is a lawn. Brick, stone, or concrete pavers laid just 1 to 2 feet wide will keep the lawn mower away from the plants and keep the plants from smothering the grass as they flop forward. Edging also acts as a unifying element for the whole plant display.

BACKDROPS ANCHOR THE PERENNIAL BORDER
A handsome fence adds strength and completeness to this border, which includes pale yellow Achillea 'Moonshine' (foreground), reddish Alstroemeria, and tall, lilac-colored Verbena bonariensis. Without such backdrops, which define the plants' shapes and highlight their colors, some borders might lose their visual impact and become harder to see.

Choosing the Right Plants

Selecting plants to fit your garden style is the most challenging and rewarding aspect of perennial gardening. The complexities of selecting perennials for their colors, shapes, and textures can appear overwhelming, but by taking a systematic approach, you can become a master.

The whole idea of composing with herbaceous plants can be a new one for many home gardeners. In the past, gardeners were able to find beauty in only a limited range of old-fashioned species of such perennials as daylilies, hostas, peonies, bearded iris, and phlox. Shrub borders were favorites, as were foundation plantings of broad-leafed evergreens and a well-trimmed lawn. Color was achieved by planting a few perennials, bulbs, flowering trees, shrubs, and, especially, annuals.

An Explosion of Perennial Choices

In recent years, gardeners have discovered in mail-order and local nurseries alike a sumptuous and sometimes bewildering array of

SAME SPECIES, DIFFERENT COLOR
A drift of Echinacea purpurea, the purple coneflower, shows up nicely against a backdrop of unfinished fenceboards (right). Lending a different character to the species is a cultivar called E. purpurea 'Alba', or white purple coneflower (above), which can be used in a color scheme where purple would clash. Echinacea purpurea is one of many venerable species that have been bred to produce new colors.

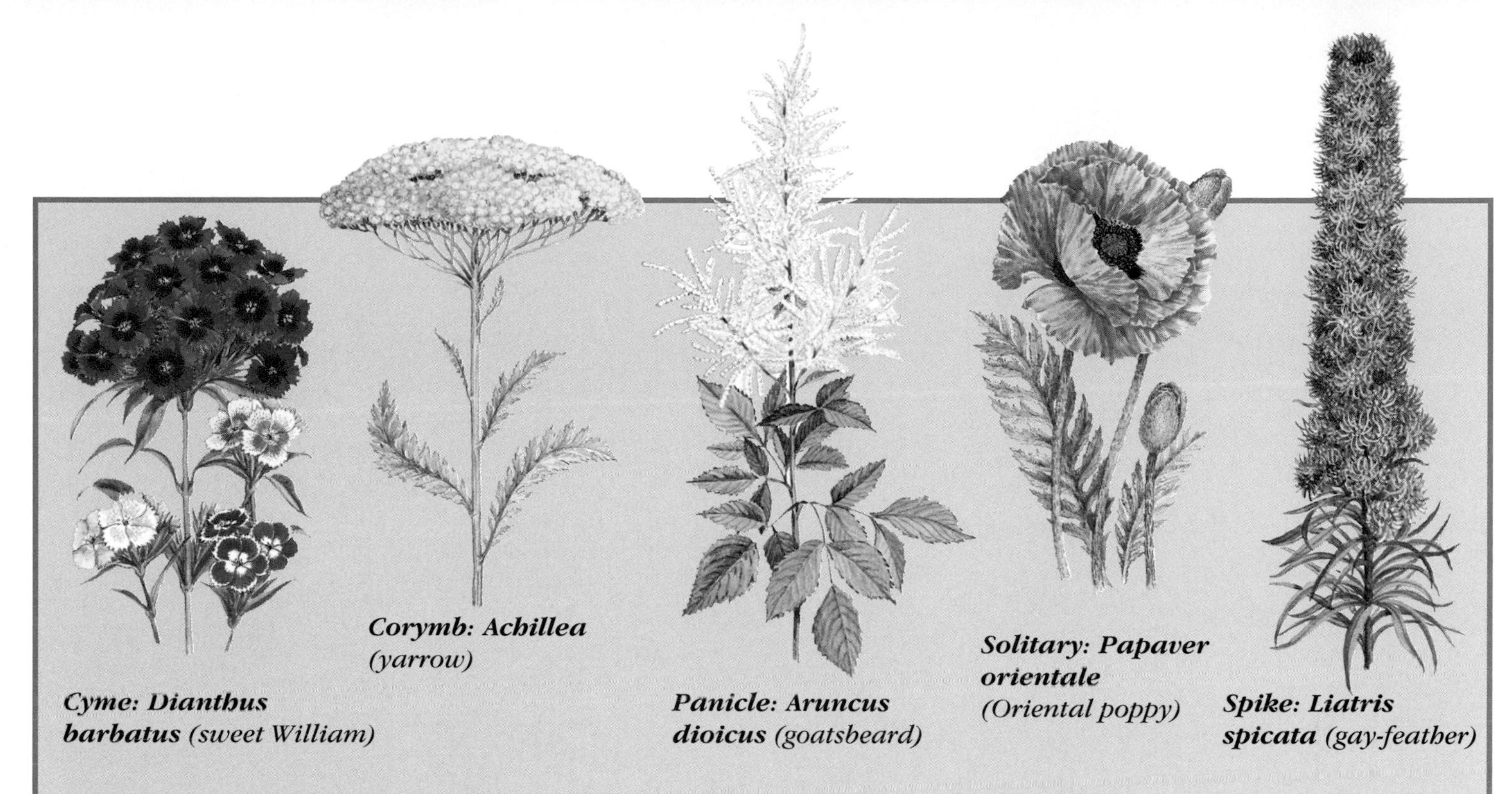

A Variety of Flower Heads

The flower heads, or inflorescences, of perennials can be grouped into several types, each lending its character to a plant and even influencing the length of its blooming season. Spikes, for example, generally have a long season, as the tiny individual flowers open in sequence. Other factors also influence the duration of flowering, such as the speed of pollination—slow pollination lengthens flower life—the number of blossoms produced, and the durability of the petals. Besides the inflorescences shown above, perennial flowers also take the form of racemes, such as *Aconitum napellus (page 113);* umbels, *Asclepias tuberosa (page 119);* and heads, *Gaillardia* x *grandiflora (page 133).*

perennials. At the same time, a distinct type of perennial garden plant, the ornamental grass, has been elevated from horticultural obscurity and now stands center stage in the perennial renaissance, particularly with the development of many fine cultivars.

The sustained popularity of all perennials has changed the face of the American garden. In an age when people want beauty and color in their garden but have little time to nurture it, well-chosen perennials provide ready solutions. Diverse and versatile, perennials can be used in any setting but are particularly well suited to looser, more natural landscape styles. They are also tougher in their ability to shrug off climatic extremes and pests and diseases.

If you do not have a ready source of free perennials from gardening friends or relatives eager to divide mature plants, or if you can't take advantage of low-cost perennials from garden-club plant sales, your initial investment in perennials can be high. But with your expenditure comes the chance to create landscapes full of color and vitality using plants that require relatively little care. You'll also save the money you would spend on replacing annuals year after year, and in time you'll have mature plants from which to propagate new ones.

Choosing Perennials for Color

The most important task perennials perform is enlivening the setting with color. It is this major ornamentation that makes the well-crafted perennial bed or border the heart of any garden plan.

If you consciously choose a color scheme for a part or all of your perennial garden, it is best to start not with a specific plant but with a specific color or colors. Once you decide on a garden of, say, soft yellows, white, and blue, you can select plants that will fall into those color bands and bloom throughout the growing season *(pages 104-109).* Interplanting fo-

Mixing and Matching Colors

***In the planting at left**, the gardener has used the neutral gray foliage of Stachys byzantina to link the harmonious colors of Veronica 'True Blue' and the pink-flowered cranesbill Geranium x oxonianum 'Claridge Druce'.*

***Red, yellow, and blue are the primary colors on the color wheel.** When equal amounts of two primary colors are mixed, secondary colors—orange, green, and violet—result. A primary color mixed with an adjacent secondary hue creates a third level of colors. Colors said to be harmonious share a portion of color; contrasting colors do not.*

liage perennials that echo or buffer the selected hues will help tie the entire arrangement together.

One color is virtually unavoidable in the garden—green. But green comes in many different shades and tints. (Shades are colors darkened by black, such as deep purple from violet; tints are colors that have been lightened by white, such as pink from red.) The careful selection of the right quality of green will enhance your color scheme. For example, the mauve-pink *Dianthus plumarius* 'Agatha' blends well with its own blue-green foliage but would jar disagreeably when paired with the yellow-green fringes of *Hosta fortunei* 'Aureo-marginata'. Successful pairing of colors is made simpler if you understand the basics of the color wheel.

Demystifying the Color Wheel

Different versions of the color wheel have been devised over the years, some reflecting the great scientific lengths to which color theory has been taken. However, most gardeners rely on the simple, standard version that starts with the three primary colors—yellow, red, and blue.

An equal mix of two primary colors produces one of the three secondary colors; hence orange is a mix of yellow and red and lies between them on the wheel, violet appears between red and blue, and green be-

Coming from opposite sides of the color wheel, *the rich blue of Nepeta mussinii and the pale yellow, umbrella-shaped blossoms of Achillea 'Moonshine' demonstrate the striking combinations that are possible with the use of contrasting colors (right).*

The robust blooms of the popular daylily *Hemerocallis 'Bejeweled' team with the dainty pink flowers of Achillea 'Rose Beauty' to produce a striking monochromatic effect (below).*

tween blue and yellow. Mixing primary colors with their adjacent secondary colors yields the further gradations yellow-orange, red-orange, red-violet, blue-violet, blue-green, and yellow-green.

Conventional wisdom holds that the best color combinations are either contrasting, meaning that they stand at opposite points on the color wheel, or harmonious, found next to each other on the wheel and sharing a common pigment. A contrasting color combination might be blue and orange, violet and yellow, or red and green. Harmonious pairs include green and yellow-green, red-orange and orange, or blue-violet and blue.

Tints and shades, as well as blends of different colors—mauve, for example, which combines red and violet—add more variables, as do such elements as the amount and strength of the light the plants receive (pastels show up better in low light, bright colors look better in full sun), the reflective qualities of the flower's petals, and the tendency for light colors to advance in the viewer's eye and dark colors to recede.

Clearly, with all these considerations to be taken into account, it is easy to become bogged down in the complexities of color. The best course is to use the color wheel to follow the basic rules of contrasting and harmonious color groupings but to let your garden plants, your eye, and your taste have the final say. If you occasionally go awry, you will

VISUAL INTERPLAY OF DIFFERING TEXTURES
The robust, coarse-veined leaves of Hosta sieboldiana look even larger next to the finer-textured foliage of Saxifraga stolonifera. Texture can provide visual interest for a garden even after the flowers have gone.

have joined ranks with even the most experienced gardeners. And remember, it is easy to move perennials from one spot to another if you have to.

Cool and Hot Colors

Besides planting for harmony or contrast, it is generally considered best to group cool colors such as violets, pinks, blues, and off-whites together. These combinations work particularly well in areas that receive filtered light or partial shade, where there will be no glaring sun to wash out the lighter hues.

Within this family of cool colors you can use yellows or reds to create accents, but for a better blending consider a red leaning toward violet rather than toward orange, and yellows that are lemon and pastel, not the pure and brilliant yellow of some achilleas or euphorbias, for example.

A garden of hot colors—reds, oranges, and pure yellows—works well in beds that receive full sun. Here, you can have fun with fiery-colored varieties of such plants as geums, poppies, daylilies, kniphofias, and gaillardias.

Foliage is an important component of color in the perennial garden. It might not present itself as vividly as flowers, but it lasts much longer. A color scheme of reds, purples, and grays, for example, might be constructed of the gray foliage of artemisia and one of the purple-leafed varieties of heuchera with coral red flowers. For a color scheme of violet, yellow-green, and gray, you might plant lamb's ears between lady's-mantle, lavender, and euphorbia. Note that gray is of immense value in the perennial garden: It calms the colors around it and, as a neutral, ties them together.

Planning for Texture and Mass

Plant foliage not only contributes color, it also gives the garden texture and mass. Many perennials are grown principally for their foliage, among them hostas, artemisia, lamb's ears, epimedium, santolina, and lamium. Many others—ajuga, lady's-mantle, and Solomon's-seal, for example—produce foliage at least as valuable as their flowers. Even such prominent flowering plants as Japanese and Siberian iris, ligularia, acanthus, and blackberry lily accompany their blooms with handsome leaf ornament.

The fineness or coarseness of the leaves gives a plant its texture. Just as light colors advance to the eye and dark hues recede, a coarse-textured plant leaps forward and a fine-textured one retreats. With judicious placement of fine-textured plants, for example, you can create an illusion of depth in a small garden.

More to the point, you can add interest to your garden through the thoughtful juxtaposition of plants of different textures. For instance, a coarse-leafed plant like ligularia would have greater impact against the fine foliage of veronica than next to an equally big-leafed plant like hosta.

If a plant's character comes from its leaf and flower texture, then its overall shape, or mass, dictates its stature. A mature miscanthus grass, for example, though fine in texture, may grow 6 feet high and 4 feet across—the size of a large shrub. Wild ginger, on the other hand, though coarse of foliage, grows as a ground cover only a few inches high.

Just as you should think about associations of different colors and textures in planning your garden, you should also consider mass. For example, a flowering mound of phlox will look more imposing when given space to show off than when it is surrounded by other perennials of similar bulk.

Putting It All Together

With all these components in mind, it is time to put your planting ideas down on paper. Assemble those ideas first according to the colors, textures, and shapes you have decided on and then select the plants to produce them. For a long border or bed, it is best to work in short sections, mindful that the most pleasing designs have some unifying element, such as a repeated pattern of color, color progression, or a recurring plant.

The perennial garden should present itself in layers—tall plants at the back, medium ones in the middle, and smaller ones up front. There are exceptions, of course: You might plant a tall perennial like macleaya at the front of a border to serve as an accent at a strategic spot. In island beds viewed from more than one side you might wish the layer-

THE SUBTLE ATTRIBUTES OF PLANT MASS
The gentle undulation of this California perennial border is achieved by combining plants of similar mass. A fan of Iris 'Victoria Falls' and the compact mounds of deep purple Spanish lavender, spiky English lavender, and fleabane, a member of the daisy genus Erigeron, echo the shapes of the background shrubs and provide a transition to the creeping thyme in the foreground.

Perennials That Attract Butterflies

Asclepias tuberosa (butterfly weed)
Butterflies: swallowtail, sulfur, gray hairstreak, spring azure, great spangled fritillary, question mark, monarch
***Aster* spp.**
Butterflies: sulfur, painted lady, American painted lady, red admiral, buckeye, viceroy, Milbert's tortoiseshell
***Centaurea* spp.** (knapweed)
Butterflies: American painted lady, common checkered skipper
***Coreopsis* spp.** (tickseed)
Butterflies: sulfur, buckeye, monarch
Echinacea purpurea (purple coneflower)
Butterfly: great spangled fritillary
***Malva* spp.** (mallow)
Butterflies: painted lady, American painted lady, red admiral, monarch
Rudbeckia hirta (black-eyed Susan)
Butterfly: great spangled fritillary
Sedum spectabile (stonecrop)
Butterflies: comma, Milbert's tortoiseshell, monarch, mourning cloak, painted lady, red admiral

Note: *The abbreviation "spp." stands for the plural of "species"; where used in lists it means that many, but not all, of the species in a genus meet the criterion of the list.*

Perennials That Attract Hummingbirds

***Aquilegia* spp.**
(columbine)
Heuchera sanguinea
(coral bells)
Lobelia cardinalis
(cardinal flower)
Lupinus 'Russell Hybrids'
(lupine)
Monarda didyma
(bee balm)

Monarch butterfly (left, top) and mourning cloak (below) on Sedum spectabile

ing to move from the center outward in all directions. And in a garden to be viewed from within the house as well as outside, you would not want tall plants blocking visual access to the rest of the flowers.

Plant in odd numbers—threes, fives, sevens—so that identical plants are not rigidly grouped and can flow easily into and among the others. You can give structure to a bed through the regular and rhythmic placement of bulkier perennials or drifts of plants, and then fill in gaps with buffers like gray-leafed neutrals or other foliage plants. By limiting the plant variety and planting individuals en masse, you will achieve a garden with less variety in color but with a simple, strong, and effective design.

Finally, as you combine plants consider scale. A bear's-breech, with its tall flower spikes and coarse leaves, would be a minor accent in a long border; next to a patio, however, it would dominate. Within the small volume of the city or suburban garden, or in small subgardens of larger properties, restraint will be rewarded.

Remember, too, that few people have the ability to produce world-class perennial gardens all at once. Mistakes are the best teachers, and with them comes an accumulation of knowledge that will, in time, produce deeply satisfying gardens.

Fragrant Perennials

Artemisia absinthium
(common wormwood)
Clematis heracleifolia 'Davidiana'
(tube clematis)
Clematis recta 'Mandshurica'
(ground clematis)
Dianthus barbatus
(sweet William)
Dianthus gratianopolitanus
(cheddar pink)
Dianthus plumarius
(cottage pink)
Dictamnus albus
(gas plant)
Geranium endressii 'Wargrave Pink'
(cranesbill)
Hemerocallis citrina and specific hybrids, including H. 'Becky Lynn', 'Betty Woods', and 'Janet Gayle'
(daylilies)
Hemerocallis flava
(lemon daylily)
Hosta plantaginea
(fragrant plantain lily)
Iris graminea 'Plum Tart'
(plum-scented iris)
Lavandula angustifolia
(English lavender)
Lupinus arboreus
(tree lupine)
Monarda didyma
(bee balm)
Nepeta cataria
(catmint)
Oenothera biennis
(evening primrose)
Oenothera caespitosa
(tufted evening primrose)
Oenothera odorata
(twisted evening primrose)
Paeonia lactiflora
(Chinese peony)
Polygonatum odoratum
(fragrant Solomon's-seal)
Polygonum polystachyum
(spiked knotweed)
Primula veris
(cowslip)
Saponaria officinalis
(bouncing Bet)
Viola odorata
(sweet violet)

Selecting Perennials for a Long Season of Bloom

Traditionally, the perennial border in an English cottage garden was viewed as the centerpiece of a fine, but relatively short-lived, display of flowers. Because English summers are warm but not hot, the border would unfurl gaily with eye-catching blocks of color emerging at one spot while other flowers were fading elsewhere. By late August, the show was over.

As American gardeners have turned to perennials in recent years, they have noticed a quite different quality to their gardens. First, the perennial garden is not just a summer garden but a place where interest can be found year round if you look for it. Second, the growth cycles of plants, individually and collectively, are so dramatic in a garden planted heavily with perennials that the landscape takes on a whole new character from month to month. No longer a static canvas of woody evergreens, the garden has become a vibrant and dynamic landscape.

There have always been peak moments in a perennial garden, of course, such as when bearded irises bloom alongside foxgloves, columbines, campanula, and dianthus. But by broadening the plant palette and observing some of nature's subtler modes of decora-

IN THE SPRING
Drifts of tulips illuminate the bare spaces of this small garden before perennials and grasses begin to stir. Blue Brunnera macrophylla at the base of the sweet bay magnolia tree will reseed after flowering. Behind the magnolia, the purple flowers of Camassia, a bulb, tower over Christmas fern.

tion, American gardeners have discovered a type of ornamental gardening that is both rich and long-lasting.

These qualities can be seen in the three photographs taken of the same garden during different seasons that appear on pages 25-27. In spring, there is an openness to the narrow townhouse backyard that will not return until winter, and then only in a completely different form. Spring bulbs carry the garden through this embryonic stage, with trees and fences providing a framework, and decorative pots and garden sculpture serving as focal points. Even when the garden is in this relatively bare state, there is a sense of the lushness and visual layering to come.

In summer, the promise of the spring is fulfilled, and the garden is transformed into an entirely different landscape: Grasses, ground covers, and foliage intermingle in a crafted jungle. Shades of green abound, changing as the sun backlights some areas and falls directly on others.

After the first frost, in late fall and early winter, some of the spatial qualities of the spring return, but the grasses and perennials remain a firm presence and take on colors associated with the season—harmonious blends of gold, tan, and ivory. The garden's heavy reliance on large grasses might not be to everyone's taste, but the arrangement illustrates the role of such gardens as well as their possibilities.

Orchestrating Seasonal Moods

Visually, the perennial garden has gloriously climactic periods and quietly reflective periods. The secret of creating a continuously satisfying garden is to discover plants that take up some of the lull between peaks of color

IN THE SUMMER
Shades of green dominate the garden in summer. The plantings produce a lush medley of texture, with delicate annuals providing color beside the steps, and the spikes of Acanthus hungaricus lending an accent in the middle ground, backed by the grasses Calamagrostis acutiflora 'Stricta' in the center and Miscanthus floridulus at right.

and that extend the blooming period both early and late, particularly toward its end.

Much of the country experiences winter frosts that kill off the top growth of herbaceous perennials for the season. Even after the freeze, though, the dead and dried forms of many perennial leaves, flower heads, and seeds have ornamental appeal, especially when dusted with frost or light snow or wearing a sparkling glaze of ice. Sedums, echinops, rudbeckia, and achillea are known for their winter appeal; for a more complete listing of perennials that will enhance the garden in winter, see page 28.

By treating these plants and others as you would ornamental grasses and not cutting them back until midwinter or later, you can prolong their value. Of course, these freeze-dried plants may be too untidy for some tastes, and some gardeners may feel that the garden—and its owner—deserve a winter vacation. But only by experimenting and experiencing the impact of these plants in winter will you know for sure if the look is right for you and your garden.

If you happen to live in the milder climates of the Deep South, the Southwest, or southern California, you can have garden color and growth year round. Perennials do well in these parts, although without periods of winter dormancy they tend to be shorter lived than they would be farther north.

Cold-Blooming Hellebores

For those who like to have some active plants while the rest of the garden slumbers, the hellebores occupy a class of their own.

Four species are grown widely in America, including two with particularly beautiful foliage—the vein-leafed Corsican hellebore,

AT SEASON'S END
After the first hard frost of late fall, the winter garden belongs to the ornamental grasses. Gone are summer's exuberant greens, replaced by the bronze, copper, and tan of the winter landscape. The smaller grasses struggle to maintain form and eventually are cut down. The giant Miscanthus floridulus, which cascaded like a fountain in summer, is stiffened upright by the autumnal frosts.

Helleborus argutifolius var. *corsicus,* with clusters of nodding, apple green flowers, and what is known as the stinking hellebore, *Helleborus foetidus.* In spite of its unappetizing name, the latter is a lovely plant bearing pale green flowers and handsome leaflets shaped like slender arrowheads. A third species, the Christmas rose, *Helleborus niger,* blooms the earliest, as its name suggests, with showy flowers that open white and grow pink with age.

The best-loved hellebore is the Lenten rose, *Helleborus orientalis.* It is the least fussy and most reliable of the group and within a few seasons after planting forms large colonies. The blooms emerge in late winter or early spring and last for weeks. Flower color varies with hybrid and age, and includes pale green, white, maroon, and pink.

The late-winter garden has a number of other perennial players, most of them—including Italian arum, lamb's ears, ajuga, and the gingers—of value for their foliage. They start the year off alone, but by the time these perennials end their frosty shift they will be in the company of a glorious explosion of spring-blooming plants.

Perennials for a Winter Garden

WINTER FLOWERS:

Helleborus foetidus (stinking hellebore)
Helleborus niger (Christmas rose)
Helleborus orientalis (Lenten rose)

WINTER FOLIAGE:

Acanthus mollis (bear's-breech)
Ajuga reptans (bugleweed cultivars)
***Artemisia* spp.** (wormwood)
Arum italicum (Italian arum)
***Dianthus* spp.** (pinks)
***Festuca ovina* 'Glauca'** (sheep's fescue)
Lavandula angustifolia (English lavender)
Macleaya cordata (plume poppy)
Saxifraga stolonlifera (strawberry geranium)
Saxifraga* x *urbium (London pride)
Stachys byzantina (lamb's ears)

OTHER ORNAMENTS: (dried flower heads, stems, and pods)

***Calamagrostis acutiflora* 'Stricta'** (feather reed grass)
Miscanthus floridulus (giant miscanthus)
Miscanthus sinensis (eulalia)
***Miscanthus sinensis* 'Gracillimus'** (maiden grass)
Pennisetum alopecuroides (fountain grass)
***Sedum* spp.** (stonecrop)

Note: The abbreviation "spp." stands for the plural of "species"; where used in lists it means that many, but not all, of the species in a genus meet the criterion of the list.

MEMORIES OF A SEASON PAST
The gardener has resisted the urge to tidy up this perennial border, reaping the rewards of a winter morning, when frost highlights the flower heads of centaurea (foreground), sedum (center of border), and the echinops right behind it. The low light adds a gentle glow to the scene, here particularly accenting the lacy artemisia.

Early Spring to Summer Bloomers

Many early-season perennials brighten the floor of the garden—candytuft, *Phlox divaricata,* allium, aubrieta, and the small blue-leafed grass *Festuca.* Ajuga is thought of as a foliage ground cover, but several varieties offer a stunning haze of blue and violet flower spikes in midspring. They pair nicely with yellow miniature daffodils.

A few weeks later, when the perennial garden has gone from the cool freshness of midspring to the warmth of summer's threshold, it reaches its glorious peak with the showiest flowers of the year—the Japanese and bearded irises, the oriental poppy, and, of course, the herbaceous peony. But it is in the sapping heat of summer that you will find tougher workhorses to sustain color, plants like daylilies, butterfly weed, macleaya, gypsophila, rudbeckia, coreopsis, hollyhock, perovskia, penstemon, echinacea, and, in warmer regions, cosmos, verbena, and California poppy.

This is also the time when the many species of ornamental grasses, which have been growing slowly through the spring, announce their presence with decorative wands of flower heads catching the slightest summer breeze.

The Arrival of the Grasses

The ornamental grasses come in many distinct forms and sizes. If properly placed in the garden, they will flourish with a minimum of fuss and a maximum of textural interest. There are cool-season species well suited to northern gardens (although most will do fine in a protected spot and with some watering in the South) and warm-season types that begin their growth cycle later and save their best displays for the fall and winter.

Small, front-of-the-border grasses include the delicate blue-green *Festuca ovina* 'Glauca'; sea oats, *Chasmanthium latifolium,* with its curious wafer-thin seed heads resembling barley; and Japanese blood grass, *Imperata cylindrica* 'Red Baron', whose thick, spiky blades turn bright red in the fall.

Other grasses grow to the size of a small shrub—about 3 feet high and 3 feet in diameter. These include the many cultivars of fountain grass, *Pennisetum alopecuroides,* with their arching wands of flower heads; the upright and refined-looking feather reed grass, *Calamagrostis acutiflora* 'Stricta'; and flame grass, *Miscanthus sinensis* 'Purpurascens'.

The giants of the grass world, often growing 6 feet or higher, make good back-of-the-border plants, accents, and screens. These include giant Chinese silver grass, *Miscanthus floridulus;* Ravenna grass, *Erianthus ravennae;* and the old-fashioned pampas grass, *Cortaderia selloana.*

Planting for Early and Late Color

Another approach to prolonging ornament in the garden is to select cultivars that have been bred to be early or late flowering within the plant's natural bloom cycle. With columbine, for example, you could have weeks of bloom by planting a range of varieties. Other candidates include astilbe, lavender, iris, and one of the most willing and flexible perennials around, the daylily.

Many gardeners also sustain color by using other classes of plants, such as shrubs for bor-

TIPS FROM THE PROS

Maximizing Your Garden Space

Successful garden designers look beyond existing site conditions to imagine what might be. Be bold in your thinking and draw ideas from books, magazines, and arboretums.

In the first year of a perennial garden, consider setting the plants closer together than is usually advised. Doing so will create a fuller look in the first season and crowd out weeds before they get a foothold. For example, when the recommended spacing between daylily plants is given as 2 feet, plant them only a foot apart. The practice will produce gaps between plant groupings, but these bare spots can be filled in with annuals. At season's end, reset the perennials at the correct intervals.

In searching out a site for a new perennial garden, take photographs of likely spots. Then lay a piece of tracing paper over the photo and draw in a possible bed or border to see how it would look at the location. You can also outline on the paper the shapes of various plants to see if you like a particular composition.

Old conifers are notorious for consuming large amounts of space at their base. If desired, this precious ground can be reclaimed for perennials by removing the lowest branches.

der structure and annuals as fill-ins. *Caryopteris,* an aromatic shrub, produces a cloud of blue flowers in the high summer. *Buddleia davidii,* the butterfly bush, has long-lasting flower spikes in a range of colors, including white, blue, and purple. The rose of Sharon is another good summer-flowering shrub that fits into the perennial border. But be careful to choose a variety that won't self-seed, or you may be saddled with an avid spreader.

The choice of annuals is vast. Some of the most successful are nicotiana (which offers the boon of being heavily fragrant at night), zinnias, marigolds, impatiens, petunias, cleome, and cosmos.

In late summer, a number of perennials come into bloom, freshening the garden after the travails of the hot months. They include cultivars of the fragrant plantain lily, *Hosta plantaginea;* veronicastrum, with its spiky racemes of tiny flowers; Joe-Pye weed; and the asterlike boltonia. Many bearded iris varieties rebloom with as much vigor as in the late spring, and the Japanese anemone is a sterling late-season plant that blooms for weeks.

The Autumn Perennial Garden

In areas of the country that experience the change of seasons, fall is an extraordinary time in the garden. The light is clear but low, casting a glow over the changing foliage color of trees and shrubs. Within this larger landscape context, the garden can become a place of serenity in the weeks leading up to the first hard frosts.

Chrysanthemums are beautiful when used in carefully planned color combinations—in reds, bronzes, and soft oranges, for example. Other perennials sustain ornament around and above them, including the many stunning species of aster, the flowering sedums, and such fall-flowering salvias as the leggy blue sage, *Salvia azurea* var. *grandiflora.* Finally, the ornamental grasses go through their own color gyrations and emerge at season's end as the main group of perennials to see the garden through the winter.

Perennials for Drying

Some perennials, such as those listed below, will dry naturally in airy, dry, dark rooms and will retain their beauty long after drying. Others, however, including peonies, hellebore, and dianthus, must be buried in a desiccant such as fine-textured sand or silica gel to keep their color and form while drying. For correct harvesting times and drying techniques, consult local garden clubs or specialty books.

Achillea **spp.**
(yarrow, particularly 'Coronation Gold', 'Moonshine', and other golden types)
Achillea filipendulina
(fernleaf yarrow, white forms only)
Achillea ptarmica
(sneezewort)
Allium **spp.**
(ornamental onion, chives)
Anaphalis **spp.**
(pearly everlasting)
Astilbe **spp.**
(astilbe)
Artemisia lactiflora
(white mugwort)
Artemisia ludoviciana
(white mugwort)
Delphinium
(delphinium)
Echinops ritro
(globe thistle)
Eryngium **spp.**
(sea holly)
Gypsophila paniculata
(baby's-breath)
Lavandula angustifolia
(lavender)
Liatris spicata
(gay-feather)
Limonium latifolium
(sea lavender)
Stachys byzantina
(lamb's ears)

Note: The abbreviation "spp." stands for the plural of "species"; where used in lists it means that many, but not all, of the species in a genus meet the criterion of the list.

Yarrow, Lamb's Ears, Sea Lavender (left to right)

Laying Out Your Garden Plan

Making decisions about the style and size of your perennial garden and the plants you would like to grow brings you one step closer to finalizing your garden plan. First, however, you must return to your base plan.

Just as trace overlays made it easier for you to record various site conditions on your base plan, they can be useful in helping you contemplate various options for your final plan. You might consider—and then reject—a number of different places on the property for your perennial garden. The overlays allow you to do that without marking the original plan. They also offer a quick and effective way to evaluate a prospective site: Will the garden get enough sun? Is it in a location where it will be enjoyed? Are the soil conditions right?

In our suburban-property example here, we decided on an informal perennial border that flows from the street-side face of the property around the end of the original log cabin. Aesthetically, the border anchors the house to the property—the cottage-garden style evokes a rustic past. Situated on the sunniest area of the property, the border can be viewed in part from within the house and frames the patio on the east side. The border also offers a coherent outside link between two doors on opposite sides of the log cabin.

Elsewhere, the historic nature of the property was bolstered by the installation of a vegetable and herb garden at the northeast corner of the house and by the new apple orchard—made possible by fixing the drainage problems in the southwest corner of the property.

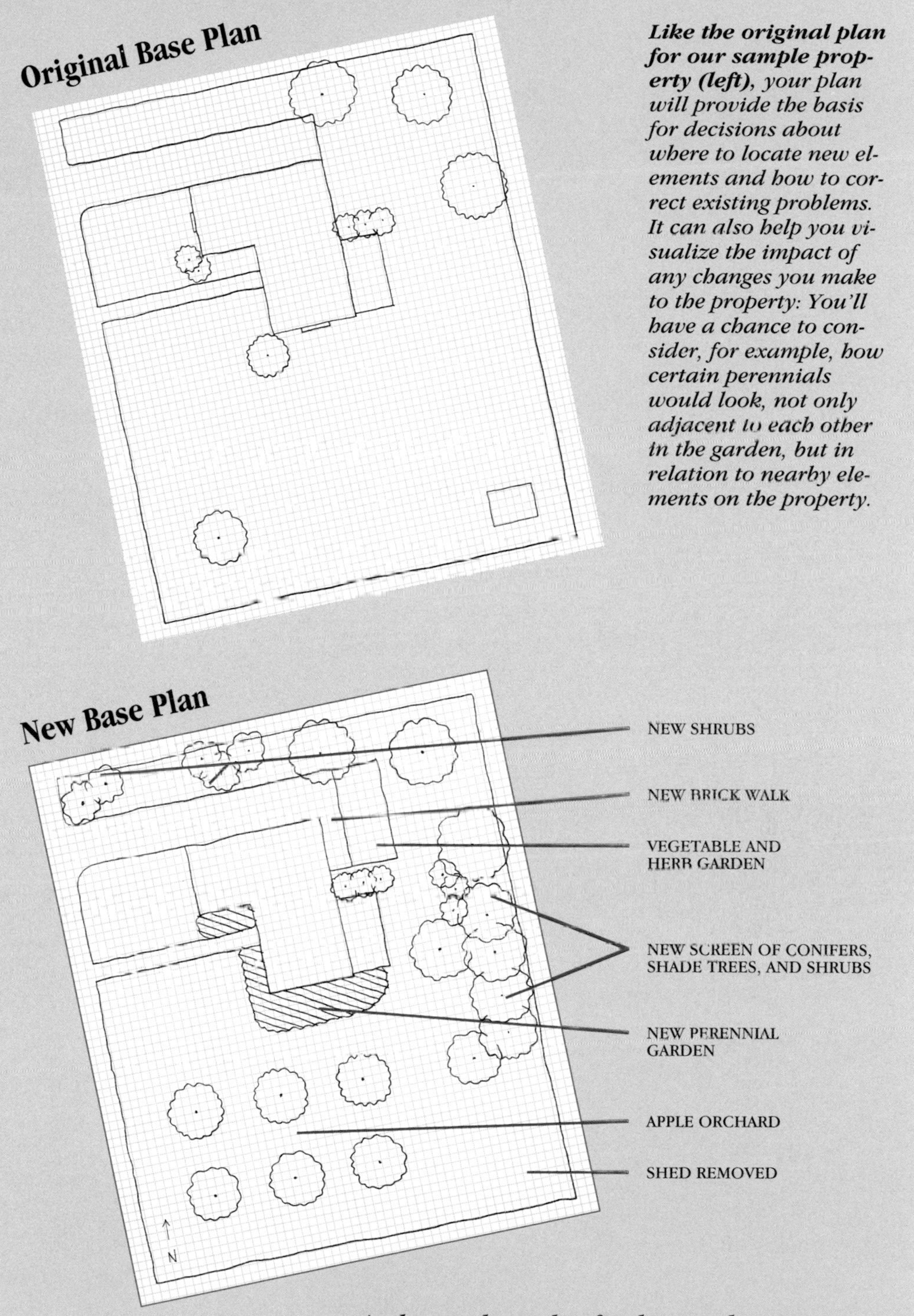

Like the original plan for our sample property (left), *your plan will provide the basis for decisions about where to locate new elements and how to correct existing problems. It can also help you visualize the impact of any changes you make to the property: You'll have a chance to consider, for example, how certain perennials would look, not only adjacent to each other in the garden, but in relation to nearby elements on the property.*

As the new base plan for the sample property shows, *numerous other changes accompany the new perennial garden. The vegetable and herb garden is placed close to the kitchen door. On the eastern boundary, a planting of conifers provides privacy for the patio and becomes a backdrop to a new shrub border.*

Turning a Paper Plan into a Real Garden

The final planting design for the sample property *(below, right),* a 9-by-20-foot bed, was intended to look relaxed and eclectic, picking up the cottage-garden theme. There is allegiance to a color band of cool and warm pinks, blues, and violets, but the occasional use of yellows and oranges *(right)* reinforces the cottage-garden air of randomness.

Even within its loose framework, the design has structure, with a layering of mass from the back of the bed to the front and careful placement of bulky perennials and shrubs. Certain plants are repeated to provide a unifying theme, among them macleaya at the back and, elsewhere, phlox.

The plants were selected to give a maximum of color and form with a minimum of maintenance. A drought-tolerant shrub, *Caryopteris,* provides blue color from high summer until frost. The macleayas present a strong vertical line and are sturdy plants with long-lasting foliage.

The garden was also designed to have a medley of texture, with coarse-leafed plants like hostas positioned to contrast with finer-leafed ones. The swordlike leaf blades of the belamcanda draw the eye into the heart of the bed, especially during the plant's summer flowering period.

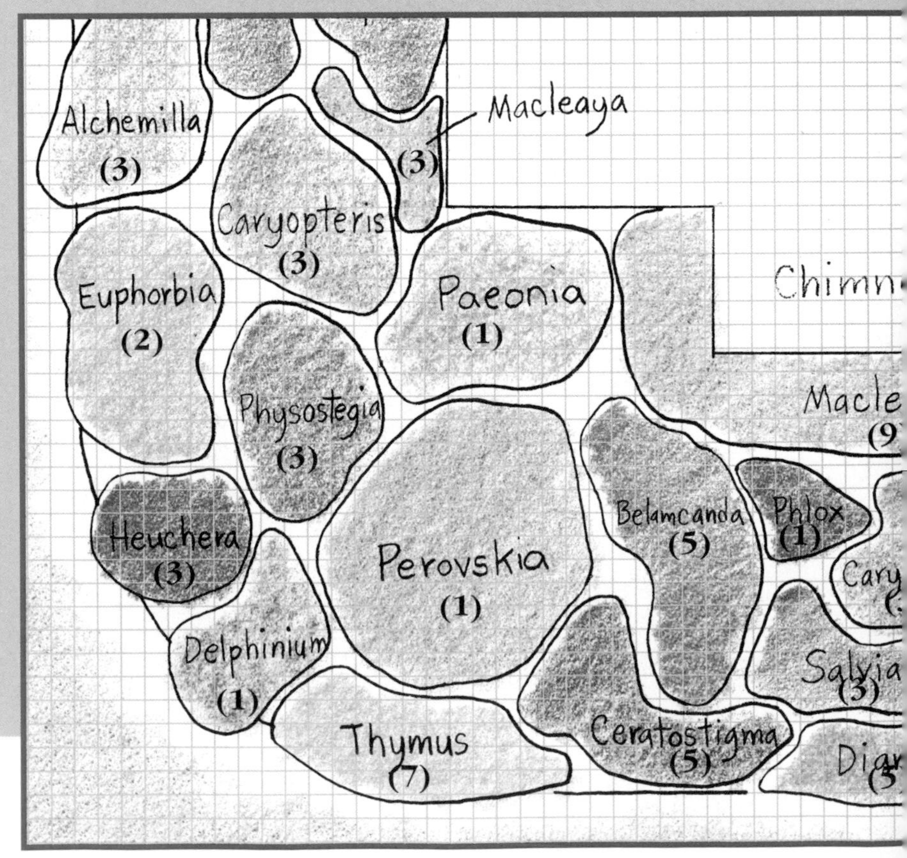

A larger-scale drawing of the garden site itself, *like this one from our sample property, will enable you to focus more intently on the color, texture, and mass of each plant or plant grouping and devise an optimum combination. In rendering the drawing, make 1 inch of your graph paper equal 1 foot. This enlarged plan also allows you to calculate how many plants you will need (right, numbers in parentheses) in following the recommended spacing, which differs by species. A large hosta, for example, might occupy 3 feet across, a liriope just 18 inches.*

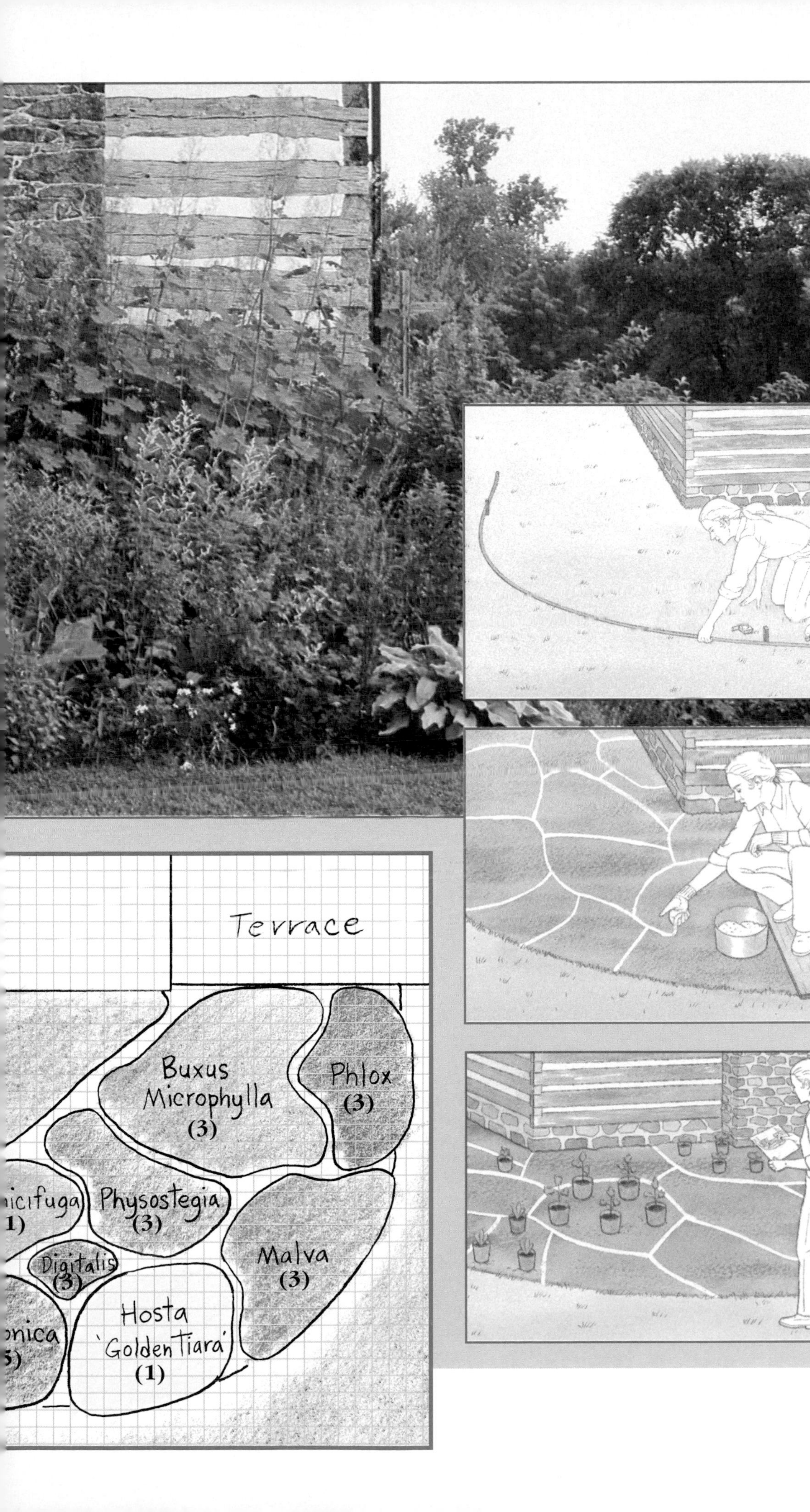

1. Measure off the dimensions of your plot *and define its perimeter using either string and stakes to create square corners or a garden hose to outline a curving edge (page 36). Next, prepare the soil (pages 36-43); if possible, do this at least several weeks before planting.*

2. With your planting guide in hand, *use a combination of measurements and eyeballing to allocate space to each group of perennials. With a gloved hand, outline each section with powdered limestone, kneeling on a board to distribute your weight and avoid compacting the cultivated soil.*

3. Set each plant in its assigned area, *working from the back of the bed forward. For a border planting like this one, place the plants with the tallest growth habit in the rear, the shortest at the front, and the others in between. Then mix them up a bit to avoid a stiff look. Resist arranging plants in rigid blocks; instead, let drifts of different plants interweave.*

CHAPTER TWO

Establishing the Garden

Putting in a perennial garden offers physical rewards and long-lasting pleasures. An autumn day's work of cultivating your plot, for example, is sure to get your blood flowing. But unless you have varieties that specifically require fall planting to look their best come bloom time, cover the soil with a layer of mulch and let the ground settle over the winter.

Just when you think spring will never come, it is heralded by the arrival of the mail-order nursery catalogs. You'll see scores of attractive perennials, each with its own cultivation needs. For example, peonies like those in the center of this border in Birmingham, Alabama, produce such beautiful flowers because their roots were carefully planted with the buds only 1 to 2 inches below the soil's surface—shallow enough for them to experience a necessary period of chill, but not so shallow they might freeze. Some of the plants you choose may have their own peculiarities. Generally, however, establishing a perennial garden requires no esoteric know-how or skills—just an understanding of the guidelines set out on the following pages.

A. ***Phlox divaricata ssp. laphamii* (8)** **B.** ***Paeonia 'Cytherea'* (2)** **C.** ***Paeonia 'Moonstone'* (2)** **D.** ***Delphinium alabamicum* (2)** **E.** ***Paeonia lutea 'Thunderbolt'* (1)**
F. ***Hydrangea macrophylla* (1)**
G. ***Rhododendron 'Treasure'* (1)**
H. ***Iris tectorum* (3)** **I.** ***Paeonia 'Pink Hawaiian Coral'* (1)**
J. ***Paeonia 'Scarlett O'Hara'* (1)**

Note:The key lists each plant type and the total quantity needed to replicate the garden shown. The diagram's letters and numbers refer to the type of plant and the number sited in an area.

Readying New Ground to Receive Perennials

The first steps toward creating a new perennial garden—deciding on the site and setting the design—take you only so far: After that it's time to go outdoors and mark off your plot *(below)*, begin preparing the soil, and choose your perennials.

Good soil preparation is the single most important factor in growing beautiful, healthy perennials. To properly ready the soil in your garden you must first understand it. Does the soil drain well? Although some perennials thrive in soil that remains continuously moist or is dry *(lists, page 39)*, most require good drainage. Look at the soil texture and color, and the health of plants that may already be growing in it. Is the soil heavy clay or loose sand? Is it poor or fertile? Adding organic amendments will condition the soil and applying fertilizer can replenish its nutrients.

Other factors, including light and exposure, will affect how your garden grows. For example, most perennials prefer full sun, meaning at least 6 hours a day with 4 of those in the afternoon. But a lush perennial garden is still possible even if your site has full or partial shade; it all depends on the plants you choose *(list, right)*.

Investing some initial time and effort in cultivating and fertilizing the soil, improving areas of poor drainage, and choosing and siting your plants correctly will pay off handsomely later. Remember, your perennials are going to be in the ground for a long time, and there will never be another opportunity to start them out right.

Appraising Your Soil

Bringing your soil to optimum readiness for planting means first knowing its present condition. You should make at least a rough de-

Outlining Your Garden Plot

For a plot with a curving edge, *use a garden hose to outline the perimeter, matching the bed's wide and narrow points to the dimensions shown on your site plan. Then mark the perimeter with powdered lime or by cutting into the soil alongside the hose with a garden spade.*

For square corners, first stake off one side of the bed. *Then set a peg 4 feet from the first stake and tie a string to it; mark the string at a point 5 feet from the peg. Tie a string to the first stake and mark it at 3 feet from the stake. Cross the two strings at the marks. Set a third stake at that point.*

The 3:4:5 ratio used to find the right angle at left, *which can be used with a garden plot of any size, demonstrates that a triangle with its three sides in the proper ratio will have a right angle opposite the longest side.*

Perennials for Full and Partial Shade

Acanthus mollis (bear's-breech)
Ajuga reptans (bugleweed)
Anemone* x *hybrida (Japanese anemone)
Anemone vitifolia (grapeleaf anemone)
Aquilegia (columbine)
Arenaria montana (mountain sandwort)
Aruncus (goatsbeard)
Astilbe (astilbe, false spirea)
Baptisia australis (blue wild indigo)
Begonia grandis (hardy begonia)
Bergenia cordifolia (heartleaf bergenia)
Brunnera macrophylla (Siberian bugloss)
Campanula poscharskyana (Serbian bellflower)
Cimicifuga (bugbane)
***Dicentra* spp.** (bleeding heart)
***Epimedium* spp.** (barrenwort)
Geranium (cranesbill)
Helleborus niger (Christmas rose)
Helleborus orientalis (Lenten rose)
Heuchera americana (American alumroot)
***Hosta* spp.** (plantain lily)
Iris cristata (crested iris)
***Lamium* spp.** (dead nettle)
Ligularia dentata (bigleaf golden-ray)
Ligularia stenocephala (golden-ray)
Lobelia cardinalis (cardinal flower)
Monarda didyma (bee balm)
Phlox divaricata (wild blue phlox)
***Polygonatum* spp.** (Solomon's-seal)
Primula (primrose)
Pulmonaria saccharata (Bethlehem sage)
Rodgersia (rodgersia)
Smilacina racemosa (false Solomon's-seal)
Thalictrum aquilegifolium (columbine meadow rue)
Thalictrum delavayi (Yunnan meadow rue)
Viola odorata (sweet violet)

***Note:** The abbreviation "spp." stands for the plural of "species"; where used in lists it means that many, but not all, of the species in a genus meet the criterion of the list.*

Aquilegia canadensis (Canadian columbine)

termination of the soil's texture—that is, the relative amounts of clay, silt, and sand particles that make up most of the mineral content of soil.

Soil with a high percentage of clay or silt is likely to be quite dense and compact, allowing little space for air and growing plant roots to penetrate and for water to slowly percolate and drain away. If you dig into these soils with a spade, they feel quite heavy; clay soil will also stick to the blade, making it difficult to turn and break up.

At the other end of the scale, soil made up predominantly of sand is so loose and porous that it cannot retain moisture or nutrients and provides poor anchorage for plant roots. It feels coarse and gritty in your hand and does not clump together well.

The soil with the best texture is loam. A mixture containing roughly 20 percent clay and 40 percent each of silt and sand, loam is easy to work, holds water and nutrients well, and allows air to reach plant roots. Loam also has an ideal soil structure, structure being determined by how well the soil particles cling together and in what shapes. The optimal structure is one in which the soil is friable—meaning that the particles aggregate into small, irregularly shaped, slightly moist clumps or crumbs that hold together well but will break up easily in your hand. Soil with this ideal structure contains countless small spaces that conduct oxygen, water, and nutrients to plant roots.

Another factor you should take into account when analyzing your soil is its acidity or alkalinity—the pH level—which you can measure using an inexpensive tester available at garden shops and home centers. Most perennials will flourish in soil ranging from somewhat acid—a pH of about 5.8— to slightly alkaline, or just above the neutral level of 7; it is in this range that soil nutrients become most available to the plants. Should the soil test excessively acid, you can raise its pH by working in a quantity of dolomitic limestone. If it is too alkaline, an application of sulfur will bring it to the desired level of acidity.

Soil Fertility

Three chemical elements are essential to plant growth—nitrogen, phosphorus, and potassium—and these all occur naturally in soil. Responsible for strong roots and healthy leaf, stem, flower, and fruit development, these elements, as well as traces of secondary elements, are the products of decaying organic matter. Compost, well-rotted cow manure, and leaf mold—soil consisting chiefly of decayed vegetable matter, particularly leaves—are good sources of organic matter, and working them into the soil of a new perennial garden may well provide all the fertilization the plot needs during its first year.

TIPS FROM THE PROS

Preparing the Ground without Toil

Some professional gardeners have devised a way of preparing a plot of land for gardening virtually without turning a single spadeful of soil. The method, called smothering, holds obvious advantages for the home gardener who wants to cultivate a relatively large area, for which the labor of digging, or even using a power tiller, would be great.

Smothering consists simply of covering up unwanted vegetation to deprive it of light until the plants die—a period of about 3 months. Once the covering is in place and the process has begun, you don't even have to wait the full time before you plant. You can cut down through the cover—indeed, you need never remove it—to plant your perennials, which will begin growing while the grass and most weeds around them are dying away.

If your chosen garden plot is covered with sod, mow the grass as low as possible, then cover the area with sheets of old newspaper—being careful to avoid using any bearing colored inks, which can deposit harmful chemicals in the soil. A covering three or four sheets thick should be enough; overlap the edges a few inches to ensure that all sunlight is blocked out. Then cover the newsprint with a layer of leaves or other organic mulch about 1 foot deep, which will weigh down the paper, improve the appearance of the plot, and eventually decompose and add humus to the soil.

Woody plants and persistent weeds will require a heavier covering—perhaps a layer of cardboard or a thickness of 30 or so sheets of newspaper, followed by the mulch. Weeds strong enough to survive smothering can be destroyed by digging them out.

Soil Amendment of Choice

If you had to select one all-purpose soil amendment that would both improve soil structure and supply nutrient-rich organic matter, the choice would undoubtedly be compost. Compost is made up of rotted plant materials such as grass clippings and fallen leaves, fruit and vegetable scraps from the kitchen, aged livestock manure, sawdust, newsprint, and any number of other organic ingredients. It also contains a teeming population of living organisms and microorganisms, the laborers who did the work of breaking down the raw materials into the black, moist, crumbly humus.

Compost is almost a panacea for imperfect soils. Not only does it add a rich supply of nutrients and beneficial microorganisms, but it can also change the structure of the soil. If a soil is loose and sandy, generous additions of compost will pull it together and make it crumbly, so that water, nutrients, and plant roots can get a foothold. If the soil is heavily compacted clay, compost will loosen and lighten it. Even the best soil can benefit from periodic additions of compost to help maintain its structure and replenish its supply of nutrients.

Choosing a Fertilizer

Although compost adds nutrients to the soil, you may need to add fertilizer periodically to meet the needs of particular plants or to help replenish depleted nutrients. Fertilizers take two forms—organic and inorganic. Organic fertilizers are derived from animal or vegetable matter. Examples of such fertilizers include compost, cottonseed meal, blood meal (from slaughtered cattle), and finely ground bone. Many gardeners prefer organic fertilizers because they arc manufactured by environmentally friendly methods, don't harm important soil microbes, and don't leave chemical residues. They also work a little slower than their inorganic counterparts, lessening the chance of burning plant roots if you happen to overfertilize.

Inorganic fertilizers are products of the petrochemicals industry. On the plus side, they tend to be faster acting and easier to use. However, they can leach out of soils quickly, requiring repeated applications that over time can become expensive. The most significant disadvantage of chemical fertilizers is that they can damage the many beneficial microorganisms that live in the soil.

Either type of fertilizer may be sold as a so-called complete fertilizer, its packaging indicating the percentages of nitrogen, phosphorus, and potassium—always in that order—that it contains. The percentages may sometimes be labeled N-P-K, the chemical symbols for these elements. A 5-10-5 fertilizer, for example, contains 5 percent nitrogen, 10 percent phosphorus, and 5 percent potassium, plus small or trace amounts of other chemicals, the remainder being inert filler. A product labeled 10-10-10 is called a balanced fertilizer. One labeled 0-20-0 is a single-nutrient fertilizer, in this case an all-phosphorus product called a superphosphate.

As a rule, perennials need relatively little fertilizer compared with that needed by vegetables, fruits, turf grasses, and annuals. But because perennials stay in the ground for so long, they may benefit from judicious applications of fertilizer from time to time.

Cultivating the Soil

Many professional gardeners recommend digging and amending the soil for a perennial garden in the fall, covering it with a mulch to hold in moisture and prevent weeds, and then waiting until spring to begin planting. During the wait the soil will settle, and winter frosts and thaws will cause it to expand and contract, improving its structure by breaking it into smaller clumps.

In areas of the country where the summers are hot and dry, it is often best to work the soil in spring and let it lie until fall. If you are too impatient to let a growing season slip by, however, it is still important to give your cultivated plot at least several weeks to begin settling before you plant it.

Make sure the soil is slightly moist before you dig, otherwise you risk destroying the soil's structure. If the ground is too wet, the pressure of digging will pack the soil into a dense mass completely impervious to water, air, and roots. If the ground is dry, the digging may cause it to disintegrate into a powder.

To determine if your soil is ready for dig-

Perennials at Home in Moist Soil

Iris pseudacorus (yellow flag)

Aruncus dioicus
(goatsbeard)
Astilbe x arendsii
(garden spirea)
Astrantia major
(masterwort)
Brunnera macrophylla
(Siberian bugloss)
Cimicifuga racemosa
(black snakeroot)
Filipendula rubra
(queen-of-the-prairie)
Filipendula ulmaria
(queen-of-the-meadow)
Hemerocallis
(daylily)
Hosta
(plantain lily)
Iris ensata
(Japanese iris)
Iris pseudacorus
(yellow flag)
***Ligularia* spp.**
(golden-ray)
Lobelia cardinalis
(cardinal flower)
Lobelia siphilitica
(great blue lobelia)
***Lysimachia* spp.**
(loosestrife)
Monarda didyma
(bee balm)
Phlox divaricata
(wild blue phlox)
Physostegia virginiana
(false dragonhead)
***Polygonatum* spp.**
(Solomon's-seal)
***Primula* spp.**
(primrose)
Ranunculus repens
(buttercup)
***Rodgersia* spp.**
(rodgersia)
Smilacina racemosa
(false Solomon's-seal)
Trollius europaeus
(globeflower)

Note: *The abbreviation "spp." stands for the plural of "species"; where used in lists it means that many, but not all, of the species in a genus meet the criterion of the list.*

Perennials at Home in Dry Soil

***Achillea* spp.**
(yarrow)
Anthemis tinctoria
(golden marguerite)
Arabis caucasica
(rock cress)
***Artemisia* spp.**
(wormwood)
Asclepias tuberosa
(butterfly weed)
Aurinia
(basket-of-gold)
Centaurea montana
(mountain bluet)
***Coreopsis* spp.**
(tickseed)
Echinacea purpurea
(purple coneflower)
Echinops ritro
(small globe thistle)
***Eryngium* spp.**
(sea holly)
Filipendula vulgaris
(dropwort)
***Gaillardia* spp.**
(blanket-flower)
Helianthus
(sunflower)
Hemerocallis hybrids
(daylily)
Iberis
(candytuft)
Liatris
(gay-feather)
***Limonium* spp.**
(sea lavender, statice)
Malva alcea
(mallow)
***Miscanthus* spp.**
(eulalia)
***Oenothera* spp.**
(evening primrose)
***Pennisetum* spp.**
(fountain grass)
Perovskia atriplicifolia
(Russian sage)
Phlox subulata
(moss pink, moss phlox)
Physostegia virginiana
(false dragonhead)
Potentilla
(cinquefoil, five-finger)
***Rudbeckia* spp.**
(coneflower)
***Santolina* spp.**
(lavender cotton)
Saponaria ocymoides
(rock soapwort)
***Sedum* spp.**
(stonecrop)
Stachys byzantina
(lamb's ears)
Verbascum chaixii
(chaix mullein)

Note: *The abbreviation "spp." stands for the plural of "species"; where used in lists it means that many, but not all, of the species in a genus meet the criterion of the list.*

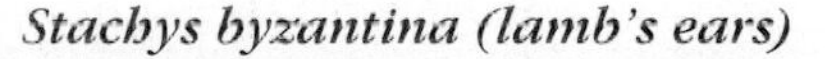

Stachys byzantina (lamb's ears)

Breaking Ground for the Garden

1. Shave off any sod with your garden spade, *cutting through the soil horizontally. Use the surplus sod to fill in bare spots on your lawn, or shake off the loose soil and save the remaining material for the compost pile. If your plot is large—and you're not in a hurry to plant—you may choose to smother the grass (page 38).*

2. To work the soil, drive your spade all the way into the soil at 4-inch intervals; *toss each slice of loosened soil forward and use the blade to break it up. Be careful not to step on the broken soil, which might compact it into a dense, unworkable mass.*

3. Use a spading fork to work amendments into the broken-up soil. *Choose from such amendments as compost, rotted cow manure, limestone, peat moss, and other materials as needed to ready the soil for your perennials.*

ging, turn over a spadeful and break up a clod. If the clod comes apart easily, you can proceed. If it sticks stubbornly together or can be formed into a ball in your hand, it is too wet; wait a few rainless days and try again. If the clump of soil crumbles to dust, it is too dry; soak the entire plot, then let it drain for 3 or 4 days before you begin digging *(above).*

Reasons for Double Digging

The procedure called double digging involves digging up and amending a layer of topsoil about 12 inches deep and then loosening and amending to an equal depth the layer of subsoil beneath it *(right).*

Professional gardeners differ on the importance of double digging. Some say it is unnecessary extra work, that you can have a fine perennial garden without it. Others say it gives the perennials plenty of loosened soil in which to sink their roots—which in the case of some plants can grow to a depth of 24 inches. Still other gardeners don't even stop at conventional double digging. After removing the topsoil and amending it, they do not merely loosen the subsoil, they dig it up and amend it thoroughly, put the original topsoil back where the subsoil was, and put the former subsoil on top.

Personal preferences aside, many experts concur that if your soil is a heavy clay with poor drainage, it is important to double dig. If you have better soil, double digging may not be absolutely necessary but will probably return a dividend in more robust, more extravagantly blooming perennials.

Reasons for Not Rototilling

Digging up a more-or-less virgin plot of ground by hand is strenuous labor, and the temptation to rent a machine to do the job can be almost irresistible. But unless you have laid out an exceptionally large plot, don't give in. Rototilling is likely to do more harm than good, for a number of reasons:

If the site for your garden is presently covered with sod, you must shave off that covering *(above)* or smother it *(page 38),* tasks the rototiller cannot spare you. If you simply tear into the sod with the rototiller, the grass you turn over will start coming up again amid your perennials.

The indiscriminate blades of the rototiller will chop the roots of perennial weeds into many small pieces, each of which may come back as a new weed. If, on the other hand, you use a spading fork to comb through the tilled soil, removing by hand as many traces of weed roots as possible, this disaster—as well as backbreaking hours of weeding—will be avoided. In addition, the blades of most rototillers cut into the soil to a depth of only about 6 inches—about half the depth needed for a well-cultivated plot. The machine is even more impractical if you plan to double dig.

Worst of all, rototillers are heavy machines that can compact the soil as they till it. Even if you use the better type, with the wheels forward and the blades in the rear, those wheels will put pressure on the soil, as will your body weight as you follow the machine along. The damage to soil structure is not worth the savings in elbow grease.

Cultivating an Existing Bed

Perennials in an established bed respond well to shallow cultivation in early spring. Use a tined cultivator with three or four prongs for the job; the sharp cutting edge of a hoe may injure shallow roots. Work over the entire surface of the bed to a depth of an inch or two, going in between groups of perennials and between individual plants. This will up-

The Deluxe Treatment: Double Digging

1. Beginning at one end of the garden plot you have laid out, *remove any sod covering as shown opposite. Then dig a trench about 1 foot wide and as deep as the blade on your spade, running from one side of the plot to the other. Remove the topsoil and heap it in a cart or wheelbarrow. Thoroughly loosen the layer of exposed subsoil with a spading fork and work in the appropriate soil amendments. Do not remove the subsoil.*

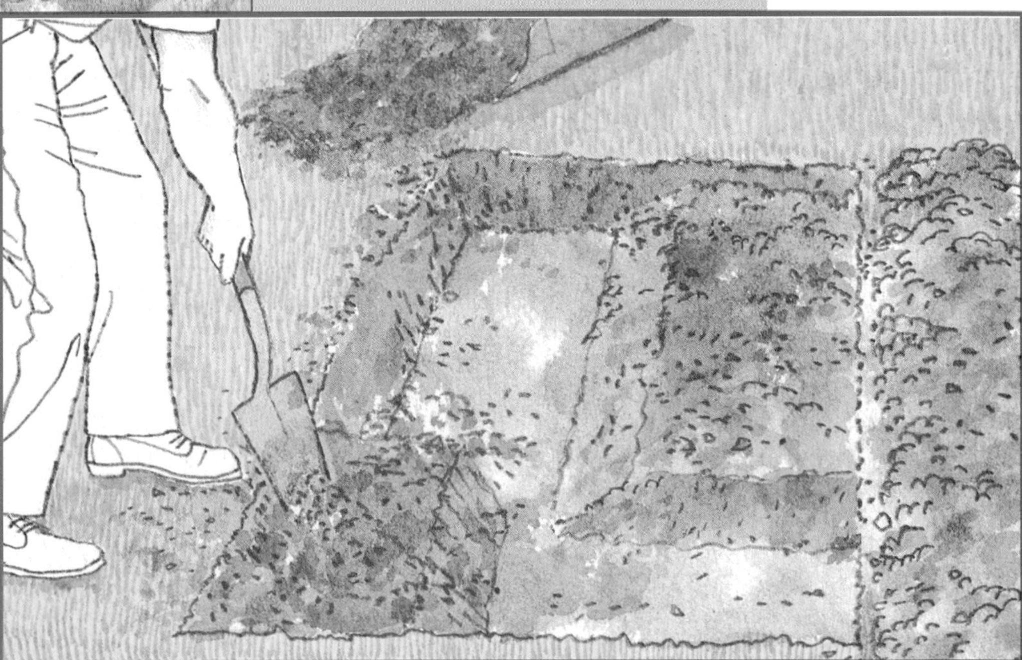

2. Dig out another trench next to the first one, *moving the loosened topsoil over to cover the amended subsoil of the first trench. Work amendments into this topsoil. Then loosen and amend the subsoil in the second trench. Repeat the process for each succeeding trench until the last one. Then amend the topsoil reserved from the first trench and use it to fill the last one.*

root weeds and allow air to get into the soil. This is also a good time to work in fertilizer around each plant. If you are using a 5-10-5 fertilizer, a level tablespoonful suffices for an initial spring feeding of a small clump. Older and larger plants may need more—the amount depends on the size of the plant and the strength of the fertilizer, but it is better to err on the side of caution. A well-established phlox, for example, should be given no more than a handful of 5-10-5. Scatter the fertilizer on the soil's surface, keeping it off the leaves and crowns so it can't burn them, and work it into the soil with the cultivator.

Solving a Drainage Problem

If your first choice of a site for your new perennial garden is fine in almost every way but suffers from poor drainage, you can consider several remedies. One, described on page 41, is to diligently double dig the plot, thoroughly loosening and then amending the heavy subsoil until it drains nicely.

Should the drainage problem persist, perhaps because the site is underlain by a layer of impervious soil called hardpan, you might want to create a simple drainage system. This approach works well when the soggy ground lies fairly close to a potential runoff area such as a gutter, a roadside ditch, or a piece of low-lying ground on your property where you can dig a catchment basin.

However, you may be confronted with drainage so poor that you have no hope of improving it except at great expense. One indication that you have such a problem is if water pools in an area after a rain and takes more than an hour or two to drain; another is if the soil is still soggy 12 to 24 hours after a rain. In either case, you can still have your garden where you want it, in the form of a raised bed. This arrangement allows you not only to get around a drainage problem but also to dodge many other site problems by creating your own soil for the bed, with perfect texture, structure, pH, and fertility.

A raised bed can be any size or shape you wish, although its widest point should be no more than about two arm's lengths; this allows you to reach into the center of the bed from either side. The bed can be a simple, neat raised island of topsoil dug and mounded up from the surrounding level ground. Or it can be bordered by a frame made of landscaping timbers, redwood or cedar planks, logs, bricks, cinder blocks, or stones.

Drying Out a Wet Patch

1. Working from the wet area toward a nearby street, *dig a trench 12 to 18 inches wide and 1 foot deep at the start. As you dig, gradually increase the depth to about 18 inches at the outlet end so that water drains in the right direction.*

2. If you lack an outlet to a street, *dig a dry well to serve as a basin for your drainage ditch: Dig a pit about 3 feet deep at a low spot. Fill it with water three times and monitor it; all water should be gone 1 hour after the last fill. Then fill the basin with gravel to where the ditch joins it.*

THE BOUNTY OF A CUSTOM-MADE BED
Set off simply but handsomely with weathered planks, this raised bed of spiky larkspur, yarrow, daisies, and lamb's ears scintillates with color and robust growth, its blooms flourishing in an environment unaffected by uncertainties of drainage, soil structure, or pH.

3. Lay a bed of gravel in the ditch and install perforated drainpipe over it. *If your system empties into a dry well, extend the pipe a few inches into the well (above). Cover the pipe inlet with a piece of woven landscape fabric to screen out silt, sand, and stones.*

4. Cover the drainpipe with a layer of gravel, *and bring the level of gravel in the dry well up even with it. Cut out strips of landscape fabric as wide as the ditch and lay them over the gravel to keep overlying soil from sifting down and clogging the openings in the pipe.*

5. Fill in the ditch and the dry well with topsoil, *mounding the soil over them to allow for settling. Finally, go back to the original zone of poor drainage and build up the area with topsoil, contouring the surface to slope gently in the direction of the drainpipe.*

Choosing Your Perennials

Selecting Healthy Plants

If you decide to purchase your perennials locally, *look for robust plants that reflect good care. In general, choose plants that are compact and bushy with bright-colored foliage (far left); if the plants are not yet in bloom, so much the better—their first spurt of energy will be spent on sending out strong roots. Tall, spindly plants with scant, pale foliage (left) may be badly root-bound or perhaps were grown in poor light. While these plants can usually be nursed to full health, perennials that show signs of disease or insect infestation should definitely be avoided (pages 96-103).*

Perennials That Resist Pests and Diseases

Achillea (yarrow)
Amsonia (bluestar)
Anchusa (bugloss)
Anemone* x *hybrida (Japanese anemone)
Artemisia (wormwood)
Asclepias tuberosa (butterfly weed)
Astilbe (astilbe, false spirea)
Aurinia (basket-of-gold)
Boltonia (boltonia)
Brunnera macrophylla (Siberian bugloss)
Coreopsis (tickseed)
Dianthus (pinks)
Dicentra (bleeding heart)
Echinacea (purple coneflower)
Echinops (globe thistle)
Eupatorium (boneset)
Geranium (cranesbill)
Hemerocallis (daylily)
Heuchera sanguinea (coral bells)
Iberis (candytuft)
Iris cristata (crested iris)
Iris sibirica (Siberian iris)
Liatris (gay-feather)
Limonium (sea lavender)
Nepeta (catmint)
Oenothera (sundrop)
Papaver (poppy)
Phlox divaricata (wild blue phlox)
Phlox stolonifera (creeping phlox)
Physostegia (false dragonhead)
Polygonatum (Solomon's-seal)
Rudbeckia (coneflower)
Sedum (stonecrop)
Trollius (globeflower)
Verbena canadensis (rose verbena)
Veronica (speedwell)

Note: *The plants listed here are naturally disease and pest resistant. But almost all perennials will be problem free if properly planted and maintained.*

Whether you are buying perennials to fill a new bed or add to an established plot, you'll want to look for two things: the healthiest plants possible and a wide assortment from which to choose. You can purchase plants locally at nurseries or garden centers, or you can order them through the mail.

Local Sources for Plants

At local nurseries or garden centers, you can shop for the best prices, widest selections, and healthiest specimens. Unlike mail-order nurseries, which may list plants for your hardiness zone that are actually borderline cases where you live *(USDA Zone Map, page 110),* local nurseries will only carry plants that are hardy in your region. At local shops, moreover, the plants will already be growing in containers, and will thus be larger and better established than the dormant plants sent out through the mail. And local nurseries and garden centers will be glad to answer questions and give you gardening tips about the plants you purchase.

Ordering Plants by Mail

Large-scale and specialty nurseries that ship to customers all over the country are likely to offer a wider choice of plant varieties than most local operations are able to do, including the very latest cultivars and hybrids—and often at lower prices.

Mail-order nurseries typically ship your order to arrive at the proper planting time in your region, but it is probably best to specify a delivery date. Most mail-order perennials are shipped in a dormant, bare-root state to save postage. Once the plants arrive, look them over; if you find evidence of disease or damage, return them immediately. Put healthy plants into the ground right away, if possible. But if you must delay planting for a few days, rewrap them and keep the roots moist until you are ready to plant. If planting is delayed more than 2 weeks, heel the plants in *(pages 48-49).*

Putting Plants into the Ground

Perennials are long-lived plants that must be given room and time to grow and flourish. This means that a newly planted perennial garden may look somewhat skimpy its first year, even after the plants are established.

Achieving Flowers the First Year

Many perennials, especially first-year seedlings and those that were planted with bare roots, will not bloom until their second year in the garden. If you have your heart set on seeing abundant flowers the first year, however, you can do several things to make that happen while waiting for your fledgling perennials to mature.

One option is to plant annuals among the perennials. If you have allowed the proper amount of space between the young perennials, you will have plenty of room to interplant colorful annuals without disturbing the roots of the long-term inhabitants. Annuals that tend to reseed, such as marigolds and snapdragons, should be deadheaded as blossoms fade to prevent unwanted seedlings the following year, to encourage abundant bloom, and to keep the plants tidy.

If you are willing to pay higher prices for your plants, you can buy container-grown perennials that are large enough to bloom the year you plant them. A third choice is to plan your garden to include *Rudbeckia fulgida* 'Goldsturm', *Coreopsis verticillata* 'Moonbeam', *Hibiscus moscheutos* hybrids, or several other perennial varieties that bloom nicely their first year in the ground. If none of these flowers appeals to you, you can get your garden started with plants donated by friends who have divided their overgrown perennials *(pages 80-85)* and now have more healthy, mature plants than they know what to do with. These too will flower the year you plant them, if you can get them into the ground before their normal bloom time.

Finally, and perhaps most gratifying of all the possibilities, you can make sure that flow-

Planting Depths for Bare-Root Perennials

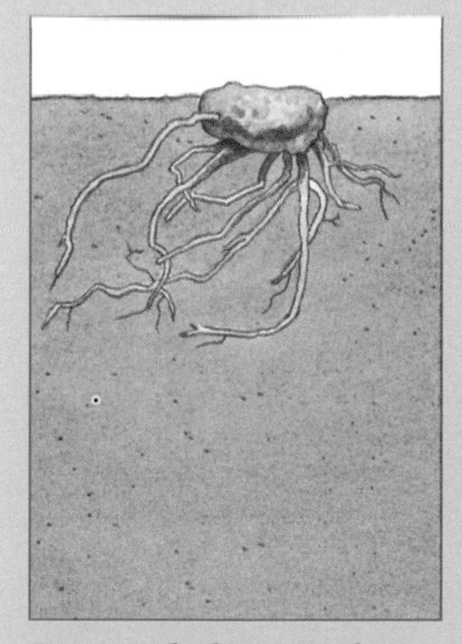

Perennials that grow from rhizomes, *such as iris and bergenia, should be planted with the roots below ground and the surface of the rhizome just emerging from the soil.*

Plant peonies with the tips of the buds just below *ground level if your area has mild winters, and up to 2 inches below the surface if you live in the North.*

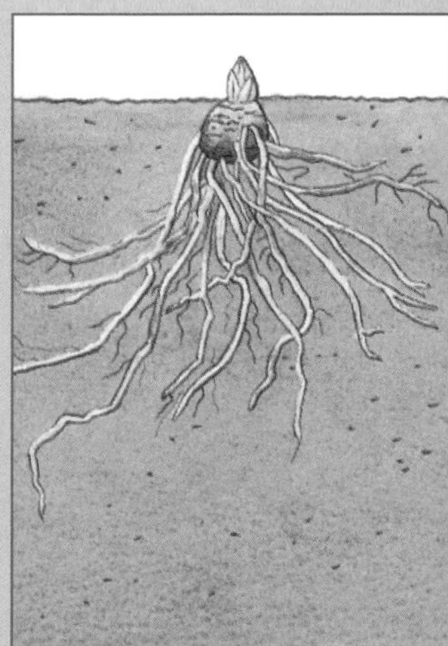

More than half of all perennials (including hostas, *above) do best when planted so that the crown—where the roots and the stem meet—is flush with the soil surface.*

Daylilies (Hemerocallis) *and other plants with a fleshy main root or taproot should be planted with the taproot straight up and down and the bud just below ground level.*

Planting Bare-Root Perennials

Unwrap the plant and check its roots, *clipping off any that are damaged or diseased (left). Place the plant in a bucket of water to keep the roots wet while you dig a hole as deep and as wide as the plant's longest roots. Form a cone of soil in the hole high enough to hold the plant at the proper level. Place the plant atop the cone, gently spreading out the roots (above). Fill in the rest of the soil, tamp down, water generously, and mulch.*

ering perennials of all kinds show up in your garden's first year by filling the garden with plants that you yourself have nurtured for a year or more in a separate nursery bed.

Planting a Nursery Bed

Setting aside a small plot of ground—perhaps a 10-by-10-foot area—for a nursery bed can pay dividends both in the quality and beauty of your perennial garden and in the money you save by raising your own stock. Almost any sunny spot will do for most perennials; a part of the vegetable garden would be ideal. And the space can be compact because you can set the plants in neat rows and much closer together than you would in the garden. With a nursery bed you can buy one plant each of as many varieties as you are interested in and watch them grow and flower. In a year, stem cuttings *(pages 86-87)* or root cuttings *(pages 88-89)* can be taken from some perennials to propagate additional plants. In a few years, others can be divided to produce the number of new plants you want.

In the meantime, you will have a chance to learn the plants' behaviors—whether they spread too fast; require staking; feel at home with your property's climate; demand little attention or much care; and, perhaps most important, produce flowers of the color, size,

Planting Container-Grown Perennials

Dig a hole slightly larger than the plant's rootball. *Then tap the bottom of the pot to loosen the plant and slide it out. With your fingers, fluff out the roots. If the plant is severely root-bound, use a knife to cut an inch or two into the rootball from its base (left).*

Without disturbing the top of the rootball, *carefully pull apart the two lower sections and tease loose as many roots as possible with your fingertips.*

Place the plant in the prepared hole, *spreading the roots out all around (left). Make sure the base of the plant is level with the surrounding soil. Fill the hole with soil, tamp it down, then water thoroughly and mulch.*

and shape you expected. You also can judge how the colors, flower shapes, and foliage types of different plants work next to each other before taking the trouble to establish them in your garden.

Siting Your Plants

Even with a garden plan to guide you, there still remains the process of actually placing individual plants for best effect. To achieve a natural, unforced look, start with an area you have marked off for a single variety, and try to site the plants randomly rather than in a straight line or some other rigid formation. It also helps to work with an odd number of plants—three, five, or seven is best.

Allow enough space between the plants to afford them room to grow and to enjoy good air circulation—important for preventing lingering dampness in flowers and foliage, which can lead to disease. Perennials that are difficult to transplant successfully when mature, such as peonies and wild (false) indigo, should be given even more space to spread out than other plants.

When to Plant

As a rule, bare-root perennials should be planted at a time that will give them a chance to establish themselves before they have to face extremes of weather. This means, usually, in the spring or fall. Most larger, container-grown plants can be planted anytime during the growing season and into the fall.

Late-season bloomers such as asters, phlox, and chrysanthemums should be planted in the spring. They need time to become firmly rooted before they can direct their energy toward flowering later in the season. For the same reason, Oriental poppies, peonies, and other early-blooming perennials should be planted in the fall for flowering the following

A FIRST-YEAR GARDEN IN FULL FLOWER
Delphiniums and foxgloves give way to yellow chamomile, dahlias, and violet sage at the front of this new 7-by-20-foot Maine border. Planted in ready-to-bloom condition, these perennials were all grown first in the gardener's own nursery bed. Annuals and biennials filled the bare spots in the bed with color.

THE DAYLILY—A PERENNIAL FOR ALL CONDITIONS
A member of a vast and hardy genus, this Hemerocallis 'Cherry Cheeks', with its 6-inch flowers on 28-inch stalks, will flourish in almost any soil. Daylilies are robust spreaders, but they are not invasive. To keep them in check, divide them about every 3 years.

spring. Hostas, pachysandra, and other foliage plants can be planted anytime, because their flowers are not their main attraction.

In regions colder than Zone 6, limit the planting of bare-root perennials to the spring so that the plants will have the summer and fall to establish deep roots before the cold sets in. Container-grown plants, however, will tolerate fall planting well if you follow up with a mulch of pine needles or salt hay to protect the roots from extreme cold over the winter.

Conversely, in the warmest zones it is best to plant bare-root perennials in the fall, giving them time to take hold before the heat of summer arrives. Container-grown plants will tolerate a spring planting if they are protected by a good mulch, which will shield the roots from the effects of extreme heat by moderating ground temperatures. Be careful not to let the mulch touch the crown, stem, or any low-growing leaves of the plants.

Planting in midsummer is not recommended, but if you must, water the soil a few days before you dig so that it will be slightly moist. After planting, water the site well, apply mulch, and keep the plants shaded from the sun for the first few days. Whatever the season, your perennials will have an easier time of it if you plant them on an overcast day.

Holding Bare-Roots for Planting

Occasionally a spring shipment of bare-root plants arrives before the soil has thawed and dried out enough to cultivate. If that happens, or if for some other reason you are unable to put the plants into the ground immediately, it is essential to keep their roots moist and covered until they are to be planted. Even the best care won't preserve bare-root perennials out of the soil for more than about 2 weeks, however. If you are delayed in planting beyond that time, pot the plants temporarily in a good growing medium such as moist sawdust, moist finished compost, or leaf mold, and set them in a cool, shady spot. You won't need to worry about the plants' roots drying out, and, in addition, potting helps get growth under way.

Heeling In Bare-Roots

Another method for holding plants until you are ready to plant them in the garden is "heeling in." An acclimatization process, heeling in is recommended only if the cold weather—and any chance of hard frost—has passed.

To heel in plants, you need to find a sheltered spot outdoors. Dig a narrow, shallow trench and lay the plants across it so that their crowns are at ground level and their roots are spread out in the trench. The plants can be placed side by side—spacing does not matter. After positioning the plants, water the roots, cover them with soil, and gently tamp the soil in place. This not only will keep your bare-root plants alive but will also give them a head start on becoming accustomed to outdoor living. Remember, though, that this is only a temporary procedure and that when the plants show signs of growing, you must dig them out and put them into the garden or nursery bed without delay.

Planting Tips

Planting can be hard work, but you need not do all of it in one day. Have the soil ready for the plants before you dig the holes; to keep roots from drying out, unpot, unwrap, or unearth each perennial just before you place it in the hole. If you are cultivating a new bed, loosen and amend the soil as needed *(pages 36-43).* When introducing new plants into an existing bed, you may wish to mix some fertilizer into the soil before digging holes for your plants. Use a product that blends organic ingredients such as dehydrated manure, blood meal, bone meal, and sunflower meal with minerals such as phosphate and potassium.

Planting depth will depend on the type of perennial and whether it is container grown or bare-root. Container-grown plants are set at the same depth at which they were growing in the pot. With few exceptions, bare-root perennials are planted with the crown—the point at which any dormant stems or new growth emerges—flush with the soil *(exceptions, page 45).* Finally, mark every spot where you have set a plant. If you trust your memory, you may find yourself digging into and ruining some slow starters when you are hoeing weeds or starting other plants.

Hemming In Fast Spreaders

Cut the bottom out of a 10-gallon or larger plastic pot—other containers, *such as old buckets with the bottoms cut out or holes punched in them for drainage, will also do. Then dig a hole large enough to hold all but the top inch or so of the container. Place the empty container in the hole and pour in just enough soil to bring the top of the plant's rootball level with the ground. Place the plant in the container, fill in around it with soil, and tamp the soil down. Water thoroughly, then mulch to hide the exposed rim of the pot.*

Perennials That Need Controlling

Achillea millefolium (common yarrow)
Ajuga (bugleweed)
Artemisia pontica (Roman wormwood)
Campanula glomerata (clustered bellflower)
Coreopsis rosea (pink coreopsis)
Coreopsis verticillata (threadleaf coreopsis)
Eupatorium coelestinum (hardy ageratum)
***Lysimachia* spp.** (loosestrife)
Macleaya cordata (plume poppy)
Monarda didyma (bee balm)
Physostegia virginiana (false dragonhead)
Polygonatum multiflorum (European Solomon's-seal)
Polygonatum odoratum thunbergii 'Variegatum' (fragrant Solomon's-seal)
Verbascum (mullein)

Note: *The abbreviation "spp." stands for the plural of "species"; where used in lists it means that many, but not all, of the species in a genus meet the criterion of the list.*

A Garden Sampler

Tall and spiky or low, lush, and spreading, perennials come in many colors, shapes, sizes, and textures. Such a rich palette can be used to design an infinite variety of gardens, from a unique, free-form prairie garden (pages 52-53) to the classic, formal bed known as the English border (pages 58-59). Whatever shape the garden takes, by combining different plant varieties you can create a succession of vivid colors throughout the growing season as one plant flowers to take the place of another. And because perennials are adaptable, hardy, and need no more than minimal maintenance, you may spend more time enjoying your garden than working in it.

A selection of perennial gardens appears on the following pages; for a list of plants and a planting guide for each garden, see pages 62-65.

A GARDEN WITH OLD-FASHIONED CHARM
Brightly colored daylilies, a low-growing prostrate blue spruce, and pinkish purple summer phlox border a rustic footbridge in this Virginia country garden.

VIVID NATIVES IN A NATURAL GARDEN
Yellow lance coreopsis, purple coneflower, orange-yellow zexmenia, and other native perennials flank the limestone steps that lead up through the front yard of a northeast Texas home. Originally a lawn, the yard was stripped of its grass to create this low-maintenance natural garden, which provides color from March until November.

A FRONT-YARD PRAIRIE GARDEN
A miniature prairie thrives in a dry, sunny location at a house in Milwaukee. Chosen for their hardiness and drought resistance as well as their contrasting leaf forms, indigenous plants such as rattlesnake master (foreground, with white flower balls) and blackroot (tall with spiky tops) require almost no maintenance and bloom in succession all summer; flower heads and seed stalks are left on the plants as food for wildlife.

PLEASING SHAPES AND COLORS IN A COOL WOODLAND GARDEN
Graceful pink and white bleeding hearts mingle with wild blue phlox to add bright splashes of color to this shady Virginia garden. Perfect for areas that get little sunlight, these perennials, with their delicate blossoms and the varied color, shape, and texture of their leaves, evoke a lush woodland setting—right down to the layer of natural pine-bark mulch. To help keep the flowers blooming from spring through midsummer, the shade garden is fertilized once a year.

A SLICE OF THE DESERT SOUTHWEST
Yellow desert marigold and purple moss verbena, planted among swaths of crushed rock and river-washed stones, re-create the informal look of the desert Southwest in this Arizona border. These brilliant spring-flowering perennials hold up well in hot, dry climates. Other native plants contribute a variety of shapes and textures to the garden, including the cut lengths of ocotillo cane in the background, which will in time take root and create a living fence. The bed is mulched with ground fir bark and requires very little care.

A SUNNY YELLOW DESERT PALETTE
The broad strokes of yellow in this New Mexico high desert garden, created with lance coreopsis, moonshine yarrow, and ice plant, are punctuated by the silver gray foliage of white sage and the red spikes of beardlip penstemon. The perennials flower from mid-May until late October; the evergreens bordering the garden contribute year-round interest.

YEAR-LONG COLOR IN AN ENGLISH-STYLE BORDER
Spiky purple Mexican bush sage, purple Peruvian verbena, and pink gloxinia penstemon contribute to the cascade of color in this gently sloped California border garden. Designed in the tradition of a romantic English border, the garden blooms throughout the year. Roses and herbs are planted among the perennials to create interesting textures while maintaining color harmony and progression. For all of its showy good looks, this garden requires relatively little attention: Dead flower heads are removed once a week, and the entire garden is fertilized once a month. The plants are also mulched with redwood shavings to which nitrogen has been added.

A GARDEN THAT GLOWS IN MOONLIGHT
Cool and inviting after the heat of a summer day, this white, green, and silver Alabama garden casts a pale glow in the evening or on a moonlit night. The luminous effect is created by a variety of perennials, including summer-blooming daisylike Japanese asters (far right foreground) and airy stalks of rose campion (right, center of border), that flower among dense silver and green foliage for up to nine months of the year. Although the lines of the borders are formal, they are softened by an overhanging edging of velvety gray-leaved lamb's ears, mingled with white pansies and snow-in-summer. Simple and elegant, the garden can be maintained with a weekly weeding, by deadheading three times a week, and by thinning the plants in autumn.

A Guide to the Gardens

COUNTRY GARDEN
pages 50-51

A. *Hemerocallis fulva 'Europa'* (3)
B. *Hemerocallis 'Stella de Oro'* (5)
C. *Hemerocallis 'Hyperion'* (3)
D. *Hemerocallis 'Ed Murray'* (3)
E. *Miscanthus japonicus* (7)
F. *Miscanthus floridulus* (7)
G. *Phlox paniculata* (9)
H. *Hemerocallis aurantiaca* (5)
I. *Picea pungens 'Glauca Prostrata'* (1)
J. *Juniperus x chinensis 'Hetzii'* (1)
K. *Macleaya cordata* (3)

NATURAL GARDEN
page 52

A. *Phlox pilosa* (3)
B. *Echinacea purpurea* (6)
C. *Coreopsis lanceolata* (6)
D. *Callirhoe involucrata* (1)
E. *Alstroemeria pulchella (A. psittacina)* (1)
F. *Wedelia hispida (zexmenia)* (1)
G. *Tradescantia ohiensis* (1)
H. *Engelmannia pinnatifida* (3)
I. *Physostegia virginiana* (1)
J. *Achillea millefolium* (3)
K. *Berlandiera texana* (1)
L. *Thalictrum dasycarpum* (2)

PRAIRIE GARDEN
pages 52-53

A. *Echinacea purpurea* (9)
B. *Veronicastrum virginicum* (18)
C. *Eryngium yuccifolium* (12)
D. *Rhus aromatica* (20)
E. *Euphorbia corollata* (14)
F. *Vibernum prunifolium* (1)
G. *Clematis texensis 'Duchess of Albany'* (1)

WOODLAND GARDEN
pages 54-55

A. *Dicentra eximia* (1)
B. *Phlox divaricata* (2)
C. *Polygonatum odoratum thunbergii 'Variegatum'* (1)
D. *Dicentra spectabilis* (1)
E. *Dicentra spectabilis 'Alba'* (1)

Note:The key lists each plant type and the total quantity needed to replicate the garden shown. The diagram's letters and numbers refer to the type of plant and the number sited in an area.

ARIZONA DESERT GARDEN
pages 56-57

A. *Verbena tenuisecta* (10)
B. *Yucca elata* (1)
C. *Baileya multiradiata* (3)
D. *Aloe barbadensis* (3)
E. *Fouquieria splendens* (several)
F. *Verbena peruviana* (1)

NEW MEXICO DESERT GARDEN
page 57

A. *Artemisia ludoviciana* (3)
B. *Coreopsis lanceolata* (6)
C. *Achillea taygetea 'Moonshine'* (8)
D. *Cerastium tomentosum* (8)
E. *Delosperma nubigenum* (11)
F. *Santolina chamaecyparissus* (5)
G. *Stachys lanata* (3)
H. *Delosperma cooperi* (5)
I. *Nepeta x faassenii* (3)
J. *Helianthus maximiliani* (6)
K. *Festuca ovina var. glauca* (5)
L. *Penstemon pinifolius* (7)
M. *Miscanthus sinensis 'Gracillimus'* (1)
N. *Caryopteris x clandonensis* (3)
O. *Achillea filipendulina* (3)
P. *Penstemon barbatus* (5)
Q. *Penstemon strictus* (7)

ENGLISH BORDER
pages 58-59

A. *Penstemon gloxinioides 'Firebird'* (6)
B. *Salvia leucantha* (2)
C. *Iris 'Babbling Brook'* (2)
D. *Erigeron karvinskianus* (6)
E. *Convolvulus cneorum* (3)
F. *Verbena peruviana* (3)
G. *Dianthus caryophyllus* (2)
H. *Oenothera berlandieri* (4)
I. *Lobelia erinus* (1)
J. *Stachys byzantina* (2)
K. *Penstemon gloxinioides 'Midnight'* (2)
L. *Chrysanthemum maximum* (2)
M. *Penstemon gloxinioides 'Apple Blossom'* (1)
N. *Rosa sp. 'Cl. First Class Prize'* (1)
O. *Aquilegia x hybrida ('McKana Hybrids')* (12)
P. *Rosa sp. 'The Reeve'* (2)
Q. *Rosa sp. 'Fair Bianca'* (1)
R. *Rosa sp. 'Mary Austin'* (1)
S. *Rosa sp. 'Graham Thomas'* (1)
T. *Rosmarinus officinalis* (1)
U. *Limonium perezii* (3)

MOON GARDEN
pages 60-61

A. *Lychnis coronaria 'Alba'* (12)
B. *Campanula latiloba (C. persicifolia) 'Alba'* (3)
C. *Salvia greggii 'Alba'* (1)
D. *Viola 'Crystal Bowl'* (18)
E. *Asteromoea mongolica* (18)
F. *Stachys byzantina* (24)
G. *Senecio 'New Look'* (2)
H. *Cerastium tomentosum* (4)
I. *Veronica spicata 'Icicle'* (3)
J. *Phlox maculata 'Miss Lingard'* (6)

Note:The key lists each plant type and the total quantity needed to replicate the garden shown. The diagram's letters and numbers refer to the type of plant and the number sited in an area.

Maintaining Your Garden

If soil is properly prepared and planting is done correctly, a perennial garden should require little upkeep. The one shown at left, in Los Angeles, is filled with many heat- and drought-tolerant plants and is covered with a layer of gravel mulch to conserve water.

Watering, fertilizing, and mulching will give the plants the moisture and nutrients they need to mature and blossom. Staking, pruning, and weeding keep a border looking its best. And checking for pests and diseases that can disfigure or destroy plants (pages 96-103) is also part of the maintenance regimen.

In areas of the country where the ground alternately freezes and thaws, the approach of winter calls for putting down a protective mulch on newly planted beds (page 71). But whatever the winter weather, most perennials should be cut to the ground at the end of the growing season. The exceptions, including evergreen perennials and chrysanthemums, should be left standing to protect the crowns of the plants from frost, wind, and sun.

A. ***Lobularia maritima (many)*** **B.** ***Eschscholzia californica (1)*** **C.** ***Stachys byzantina (1)*** **D.** ***Achillea millefolium) (many)*** **E.** ***Stipa tenacissima (1)*** **F.** ***Pennisetum setaceum 'Cupreum' (3)*** **G.** ***Oenothera berlandieri (many)*** **H.** ***Alcea rosea 'Chater's Double' (1)*** **I.** ***Salvia leucantha (1)*** **J.** ***Salvia chaemaedryoides (3)*** **K.** ***Linum grandiflorum 'Rubrum' (1)*** **L.** ***Artemisia 'Powis Castle' (1)*** **M.** ***Verbena bipinnatifida (many)***

Note: The key lists each plant type and the total quantity needed to replicate the garden shown. The diagram's letters and numbers refer to the type of plant and the number sited in an area.

Routine Care for Your Perennials

A garden presents many chores, but not all are time-consuming or labor-intensive. A weekly watering, a daily check for weeds, and periodic mulching and fertilizing are all that's needed to keep the garden in top shape.

Water Needs

As a rule of thumb, perennials require from 1 to 1½ inches of water, either from rainfall or from watering, every 7 to 10 days. Drought-tolerant plants *(opposite)* survive on less and may actually be damaged by too much water; plants that are adapted to moist soils may need more. In all cases, water only as needed. Persistent overwatering can suffocate roots and kill them.

Tools for Watering

For most gardens a simple low-flow overhead sprinkler head, *like the one illustrated at left, is a good choice. It should release water at a rate of only about 1 inch in a 6-hour period, approximating a gentle rain.*

In areas of summer drought, *use a soaker hose made out of recycled tires (left) rather than an overhead sprinkler. Attached to a regular garden hose, it lets water seep out of pinpoint holes into the ground. For a narrow planting, snake the soaker hose down the center of the bed. Cover the bed with mulch both to conserve water and to conceal the hose.*

When to Water

Before watering, dig a hole 2 inches deep to check your soil's moisture level. If only the top inch is dry, don't water. If the soil is dry to a depth of 1½ to 2 inches, it's time to water.

A long, slow soaking is best. Depending on your soil type, the kind of watering device you have, and the water pressure, it may take 6 hours or more to deliver the recommended inch of moisture to your plants' deepest roots. Aim to deposit water at the rate of no more than 1 inch in 6 hours; watering any faster could cause wasteful runoff.

It is all right to water at any time of the day if your irrigation method emits water close to soil level. If you are using an overhead sprinkler and conserving water is a concern, some experts advise watering in early morning, rather than in the heat of the day, to reduce evaporation.

Choosing a Watering Device

A low-flow sprinkler *(left, top)* that approximates a gentle rain is the simplest and least expensive watering device. It is often said that overhead sprinkling causes diseases and mildew. But if perennials are watered as recommended—slowly, deeply, and infrequently—such problems rarely occur.

Soaker hoses and drip-irrigation systems release water directly into the soil. These devices are preferable for areas prone to summer drought such as California and Texas and also for beds too narrow to be sprinkled without a lot of waste.

Perennials That Can Survive Up to Four Weeks without Watering

Acanthus
(bear's-breech)
Achillea
(yarrow)
Allium
(flowering onion)
Amsonia
(bluestar)
Anaphalis
(pearly everlasting)
Anthemis
(golden marguerite)
Aquilegia
(columbine)
Arenaria
(sandwort)
Artemisia
(wormwood)
Aruncus
(goatsbeard)
Asclepias
(milkweed)
Aster
(aster)
Aurinia
(basket-of-gold)
Baptisia
(wild indigo)
Belamcanda
(blackberry lily)
Campanula
(bellflower)
Centranthus
(red valerian)
Ceratostigma
(plumbago)
Coreopsis
(tickseed)
Dianthus
(pinks)
Echinops
(globe thistle)
Epimedium
(barrenwort)
Eryngium
(sea holly)
Gaillardia
(blanket-flower)
Geranium
(cranesbill)
Hemerocallis
(daylily)
Iberis
(candytuft)
Iris
(iris)
Kniphofia
(torch lily)
Lavandula
(lavender)
Liatris
(gay-feather)
Limonium
(sea lavender)
Lupinus
(lupine)
Macleaya
(plume poppy)
Nepeta
(catmint)
Oenothera
(evening primrose)
Papaver
(poppy)
Pennisetum
(fountain grass)
Perovskia
(Russian sage)
Physostegia
(false dragonhead)
Platycodon
(balloon flower)
Potentilla
(cinquefoil)
Rudbeckia
(coneflower)
Salvia
(sage)
Sedum
(stonecrop)
Solidago
(goldenrod)
Verbascum
(mullein)

Evening Primrose

Controlling Weeds

The best way to keep weeding to a minimum is to weed thoroughly before planting and to mulch afterward *(page 71)*. As the perennials fill out the bed, fewer weeds will appear because the plants shade the soil and prevent them from growing.

Early in the season, remove emerging weeds to make sure none sets seed. Sometimes simply pulling the weed out by hand will be sufficient, but if it is large or has brittle roots or a long taproot, it should be dug out to ensure that no piece is left in the ground to sprout. Take care not to hit the crown of any nearby perennial; nicks in this vulnerable area, where the stem and the roots meet, are often entry points for fungus and bacteria infections.

Make frequent checks for weeds at the base of the plants, where the mulch is thinnest. A new crop of weeds may spring up

Watering Correctly

The frequent application of small quantities of water creates *shallow-rooted plants with weak, leggy stems, like those of the aster illustrated above.*

Thorough but infrequent watering, *at least 6 hours every 7 to 10 days, produces perennials with deep roots, lush foliage, and plentiful blossoms. Such plants are more drought tolerant and resist winter injury.*

after a rain or a routine watering and should be removed promptly. To avoid spreading weeds around the garden, always throw them into the trash, not into the compost pile, if they've set seed.

The Right Way to Mulch

***Spread a 2- to 4-inch layer of organic mulch** on your bed, taking care to keep it an inch or so from the crown of each plant, where the stem and the root meet. Mulch piled against the crown may foster rot.*

When to Fertilize

If the soil has been adequately prepared *(pages 36-43)* and an organic mulch *(chart, right)* applied over the bed, plants shouldn't need much fertilizing; one application of organic fertilizer before the growing season begins will usually be enough. Supplement that with a second application in midsummer or early fall if plants show stunted growth, yellowing leaves, or small, sparse flowers. Instead of using a granular fertilizer on a flagging perennial, give the plant a quick, temporary boost by sprinkling or lightly spraying its leaves with a liquid infusion of seaweed or fish emulsion.

Fertilizing should be done with a light hand, especially in the case of chemical fertil-

***AN OAKLEAF MULCH** The layer of oak leaves spread among the hostas, ferns, yellow-flowered sedum, and low-growing ajuga (foreground) in a Baton Rouge, Louisiana, garden keeps weeds down and the soil moist. As the leaf mulch decays, it also supplies the perennials with nutrients.*

	TYPE OF ORGANIC MULCH											
	COMPOST	SHREDDED LEAVES	SHREDDED BARK	HAY OR STRAW	GRASS CLIPPINGS	NEWSPAPERS	PINE NEEDLES	SEAWEEDS	FRUIT POMACE	PEANUT HULLS	COCOA HULLS	WOODCHIPS
SUPPRESSES WEEDS	✔	✔	✔	✔	✔	✔	✔	✔	✔	✔	✔	✔
KEEPS SOIL COOL	✔	✔	✔	✔			✔	✔	✔	✔	✔	
CONDITIONS SOIL	✔	✔	✔	✔	✔		✔	✔	✔	✔	✔	
FERTILIZES SOIL	✔	✔		✔	✔			✔	✔			
BEAUTIFIES BEDS	✔	✔	✔		✔		✔			✔	✔	✔
KEEPS SOIL MOIST	✔	✔	✔	✔	✔	✔	✔	✔	✔	✔	✔	✔
ADDS HUMUS	✔	✔	✔	✔	✔		✔	✔	✔	✔	✔	

Materials not to use: sawdust, ashes, fresh manures, grass clippings from lawns treated with herbicides, etc. (anything toxic).

izers, which can burn roots. In addition, a nitrogen-rich fertilizer, whether chemical or organic, can cause excess vegetative growth and, as a consequence, make staking necessary *(pages 72-74)*. Be especially sparing with chemical fertilizers late in the season, since a burst of growth then may not have time to mature and will be damaged by winter cold.

Beneficial, Attractive Mulch

A covering of organic mulch conserves water, discourages weeds, adds humus and nutrients to the soil, and gives a finished appearance to your bed or border. Gravel and crushed stone can also be used as mulches, but they provide virtually no nutrients. Black plastic and woven landscape fabrics are excellent for thwarting weed growth but are unattractive; they are best reserved for the vegetable garden.

Depending on the height of your plants, a layer of mulch 2 to 3 inches thick is sufficient if you are using a fine-textured mulch. In the case of a bulkier mulch, such as woodchips, layer the mulch 4 to 6 inches deep. Replenish the mulch as it decays and thins during the growing season. This is especially important in the South, where the high heat and humidity accelerate the decomposition process.

A Mulch for Winter

In areas where the ground alternately freezes and thaws in winter, apply a winter mulch to newly planted beds after the soil has frozen in order to keep the temperature constant; otherwise, the expansion and contraction may heave a plant out of the ground, breaking the roots and exposing them to freezing air. The best choices for winter mulching are airy materials such as pine boughs, straw, and salt hay, laid down over what remains of the permanent mulch.

Where the climate is mild year round, or where snows start early and stay late, a winter mulch isn't necessary. Snow, far from being harmful, is actually the best natural winter protection for perennials.

In early spring, move the winter mulch away from the crowns of the plants when the first new sprouts appear. Remove the mulch completely only after the danger of a hard frost has passed.

Staking Perennials to Add Support

The majority of perennials have stems that are strong enough to remain erect when their blossoms open. Nevertheless, you may find that in some cases you will need to devise simple supports to keep your plants standing upright and the garden looking orderly.

Why Plants Fall Over

In general, plants over 2 feet in height are more likely to need such support—or staking—especially those with large, heavy blossoms. A severe thunderstorm can easily flatten top-heavy plants to the ground and snap off the blooms. Also, recently planted perennials that haven't had time to develop sturdy stems may need temporary support until they become established.

However, an apparent need for staking may actually indicate a separate problem. Weak stems, for example, may be a sign that the plants need better care. In the case of an old, overgrown clump, division may be the solution *(pages 80-85)*. Other common sources of trouble include overwatering and a soil oversupplied with nitrogen and deficient in phosphorus and potassium.

Location also plays a role. Plants exposed to wind will be more susceptible to toppling than those in a sheltered spot, and a sun-loving plant set in the shade may grow lanky and lean toward the light. In either case, transplanting when the perennials are dormant should help solve the problem.

Staking Methods

When staking is necessary, pick a method matched to the perennial's growth habit. Use single stakes to brace the unbranched stems

Three Ways to Stake

1. For a single-stemmed perennial, *use a stake about three-fourths the mature plant's height. Loop twine around the stem halfway up and tie it to the stake (left).*

2. When the plant is about two-thirds grown, *add another loop of twine above the first one. Add a third tie at the base of the flower head when it is about to bloom (far left).*

When a bushy perennial is several inches tall, *cut four or five stakes to the height of the mature plant's foliage and drive them into the ground (below). Loop twine from stake to stake 6 to 8 inches above the ground. When blooms appear, add a tier of twine just below the flowers.*

TWO UNOBTRUSIVE FRAMEWORKS
The foliage and blossoms of blue bellflowers and white feverfew hide the bamboo stakes that keep them from sprawling (left). In the photograph below, a framework of twiggy branches is barely visible beneath a stand of yellow yarrow.

To stake a fine-textured perennial such as baby's-breath (above), *choose several twiggy branches about 6 inches shorter than the plant's mature height and sharpen their ends. Push the branches into the ground around the plant, angling them toward its center.*

of tall perennials such as pompon, cushion, and decorative chrysanthemums and the delphinium illustrated overleaf. Bamboo canes, a half-inch in diameter and painted green, are ideal for blending in with the foliage of a fully grown plant, although steel stakes, sometimes coated with dark green plastic, are also available.

Push the cane gently into the ground beside the stem; if the stem's natural inclination is to bend a little, angle the stake to follow it. Use twine, which may be green or tan colored, to tie the stem to its support—or you may use raffia fiber, paper- or plastic-coated thin wire, or green-tinted plastic gardening tape, which is slightly elastic. Knot the twine around the stake, securing it tightly, then loop the twine loosely around the plant so that it does not constrict the stem.

For dense, bushy perennials such as heliopsis, Shasta daisies, and peonies, you can buy wire hoops or frames at garden centers. These supports are circular, square, or rectangular in shape, with three or four long legs. When the clump of growing foliage is about a foot tall, place the support over the plant and push its legs several inches into the ground until the frame is at the height of the plant growth.

A homemade frame of twine and stakes *(page 72)* is just as effective and much less expensive than wire hoops. For groups of spiky perennials such as delphiniums, you may choose to stake them on a frame rather than tie each stem individually. Simply use four or five canes that are about three-fourths as tall as you expect the plant to grow, and push them into the ground around each cluster. As flowers begin to bloom, tie twine to the stakes at height intervals of 12 inches and weave it among the stems.

For staking bushy plants and for baby's-breath and other fine-textured perennials, try using twiggy branches *(page 73)*. Birch, oak, buddleia, and vitex are good choices.

When to Stake

The key to successful, unobtrusive staking is planning ahead. Put the stakes in place early in the season, while the plant is still growing upright and before flower buds appear. As the plant fills out, its foliage will hide the stakes *(page 73, top)*.

TIPS FROM THE PROS

André Viette, an internationally known horticulturist and past president of the Perennial Plant Association, grows more than 3,000 varieties of perennials at his nursery in Fishersville, Virginia. He doesn't stake any of them. Weak stems, he says, are often the product of improper watering and fertilizing. Viette recommends watering deeply, rather than lightly and more frequently, and favors organic fertilizer *(pages 70-71)* that is high in phosphorus and low in nitrogen.

Other ways that experienced gardeners circumvent the task of staking include:

-Cutting back tall-growing perennials such as asters when they are about half grown to limit their ultimate height.

-Planting a support of strong-stemmed annuals such as larkspur among newly planted perennials with still-floppy, immature stems.

-Designing a perennial border to have a cottage-garden look, suitable for plants with sprawling, informal growth habits.

-Choosing tall perennials with sturdy stems that don't need staking. This group includes:

Aconitum napellus (monkshood)
Artemisia lactiflora (white mugwort)
Aruncus dioicus (goatsbeard)
***Astilbe* x *arendsii* 'Professor Weilen'** (astilbe)
Dictamnus albus (gas plant)
Echinacea purpurea (purple coneflower)
Hemerocallis cultivars (daylily)
Iris sibirica cultivars (Siberian iris)
Liatris pycnostachya (gay-feather, blazing star)
***Ligularia stenocephala* 'The Rocket'** (narrow-spiked ligularia)
Macleaya cordata (plume poppy)
Miscanthus sinensis cultivars (eulalia)
Perovskia atriplicifolia (Russian sage)

Matching the Method to the Plant

TALL FLOWER STEMS:
Single Stakes

Chrysanthemum (pompon, cushion, decorative)
Delphinium (*elatum* hybrids)
Digitalis (foxglove)

BUSHY PLANTS:
Stakes and Twine or Twiggy Branches

***Anchusa azurea* 'Dropmore'** (bugloss)
Aster novae-angliae (New England aster)
Campanula lactiflora (milky bell-flower)
Centaurea montana (cornflower)
Chrysanthemum morifolium (florist's chrysanthemum)
Chrysanthemum nipponicum (Nippon daisy)
Chrysanthemum parthenium (feverfew)
Chrysanthemum* x *superbum (Shasta daisy)
***Clematis heracleifolia* 'Davidiana'** (clematis)
Gaillardia* x *grandiflora (blanket-flower)
***Helenium autumnale* 'Bruno', 'Riverton Beauty'** (sneezeweed)
Helianthus* x *multiflorus (sunflower)
Heliopsis (false sunflower)
Paeonia lactiflora (peony)
Salvia azurea* ssp. *pitcheri (sage)
Solidago (goldenrod)
Thalictrum delavayi (Yunnan meadow rue)
Thalictrum rochebrunianum (lavender mist meadow rue)
Thalictrum speciosissimum (dusty meadow rue)

FINE-TEXTURED PLANTS:
Twiggy Branches

Achillea millefolium (yarrow)
***Clematis integrifolia* 'Caerulea'** (clematis)
***Coreopsis grandiflora* 'Badengold', 'Mayfield Giant'** (tickseed)
***Gypsophila paniculata* 'Bristol Fairy', 'Perfecta'** (baby's-breath)
Limonium (sea lavender, statice)
Linum (flax)
Physostegia (false dragonhead)
***Veronica latifolia* 'Crater Lake Blue'** (speedwell)

'Fanfare' Delphinium

Enhancing the Bloom

Applying a handful of special pruning techniques at the right time and to the right plant will increase the number or size of the blooms your perennials produce. Such methods—including pinching, thinning, disbudding, deadheading, and cutting back—variously keep a plant looking its best and direct energy that would otherwise be expended on seed production into creating more flowers.

Many perennials benefit from a combination of pruning methods. When delphiniums are in bloom, for example, deadheading, or removing faded blossoms, prolongs the display. When flowering stops, cutting back the stalks to the rosette of leaves at the base of each plant makes the plants look neater and often stimulates a second flowering.

Why Deadhead?

Removing individual flowers or flower clusters as they begin to droop and fade is an important chore, and not for appearance alone. Some perennials, such as pincushion flower and Stokes' aster, may stop blooming if they aren't attended to promptly, and a hybrid perennial allowed to go to seed may in time be crowded out by its inferior offspring.

Not all perennials require deadheading—the blossoms of linums, geraniums, and pen-

Pinching Stem Tips

Using your fingers, pinch off emergent stem tips just above the topmost unfurled leaves. *The net result will be three or four new branches, smaller but more plentiful flowers, and a stockier plant. This technique works well with plants that can develop numerous stems and buds, and that look attractive when bushy. Chrysanthemums can be pinched two or three times, up until the flower buds develop.*

Perennials to Pinch

Anaphalis
(pearly everlasting)
Anthemis
(golden marguerite)
Artemisia
(wormwood)
Aster
(aster)
Boltonia
(boltonia)
Centaurea
(cornflower)
Chrysanthemum morifolium
(florist's chrysanthemum)
Chrysanthemum nipponicum
(Nippon daisy)
Chrysanthemum* x *superbum
(Shasta daisy)
Echinacea
(purple coneflower)
Erigeron
(fleabane)
Eupatorium
(boneset)
Gaillardia
(blanket-flower)
Gillenia
(bowman's root)
Heliopsis
(false sunflower)
Nepeta
(catmint)
Perovskia
(Russian sage)
Phlox paniculata
(summer phlox)
Physostegia
(false dragonhead)

Deadheading Spent Flowers

For perennials with flowers at the tips of leafy stems, cut just below the fading flowers (right) to stimulate new buds. For plants with leafy flower stems and a rosette of leaves at the base of the plant, cut back to just above the topmost unopened bud. If there are no buds, cut the stem off just above the foliage rosette. For perennials with bare stems, cut off close to the ground to encourage new growth.

Perennials to Deadhead

Achillea
(yarrow)
Anthemis
(golden marguerite)
Armeria
(thrift, sea pink)
Campanula
(bellflower)
Centaurea
(cornflower)
Chrysanthemum morifolium
(florist's chrysanthemum)
Chrysanthemum* x *superbum
(Shasta daisy)
Delphinium
(delphinium)
Digitalis
(foxglove)
Echinops
(globe thistle)
Eupatorium
(boneset)
Gaillardia
(blanket-flower)
Heuchera
(alumroot)
Lobelia
(cardinal flower)
Nepeta
(catmint)
Penstemon
(beardtongue)
Phlox paniculata
(summer phlox)
Platycodon
(balloon flower)
Salvia
(sage)
Scabiosa
(pincushion flower)
Sidalcea
(false mallow)
Stokesia
(Stokes' aster)
Verbena
(verbena)
Veronica
(speedwell)

stemons, for instance, fall off by themselves. Others, such as rudbeckia and 'Autumn Joy' sedum, have ornamental seed heads that enliven a garden in the fall and winter *(below)*.

Pinching for More Blooms

Perennials that bloom in midsummer or later benefit from having their stem tips pinched back early in the growing season. In response to pinching, a stem produces several branches that together may yield double or even triple the number of blooms on an unpinched stem. The technique also makes plants shorter and more compact—and thus less likely to need staking.

Pinching carried out early in the growing season has little or no effect on a plant's blooming schedule. If, however, you want to delay a plant's flowering, pinching in midsummer is desirable. The technique is not appropriate for spring perennials because they don't have enough time to form new flower buds before their blooming season ends.

Thinning for Larger Flowers

If you'd prefer fewer but larger flowers to more numerous, smaller ones, remove up to a third of the plant's stems, cutting them off at the base. Perennials that bloom in midsummer should be thinned in early spring, and

'Autumn Joy' Sedum and Eulalia

Coneflower and Fountain Grass

Eulalia

A Reason Not to Deadhead

The following perennials have attractive seed heads that will enhance the garden in fall or winter:

Acanthus
(bear's-breech)
Allium
(flowering onion)
Aruncus
(goatsbeard)
Asclepias
(milkweed)
Astilbe
(astilbe)
Baptisia
(wild indigo)
Belamcanda
(blackberry lily)
Calamagrostis
(reed grass)
Dictamnus
(gas plant)
Echinacea
(purple coneflower)
Echinops
(globe thistle)
Eupatorium
(boneset)
Iris sibirica
(Siberian iris)
Miscanthus
(eulalia)
Paeonia 'Krinkled White', 'Seashell'
(peony)
Papaver
(poppy)
Pennisetum
(fountain grass)
Perovskia
(Russian sage)
Rudbeckia
(coneflower)
Sedum 'Autumn Joy'
(stonecrop)
Solidago
(goldenrod)

fall bloomers in midsummer. As with pinching, this method isn't suitable for spring bloomers—it merely reduces the number of flowers, with no payoff in size.

Thinning is particularly useful for restoring the display of phlox, sunflower, and rudbeckia that are several seasons old and that, if left unattended, may produce a dense mass of stems with undersized blooms.

Disbudding for Showy Blooms

For peonies, chrysanthemums, and other perennials whose flower buds appear in groups, removing all but the central bud yields a single blue-ribbon blossom *(right)*. This showy flower is likely to make the stem so top-heavy that staking is required *(pages 72-74)*. For a different effect, pinch off the central bud but leave the side buds to develop into a spray.

Cutting Back for Shape, Bloom

Cutting back may be performed at two different times in a perennial's growing cycle, and for different reasons. In both cases, all of the stems should be reduced in height by one-third to one-half. Performed early in the growing season, cutting back results in shorter plants that bloom later than usual. Carried out later in the season, as soon as a plant stops flowering, the shearing stimulates fresh new foliage and, in the case of catmint, bellflowers, and many other perennials, a second wave of bloom.

'Gay Paree' Peony

Removing Side Buds

1. With your thumb and index finger, *pruning shears, or a knife, pinch off all the small side flower buds surrounding the central bud at the tip of each stem (below).*

2. Cut off any other groups of buds and *all side branches along the stem (below, right). Remove any new growth promptly.*

Perennials to Cut Back for a Second Flowering

Achillea millefolium (common yarrow)
Anthemis (chamomile)
Aster x frikartii (Frikart's aster)
Campanula carpatica (Carpathian harebell)
Centranthus (red valerian)
Coreopsis lanceolata (lance coreopsis)
Coreopsis verticillata (threadleaf coreopsis)
Delphinium (delphinium)
Echinops (globe thistle)
Nepeta (catmint)
Phlox paniculata (garden phlox)
Stokesia (Stokes' aster)
Veronica spicata (spike speedwell)

Globe Thistle

CHAPTER FOUR

Propagating Perennials

Healthy gardens are never static, because the plants within them change as they grow. Herbaceous perennials, such as the Siberian iris and astilbe in the Purcellville, Virginia, garden at left, expand and sprawl as they reproduce season after season. Using home-propagation methods, you can gently guide plant-reproduction processes to your advantage.

Propagating perennials not only gives you new plants at no cost and improves the health of the older ones; it also pays dividends in extra flowers. Many perennials bloom most abundantly in the early stages of their lives. As you grow new plants from predecessors whose flower power is waning, you will keep a fine show of flowers in your garden.

The following pages lead you through four propagation techniques. As you experiment, it pays to be philosophical. Not all your efforts will succeed, and many new plants will die aborning. Others, because of genetics, soil chemistry, and angles of light in different areas of the garden, won't look exactly like their parents. But pride will surely replace any initial disappointment when you gaze on the blooming perennials you raised from seed or coaxed from tiny fingerlings of root.

A. *Iris sibirica* 'Fourfold White' (5)
B. *Phlox paniculata* (5)
C. *Astilbe* 'Deutschland' (9)
D. *Iris sibirica* 'Caesar's Brother' (9)
E. *Iris sibirica* 'Dreaming Spires' (9)
F. *Matteuccia struthiopteris* (12)
G. *Rhododendron catawbiense* (7)

Note: The key lists each plant type and the total quantity needed to replicate the garden shown. The diagram's letters and numbers refer to the type of plant and the number sited in an area.

Plant Multiplication the Fast and Easy Way

THE DUSTY PINK BLOOMS OF SEDUM 'AUTUMN JOY' *turn russet in the fall, then stand through the winter as seed-head accents. Trouble free if grown in well-drained soil, sedums are easy to propagate by division or from stem cuttings (pages 86-87).*

Most herbaceous perennials enthusiastically colonize their surroundings, spreading new roots and shoots outward every year. Though their stems and leaves may die back each fall, the roots are dormant through the winter, then thrust out new growth in both roots and shoots every spring. Perennials are slow to mature, and generally spend more than one season growing roots and foliage before they bloom or propagate in any other way. This is the vital habit distinguishing them from the annuals, which throw their energy into growing fast, blooming, and scattering seed in the single season before they die.

Because nurseries have to work with nature's timing, the perennials they propagate and sell must be carefully tended for a year or more before coming to market. This makes perennials a costly crop for nurseries—one reason they carry higher prices than annuals. If you are growing perennials in your garden, however, propagation is already taking place. To propagate your own plants, you have only to take charge of the process.

Propagation by Division

The simplest propagation practice in perennial gardens is division, which takes direct advantage of the plants' tendencies to spread. Division is simply separating young, already rooted offshoots from mature perennials and placing them elsewhere in the garden. The independent plants produced are called divisions, or slips. New plants created by this method develop the same growth traits and flower color as the originals, so you can confidently fill flower beds with your favorites. Another bonus from division is that most slips establish themselves quickly and bloom the same season or the following one.

Dividing for Healthy Plants

Division is also a means of maintaining your mature perennial plantings; many perennials look their best only when regularly divided. Gaillardias and chrysanthemums tend to deteriorate at their centers, while growing actively around the edges. You may wind up with unsightly, dead-looking patches in the midst of your lovely blooming clumps unless you dig the plants out, trim old growth away, and reset new growth in its place.

Other perennials, such as rudbeckia, outgrow their spaces, crowd their neighbors, and make the whole flower bed more susceptible to disease. Division of such plants thins the invaders, permits air to circulate through the bed once more, and lets you develop a colorful new border with your fledgling plants elsewhere in the garden.

Division is also the easiest way to keep some of the shorter-lived perennials growing in your garden year after year. Members of the genus *Dianthus*—sometimes called pinks—generally last only a few years. You must replace the plants with offspring if you want to keep them growing in your garden.

When to Act

Although a few plants, like the globe thistle and the gas plant, will remain the same size in the same place for years, they are exceptions in the world of perennials. Most genera actively grow outward from their centers as they deplete soil nutrients there and develop new roots away from the plants' centers. This pattern produces a natural crisis, and when it arrives, perennials send out clear distress signals. These include a dead, woody portion at the center of the clump, fewer blooms, and fewer stems emerging in the spring. Crowns or rhizomes may be forced out above the surrounding soil, and a plant may grow so large that there is no air space around it in the bed. The remedy is division.

Perennials in need of division should be tackled while they are dormant or growing vegetatively, not when they are preparing to bloom. For most plants, this means early spring to early summer, as soon as the growing crowns can be seen. (Exceptions include plants like doronicum, primrose, iris, and other early-spring bloomers, which should be divided after flowering.) When performing any divisions, work on a cool, cloudy day—it helps keep the plants' roots moist while they are exposed to the air.

How to Begin

Division starts at the roots of the plant, since offshoots must have their own roots already formed if they are to live on their own. The root systems of perennials fall into several categories—fibrous, fleshy, and rhizomatous.

Most perennials have fibrous roots. These resemble slender, outspread fingers, and grow relatively close to the soil surface. A few plant types, notably *Hemerocallis* (daylilies), have thick, fleshy roots that can closely intertwine. Another handful of perennials, including iris, grow from rhizomes—hard, tuberous stems planted just below the soil's surface.

Plants Recommended for Division

FIBROUS ROOTS:
Acanthus (bear's-breech)
****Achillea*** (yarrow)
Ajuga (bugleweed)
Alchemilla (lady's-mantle)
Allium (flowering onion)
Amsonia (bluestar)
****Anchusa*** (bugloss)
Anemone (windflower)
Arabis (rock cress)
Arenaria (sandwort)
Armeria (thrift, sea pink)
****Artemisia*** (wormwood)
Aruncus (goatsbeard)
Astilbe (astilbe, false spirea)
Brunnera (brunnera)
Campanula (bellflower)
****Centaurea*** (knapweed)
Delphinium (delphinium)
****Dianthus*** (pinks)
Dicentra (bleeding heart)
Doronicum (leopard's-bane)
Geranium (cranesbill)
****Geum*** (avens)
Hosta (plantain lily, funkia)
Iris sibirica (Siberian iris)
Lamium (dead nettle)
Ligularia (golden-ray)
Limonium (sea lavender, statice)
Lobelia (cardinal flower)
Lychnis (catchfly, campion)
Monarda (bee balm)
Nepeta (catmint)
****Oenothera*** (sundrop, evening primrose)
Phlox paniculata (summer phlox)
Polygonum (smartweed, knotweed)
Potentilla (cinquefoil, five-finger)
****Primula*** (primrose)
Pulmonaria (lungwort)
****Rudbeckia*** (coneflower)
Sedum (stonecrop)
Smilacina (false Solomon's-seal)
****Solidago*** (goldenrod)
Stachys (lamb's ears)
Stokesia (Stokes' aster)
Thalictrum (meadow rue)
Tricyrtis (toad lily)
Trollius (globeflower)
Veronica (speedwell)
Viola (violet)

FLESHY ROOTS:
Hemerocallis (daylily)
Kniphofia (torch lily, tritoma)

RHIZOMES:
Bergenia (bergenia)
****Iris*** (iris)

**Regular division necessary for health of plants.*

Choose your division method to match the root type of your plants *(list of plants, above; division methods, pages 82-85)*. For every method, the overall procedure is the same: Gather your tools and prepare replanting sites ahead of time; work fast; protect roots from drying out; and pamper the slips while they acclimate.

Before beginning the actual work of dividing, consider both the parent plant and your intentions for the offspring. Do you want to populate the garden with many shoots, even if some will not bloom this year? Or do you want to turn last year's single clump into three distinct blooming plants? Or is your aim to rejuvenate the parent by maintenance division, whether or not you end up with more individual plants? Starting out knowing what you want will shorten the handling time for the plants—and the less time they're out of their natural element, the better.

Ready the soil in the area where you will

put the new divisions, so that they can go into the ground immediately. Preparation should include adding a soil amendment such as compost, peat, or sand as necessary to ensure good drainage and improve soil structure *(pages 36-41)*. Judging by the size of the parent plant, allow plenty of space around the hole you dig for each new shoot, so that the plant will not be crowded when it is mature. If the ground is not wet from a recent watering or rain, water anything you plan to divide at least an hour before you start work.

Making the Cut

The simplest way to divide a perennial with a healthy center is to slice off the new growth from the sides with a spade or sharp knife, leaving the main clump undisturbed in the ground. This is also a good way to handle invasive plants that seem to have no recognizable center. Cut so that each section of new growth includes one or two visible growing crowns or shoots, and an intact portion of root. Daylilies, phlox, centaurea, and bleeding heart are among those you can divide this way. If a plant looks poorly at the center, or if you want many divisions, dig it out of the bed, using the technique shown below.

After Division

Both your new divisions and the parent plants require a little extra care after the main procedures are complete. Set the new divisions into prepared holes, spreading out the roots and positioning the crowns at ground level, not below. Press soil firmly over the roots, eliminating air pockets and giving the roots good contact with the soil. If you have lifted the parent plants from the soil, take this opportunity to work up the soil there, too, and add compost to the holes before resetting the plants in them.

How to Divide Perennials with Fibrous Roots

While the main goals of division are to separate offshoots for distribution and to rejuvenate aging perennials, the viability of all the plants afterward is crucial. Give them the best chance to thrive by minimizing root damage, preserving a balance between the top growth and the roots, and treating new transplants tenderly after separation and moving.

The tools for division will vary with the type of plant you're working on, but you probably already have the equipment on hand. You'll need a spade or a shovel for digging large clumps and a trowel for small, shallow-rooted ones; a bucket of water or a hose for rinsing soil off the roots; and an old kitchen knife or cross-bladed shears. Wet burlap is useful to cover dug-up plants when you're not working on them.

Keep spades, knives, and shears sharp so you can make clean cuts. Having all the equipment at your fingertips before you start speeds the operation and spares the plants stress.

1. Dig deeply around the plant with a sharp shovel or spade, along a line below the tips of the foliage. *Don't use a fork for this job—it is too likely to sever roots. To test whether you have freed the root mass, grasp the foliage at its base and rock the plant gently. Dig deeper anywhere roots are still holding on.*

2. Lift the plant carefully from the ground, supporting the roots with your hands (left). *Shake and rinse off the soil until you can clearly see the roots and the crowns—where roots join stems. Cut out and discard any old, woody tissue, rotted soft tissue, or areas of insect damage on roots or foliage.*

If you are dividing in late summer or fall, when perennials have full complements of foliage, prune back the stems and leaves of plant divisions by about half after planting. This restores balance to the plant, giving the smaller root system less top growth to nourish and reducing water loss through respiration. If you are dividing in early spring, before plants have developed much top growth, cutting back is unnecessary.

Water all your new plantings thoroughly and keep the soil moist for the next few days. Providing shade from full sun for a week also helps—an old lawn chair or pruned-off evergreen branches strategically placed can intercept the burning rays. Because the smaller root systems of divisions are especially vulnerable to drought in dry spells and to frost-heave damage in winter, protect them with ample mulch through their first seasons.

Divisions well established in their transplant locations will soon show new growth. When they do, they should share in your normal maintenance procedures, including fertilizing and pinching back to encourage bushy growth. If it's still early in the growing season, you may well see blooms this year on the newly divided plants of most genera.

Fleshy-Rooted Plants

Hemerocallis, Kniphofia, and a few other perennials grow from fleshy rootstocks, which tangle together underground and can be more difficult to separate than fibrous roots. Where the plant clumps are large and unwieldy, some experts recommend dividing them as they stand in the flower bed *(page 84)*. This approach may cause some foliage and root damage, but daylilies are very resilient; most divisions that have two or three fans of foliage will take hold and bloom happily next season. To divide smaller clumps of daylilies, dig them up completely, like fibrous-rooted perennials. Wash and examine the

3. Separate the plants into smaller clumps. *Some roots—like those of primroses or Siberian iris—can be pulled apart by hand, as at left above. Some, like those of phlox, can be teased apart with a hand fork. For solid, tangled roots use a knife, spade, or other sharp instrument to separate stubborn masses (above, right). Cut down among the roots to divide the various growing crowns and stems. Each division should have a growing crown or two and some fibrous roots attached. After you have severed your divisions, examine each one again, removing any dead or rotted sections. It's a good idea to thin out matted roots; this will stimulate strong new root growth. Trim off broken or very long roots.*

Three Ways to Divide Daylilies

Daylilies—the most widely grown of the fleshy-rooted perennials and the most frequently divided—spread exuberantly from single, original plantings to form densely packed clumps. Although they keep blooming when crowded, you'll have even more of a good thing after dividing them *(below)*.

The best time to work on daylilies is in early fall, after flowering has finished for the season, but well before frost. Before digging up any plants, prepare holes in which to replant the divisions. Obviously, you will have to cut roots inside a clump, but as you dig to free the edges, keep clear of the roots by digging around the clump just outside the leaf tips. A sharp edge on your shovel or knife makes the job a bit easier on both you and the plant.

Large clumps of daylilies can be divided right in the ground. *Plan your cuts so that each division will include one to three foliage fans and the root tissue below. Drive a sharp spade or shovel down firmly between the fans, cutting through the roots (below). Then dig up the sections, working from the outside of the clump toward the center.*

To shave outer fans off the edges of a large clump without disturbing or replanting the lilies at the center, *angle the spade as you drive it in between fans, keeping one to three fans in each group (below). Go deep enough to cut the roots, then dig around and under the cut sections and lift them away from the sides of the main clump.*

To divide small clumps of daylilies, *dig them out of the ground with a spade or shovel, digging in a wide circle just outside the foliage tips to avoid roots. Lift the entire clump from the hole, supporting the center of the clump as you lift. Rinse hardened soil from the roots, then cut them apart with a sharp knife, or divide them with your spade as they lie on the ground (below).*

roots before cutting them apart; slice off any soft, rotted tissue and discard it.

Replant your fleshy-rooted divisions in prepared holes; spread the roots out horizontally and press the soil firmly around them. To minimize water loss through respiration, trim off half the foliage on each fan. Keep the new plants well watered for a few days while they adjust to their new spot.

Dividing Rhizomatous Perennials

Bearded iris and bergenia grow from rhizomes—stems that grow horizontally underground and store nourishment that is drawn in through small feeder roots. Irises in particular show their need for division and renewal by diminished bloom. Really crowded specimens of both iris and bergenia will push their rhizomes up out of the soil, sometimes causing the plant to keel over, pulling exposed rhizomes completely out of the soil.

The best time to divide rhizomatous plants is after they have bloomed. Because rhizomes lie close to the surface, they are easy to dig up with a garden fork or spade, but you must loosen the soil thoroughly to minimize breakage of the feeder roots. Some rhizomes are prone to rot and to infestation by root maggots. Before you dig, sterilize your tools in a solution of one part chlorine bleach to 10 parts water; once you've dug up a rhizome, dip it in the bleach solution as well. Use a sharp knife to divide the rhizomes, and shears to trim the foliage. Replant the divisions in shallow, trenchlike holes that have soil mounded up in the center. Spread the feeder roots out evenly over the mounds.

Layering to Form New Roots

Another strategy for dividing some perennials is to encourage a plant to form roots where none exist—along stems—and then separate the root-studded stem as a new plant. This is done by an old-fashioned technique called layering. Layering lets you create divisions during the growing season while leaving plants in place in their beds—even while they bloom. And it takes almost none of your valuable gardening time.

Plants that respond well to layering include those with creeping stems or stems that are upright but flexible and long enough to be bent to the ground without breaking. *Dianthus, Geranium, Campanula, Arabis,* and *Phlox subulata* are all good candidates.

The best time to begin the process is spring, as soon as stems have grown to several inches long. Start with a plant that has some space in the bed around it, since you will be staking the stems down on the soil. You may need to pin down stems if they are too firm to stay down obediently; fence staples, hairpins, or a small rock will do the job.

Choose an outer stem and trim off all but the top few leaves. Bend the stem down to the soil surface so that the leafless part touches the ground. Loosen the soil there and bury the stem about 2 inches deep, pinning it in place if necessary. Keep the stem tip, with its remaining leaves, above the ground, staking it to hold it erect. Water the area thoroughly and mulch to help keep the moisture in. If you want more rooting stems, you can repeat this treatment all the way around the plant, if the plant and the surrounding space are large enough. Now all you have to do is keep the layered area moist while you wait for roots to form along the buried section of stem.

How long the rooting takes will vary according to climate and the type of perennial you're layering. Even while stems are staked and buried, their tips may bloom for you. It is easiest to leave the whole setup alone, if you can, until the next spring. Then dig up the rooted stems, sever them below the roots, and plant the new individuals as you would any other rooted division.

Dividing and Planting Rhizomes

Since a rhizome is a specialized form of stem growing horizontally underground, it needs gentle uprooting and careful replanting. The technique is shown here with iris rhizomes. Use these same steps to divide bergenia, but don't trim back its foliage; instead, remove a couple of leaves entirely before replanting.

1. Loosen the soil thoroughly around the plants and lift the rhizomes with a garden fork (above) or shovel, *taking care not to break tender feeder roots. Shake or rinse the soil off and examine the rhizomes for damage. If you find iris-borer holes (page 97), rotted spots, or dried-out hollows, cut off and discard these areas.*

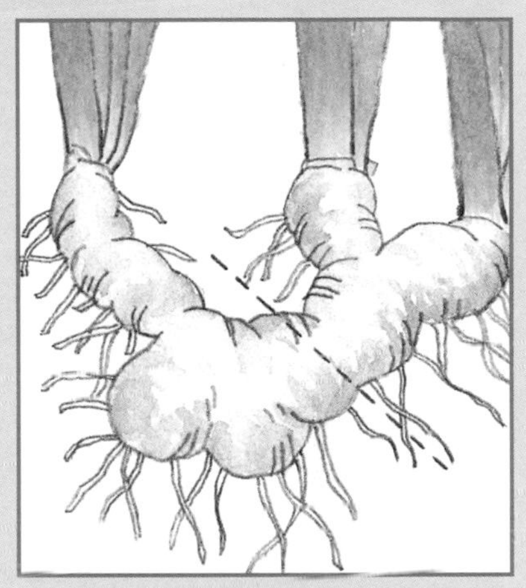

2. Separate the rhizomes, starting with those that split into sections naturally in your hand. *Cut others apart with a sharp, clean knife, separating V-shaped pieces and preserving the feeder roots. Dip the divided rhizomes in a diluted bleach solution and let them dry briefly in the shade before you replant.*

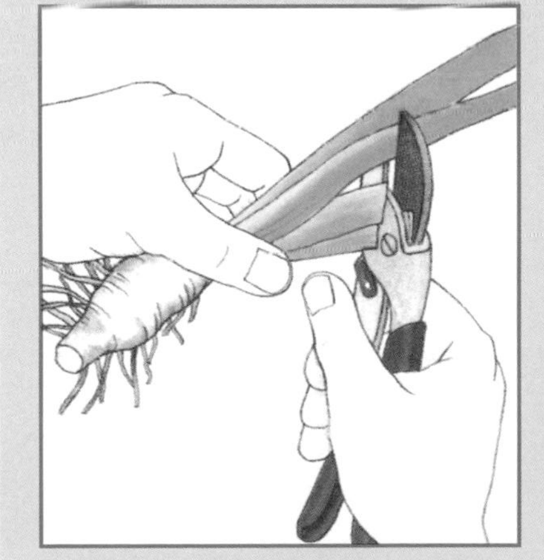

3. Trim the foliage fans to a third of their height, or about 4 inches long, *to reduce respiration and water loss while the divisions adjust. You can give the plant a more natural look by angling the cuts and by making the outer leaves shorter than the center leaf. Remove any withered or diseased foliage.*

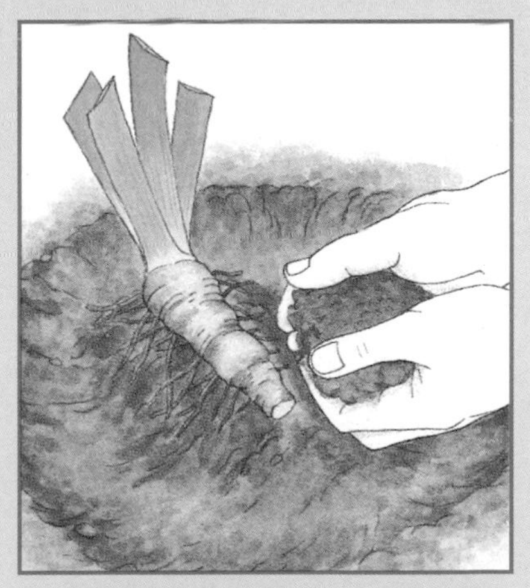

4. Set divided rhizomes on soil mounded in the middle of prepared holes, *with the fans parallel and the feeder roots spread over the mounds; the tops of the rhizomes should just peek through at the soil surface. Tamp 2 to 4 inches of soil firmly over the feeder roots and water the area well.*

Propagation through Stem Cuttings

Dividing your perennials at the roots is not the only way to produce exact replicas of them. Cuttings taken from the stems or side shoots of a wide range of plants can be encouraged to form roots and become independent individuals. These new plants almost always bloom in the very next growing season.

Stem cuttings are a good means of getting offspring from a plant that doesn't need dividing, from one that you don't want to dig up, or (with proper permission) from one that doesn't belong to you. And plants that are hard to divide because they grow from taproots, like lupines or wild indigo, are good candidates for stem-cutting propagation. Perhaps you want a great many more of some specimen. Dividing the roots of that special chrysanthemum might yield only four rooted pieces, whereas stem cuttings could give you perhaps 20 rooted sections to transplant.

Stem cutting is also a good fallback procedure for the gardener who missed the proper time to propagate by division: Cuttings can be taken almost anytime the plants are growing strongly, either before or after flowering.

Of course, like every other method, this one has its drawbacks as well as its advantages. It is more labor-intensive than propagation by simple division. Cuttings require lots of attention from you; in the early stages, you may need to check them several times daily. Stem cutting is also a long-term proposition—it may take several months from the time you cut stems to when you set the new perennials in their permanent beds. In addition, fungus disease flourishes among cuttings, lowering the success rate—in some batches, every one of your leafy babies may mysteriously wilt and die. But with care and attention to details, you can multiply your stock of a fine plant manyfold by cultivating stem cuttings.

TIPS FROM THE PROS

Secrets of Successful Stem Cutting

Experts suggest the following strategies for bringing stem cuttings to transplant size. Though even professional nurseries suffer losses, their methods can help you get good results.

1. Choose strong, healthy plants to cut from. A plant stressed by poor conditions or insect damage, or weakened by disease is a poor risk.
2. Work quickly: Cut only a few stems at a time and process them completely before cutting another batch.
3. Work in clean conditions. Scrub all your equipment with a diluted bleach solution—10 parts water to one part bleach—including the containers you will use for planting the stem cuttings.
4. Use a rooting hormone and a spray compound (Wilt-Pruf is one) to reduce moisture loss through leaf respiration.
5. Set plants to root in several separate containers rather than in one large one. This prevents wholesale disaster if you happen to overwater or underwater the container and inhibits the spread of disease from one group of cuttings to another. (Plastic dishpans make good rooting containers; they are easy to handle and have good depth.)
6. Provide bottom heat from an electric plug-in cable or mat (available at nurseries and garden centers).
7. Watch over your cuttings once they're prepared. You may need to attend to them more than once a day.

Preparations for Cutting

Before making your stem cuttings, there are a few thing you'll need to do. Several hours ahead of time, water the plants well so the stem tissue will be firm. Then mix up a solution of 10 parts water to one part bleach and use it to wash a sharp cutting knife, a cutting board, your work surface, and the containers that will hold the stem cuttings. Fill the containers with a 4-inch layer of a sterile growing medium: A commercial blend, or a 50/50 mix of perlite and vermiculite works well. Don't use houseplant potting soil or topsoil, and don't use soil brought in from the garden. Water the sterile medium until it is well moistened but not soggy.

Each container will need an incubator tent to cover the planting, so have on hand plastic food wrap or large plastic bags. Also gather wooden or wire supports to insert at the rims of the containers; these will keep the plastic from touching the cuttings.

When your preparations are complete, examine your plants for erect but bendable stems. As you snip these stems, put them into a moistened plastic bag to keep them damp while you work.

All-Important Follow-Up

Place your containers of cuttings in a bright but shaded location—under a large tree is a good place in the summer. Temperatures of 65°-75°F are ideal. Cuttings taken late in the season may need bottom heat from an electric mat or cable, available at nurseries and garden centers, to encourage them to root.

Check the containers regularly, opening each plastic tent at least once a day for air flow. If large drops of water appear on the plastic, punch a few small air holes. If the surface of the planting medium feels dry or any cuttings shrivel, carefully add a little water without disturbing the cuttings. If any leaves drop, remove them immediately; they may be hosts for disease organisms. If an entire cutting dries up, remove it as well.

Roots should form in 3 to 4 weeks, or even sooner. New growth on the foliage tips indicates roots are developing, as does resistance to a gentle tug on the tops of the cuttings. When roots have formed, remove the plastic covers and allow the plants to harden off—become used to the outdoor conditions—for several days before you transplant them.

Transplant rooted cuttings directly into flower beds if frost is still several weeks away. If the growing season has ended, leave small plants together in the container, but give them some shelter—a cold frame or a heavy mulch if your climate is mild. If the cuttings have grown large, separate them into individual pots before sheltering them. Rooted cuttings can safely be planted with other perennials the next spring.

How to Propagate from Stem Cuttings

***1. Locate a number of strong plant stems.** Then, using a sharp, clean knife or cross-bladed plant shears, slice off a few 5- to 6-inch segments, making slanting cuts about ¼ inch below a leaf joint or node. Trim off the lower leaves, leaving a rosette of leaves at the top of each cutting. Place the cuttings in a moistened plastic bag.*

***2. Pour some commercial rooting hormone powder onto a piece of paper.** Following the manufacturer's instructions, dip the cut end of each stem into the powder. Do not dip the stems into the container, as this could contaminate the powder. Tap off any excess and lay the stems aside.*

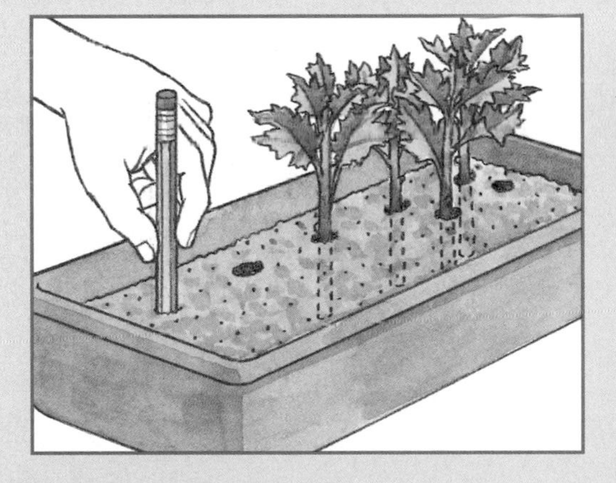

***3. Use a pencil to make holes at least 3 inches deep in the planting medium;** space the holes far enough apart so the leaves of the cuttings won't touch. Set the cuttings in the holes, pressing soil around each stem so it stands upright. Add wooden or wire supports to the rim of your container, and wrap the pot with plastic sheeting to seal in humidity. Tape down the plastic or tuck it underneath the container. Make sure the plastic doesn't touch the cuttings or the soil surface.*

Perennials to Propagate from Stem Cuttings

Amsonia (bluestar)
Anthemis (chamomile)
Arabis (rock cress)
Aster (aster)
Baptisia (wild indigo)
Boltonia (boltonia)
Ceratostigma (plumbago)
Chrysanthemum (chrysanthemum)
Clematis (clematis)
Delphinium (delphinium)
Dianthus (pinks)
Echinops (globe thistle)
Erigeron (fleabane)
Eupatorium (boneset)
Helenium (sneezeweed)
Helianthus (sunflower)
Heliopsis (false sunflower, oxeye)
Iberis (candytuft)
Lamium (dead nettle)
Lavandula (lavender)
Linum (flax)
Malva (mallow)
Monarda didyma (bee balm)
Nepeta (catmint)
Perovskia (Russian sage)
Phlox divaricata (wild blue phlox)
Phlox paniculata (summer phlox, garden phlox)
Physostegia (false dragonhead)
Salvia (sage)
Sedum (stonecrop)
Verbena (verbena, vervain)
Veronica (speedwell)

Propagation through Root Cuttings

Perennial plants employ what is perhaps their subtlest reproductive tactic underground—growing new shoots from broken-off pieces of their roots. Nursery professionals, taking advantage of this tactic, propagate root cuttings to obtain many offspring from one choice specimen. The practice is unusual among home gardeners, but it is simpler than coddling stem cuttings. If you are patient enough to wait months to see growth, you can process root cuttings during the garden's slow time, when plants are dormant, but results come quicker in early spring, just as vegetative growth is starting up.

Root-cutting propagation is recommended for the perennials that don't need regular dividing, that dislike the disturbance that division during the growing season entails, or that don't send up multiple stems to provide material for stem cuttings. It is also used on plants that don't produce good seeds and on hybrids that don't come true from seed.

The method has disadvantages, of course. The list of perennials suitable for root cutting is modest, and root cuttings from some may not grow up exactly like their parent cultivar. As with stem cuttings, fungus disease is a menace. And the offspring from root cuttings usually take a season longer than divisions or stem cuttings to reach blooming size.

But if you enjoy trying out different techniques, if you have a cold frame, unheated room, or basement, and if you can be patient, you may take much pleasure in growing root-cutting descendants from such favorites as Japanese anemone.

Preparation for Root Cutting

Many experts believe the best time to take root cuttings is early spring, when the parent plants are just coming out of dormancy, with all their systems geared toward growth. Others suggest working while plants are dormant, usually from late fall to early spring. Though less comfortable for the gardener, this may be the treatment of choice for plants that resent being moved and show it by dying back or refusing to bloom. To make replant-

How to Start Root Cuttings

For most genera, the best way to take many root cuttings is to dig up the entire plant and deal with the roots as they lie on the ground *(right)*. However, those that recover slowly from the shock of being moved—such as poppies, asclepias, baptisia, gypsophila, and limonium—should stay in the ground as you work on them. Simply expose the roots on one side, cut some off close to the crowns, then go on to Steps 2 and 3, opposite.

The wiry, fibrous roots of perennials such as sea holly, stokesia, or mullein may not provide 5-inch lengths or stand erect for vertical planting. Snip 1½- to 2-inch segments, lay them horizontally on the planting medium, and cover them with a half-inch of soil.

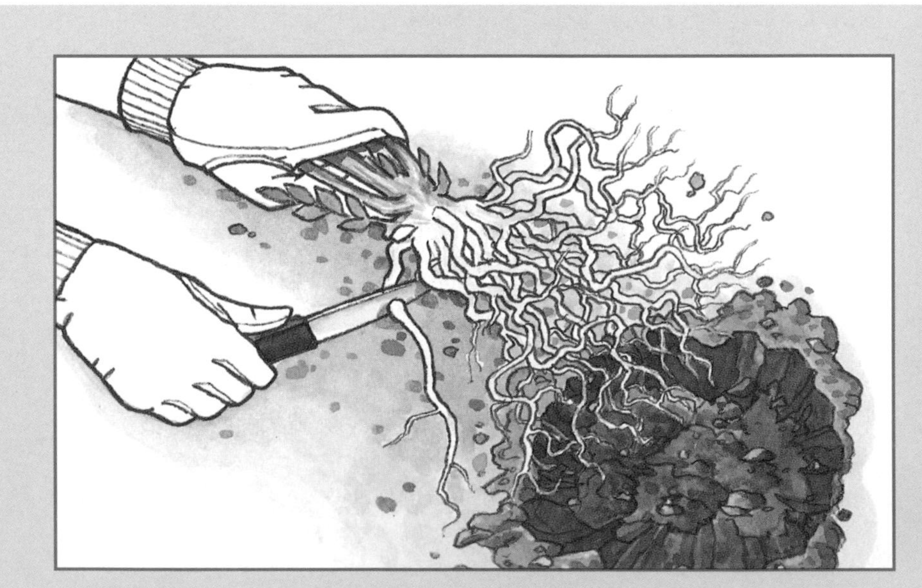

1. Choose healthy roots—tan-colored, mature roots rather than white ones*—at least ¼ inch thick and 5 inches long. Holding the base of the plant steady and working close to the tops of the roots you want, sever each root with a sharp knife. You can take up to half of the outer roots without damaging the plant. Replace the plant in its hole, firming soil around the remaining roots to prevent air pockets. Place the severed roots in a plastic bag to prevent their drying out.*

ing easy after root cuttings are taken, work when the soil is neither frozen nor too wet.

To take root cuttings, you will need a sharp spade or shovel, a bucket of water or a hose for rinsing roots, a sharp knife or cross-bladed shears, a cutting board or work surface, and containers at least 4 inches deep. Sterilize all equipment and containers in a solution of one part bleach to 10 parts water. Then fill the containers with a moistened sterile potting medium—a 50/50 combination of seedling mix and perlite is good. Next, loosen the rootball, lift the plant, and clean the roots as you would for propagation by division *(page 82)*. The steps unique to root-cutting propagation are shown below.

Caring for Cuttings

Once your root cuttings are tucked into the potting medium, check them occasionally to make sure the soil is still slightly moist; never overwater it. As spring advances, successful root cuttings will send up shoots and leaves. You can then pot these in individual containers or set them out in a nursery bed to grow to flowering size. Poppies, asclepias, baptisia, and limonium will do best if planted immediately in their permanent homes.

Perennials to Propagate by Root Cuttings

Acanthus (bear's-breech)
Anchusa (bugloss)
Anemone japonica (Japanese anemone)
Asclepias (milkweed)
Baptisia (wild indigo)
Brunnera (brunnera)
Catananche (Cupid's-dart)
Ceratostigma (plumbago, leadwort)
Dicentra (bleeding heart)
Echinacea (purple coneflower)
Echinops (globe thistle)
Eryngium (sea holly)
Gaillardia (blanket-flower)
Gypsophila (baby's-breath)
Heuchera (alumroot)
Ligularia (golden-ray)
Limonium (sea lavender, statice)
Papaver orientale (Oriental poppy)
Phlox paniculata (summer phlox)
Stokesia (Stokes' aster)
Verbascum (mullein)

Dicentra spectabilis (common bleeding heart)

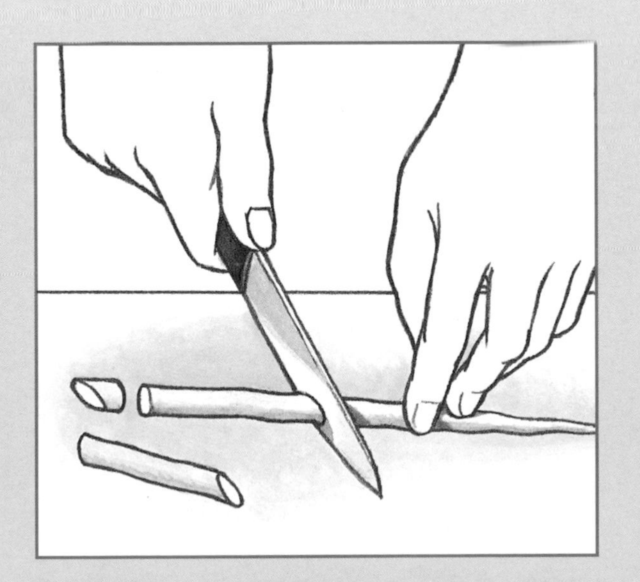

2. Working on your sterilized cutting board, slice the roots into segments about 2 inches long, *making a straight cut across the top of each segment and a diagonal cut across the bottom. These distinctive cuts enable you to know which way the root originally grew, and to plant it with its top end up.*

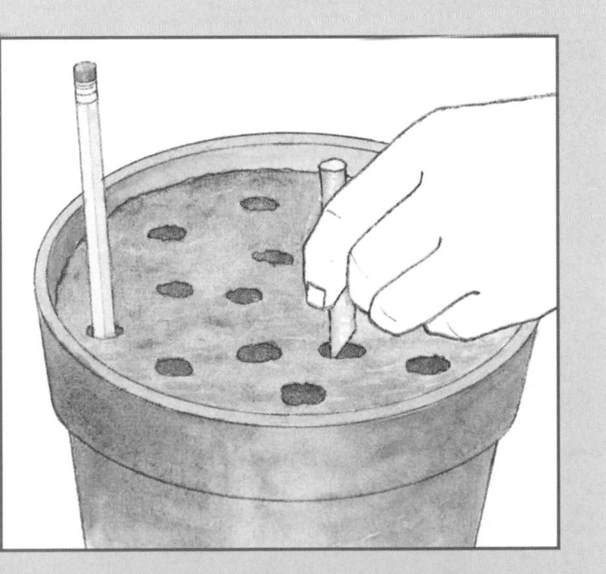

3. Poke narrow holes about 2 inches deep and 2 inches apart in the growing medium and insert root segments, diagonal cut down. *Set the straight-cut top ends just below the soil surface and tamp the medium gently around them; cover the tops lightly with soil. Set the containers in a cold frame or unheated indoor area.*

Growing Perennials from Seed

PERENNIAL FAVORITES GROWN FROM SEED
The purple and blue spires of delphinium form a striking backdrop for daisylike coreopsis. Plan to sow seeds for these classic border plants indoors in winter, so you can admire the flowers in June.

The product lists of commercial seed houses show that many perennials can be propagated from seeds. Most of the offerings, however, promise to reproduce only the genus and species, not named cultivars. This is because most of these cultivars are hybrids that produce either no seeds or seedlings that tend to revert to their ancestral types. If you like perennials but are not fussy about which cultivars you grow, you can develop beautiful beds with plants raised from seed. Many genera will even bloom their first summer if started indoors during the winter; others don't flower until their second or third season.

Experts recommend buying seeds from commercial seed houses, where strict procedures of quality control result in high germination rates and fewer disappointed gardeners. Whether you shop from catalogs or in stores, purchase your seeds early in the season and keep them in a cool, dry place until you're ready to sow them.

Consult the seed packet for the best time for planting. Some seeds do best if planted outdoors in the fall so that they can experience those natural conditions that trigger their germination in spring. If you start such seeds indoors, you may have to treat them to an artificial winter—soaking, scarifying (scratching), or stratifying (chilling) the seeds as the packet directs.

Soaking seeds is a very easy procedure. Spread them loosely in a baking dish or other watertight container and cover them with hot tap water. Soak for several hours or overnight to soften the seed coat before planting.

To scarify seeds, place them on a flat sheet of sandpaper and, using another sheet of sandpaper wrapped around a wood block, rub the seeds firmly back and forth. This scrapes and thins the seed hulls, mimicking the natural action of sand and soil particles abrading seeds planted outdoors.

Perennials to Grow from Seed

Allium
(flowering onion)
Anemone
(windflower)
Anthemis
(chamomile)
Aquilegia
(columbine)
Asclepias
(milkweed)
Aster
(aster)
Baptisia
(wild indigo)
Belamcanda
(blackberry lily)
Catananche
(Cupid's-dart)
Centaurea
(knapweed, cornflower)
Centranthus
(red valerian)
Coreopsis
(tickseed)
Delphinium
(delphinium)
Dictamnus
(gas plant) (3-4 years to bloom)
Doronicum
(leopard's-bane)
Echinacea
(purple coneflower)
Erigeron
(fleabane)
Eupatorium
(boneset)
Gaillardia
(blanket-flower)
Gypsophila
(baby's-breath)
Hibiscus
(rose mallow)
Limonium
(sea lavender, statice)
Lobelia
(cardinal flower)
Lupinus
(lupine)
Penstemon
(beardtongue)
Platycodon
(balloon flower)
Rudbeckia
(coneflower)
Scabiosa
(pincushion flower)
Stachys
(lamb's ears)
Stokesia
(Stokes' aster)
Verbena
(verbena, vervain)

Starting Seeds and Transplanting Seedlings

1. Sow commercial seeds per packet directions. *For homegrown seeds, sow larger seeds ½ to 1 inch apart, depending on size; cover with ⅛ inch of soil and tamp them flat. Press small seeds lightly into the soil. Sow in rows, with one kind of seed per pot. Make a tent of a plastic bag, propped up with a stick and pricked for ventilation. Water well from the bottom tray, then feel the soil daily and water if it is dry. When seedlings appear, remove the plastic; monitor moisture daily as the seedlings grow.*

2. When the seedlings show their second pair of leaves, prepare individual pots filled with seedling mix. *Then lift the seedlings by the second pair of leaves, not by the fragile stems, and quickly place the seedlings in the pots. Tamp the soil down firmly, water it well, and shield the pots from strong sun for a few days. Harden off indoor seedlings in a cold frame (below) before setting them out in beds to mature.*

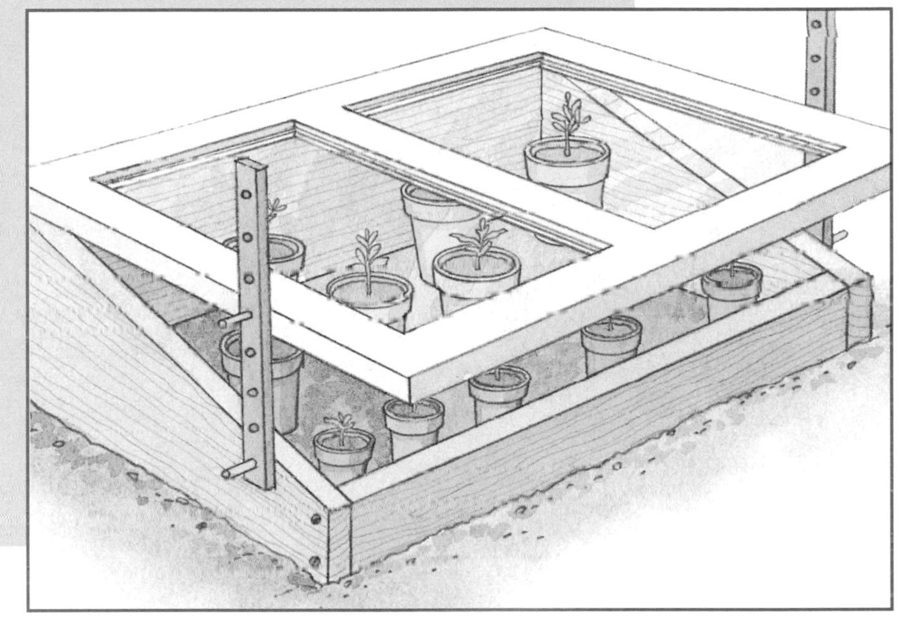

If your packet instructions call for stratifying seeds, sow them between layers of damp growing medium and store them in the refrigerator or a sheltered outdoor area—a cold frame is ideal—for 6 to 8 weeks. Then you can bring them in to sprout in the warmth of your artificial indoor springtime.

Starting Seeds Indoors

You'll need clean containers (pots, flats, plastic bins with holes punched in the bottom, or seed-start kits) filled with sterile seedling mix; do not substitute houseplant potting soil. Leave at least an inch between the soil surface and the top of the container. Place the containers on a large tray so you can water from the bottom, encouraging seedling roots to grow strongly downward. Seeds don't care where you start them, but they sprout best at temperatures of 65°-75°F. Though most seeds will germinate without light, you should move the containers into full sun or bright light as soon as seedlings appear.

Using Homegrown Seeds

To collect seeds from your own plants, wait until the flowers have faded and drooped. On a dry day, snip off flower heads and spread them on a screen or sheet of clean paper. Place them in a shady spot—the less humid the better—and turn the heads over every day, letting them dry out for a week. When the flowers feel brittle, shake or rub the seeds loose over the paper, and store them in a cool, dry place until planting time.

To check the viability of seeds before planting them, spread out a sampling of the seeds on three layers of well-dampened paper towels. Roll up the towels, tie the roll with twist ties or string, and enclose it in a plastic bag to keep it damp. Leave the bag in a warm place (65°-75°F) for a week, then unroll the towels weekly to check for germination. If nothing has sprouted after 2 months, discard both the sample and the rest of that batch of seeds.

Answers to Common Questions

CHOOSING PERENNIALS AND PLACES TO PUT THEM

Why are cultivated varieties more desirable than the parent species when picking perennials for a garden?

As a result of horticultural breeding programs, random mutation, and plant selection, many cultivated varieties—or cultivars—have one or more characteristics that render them superior to the parent species. They may flower more abundantly and over a longer period than the species, for example, or have different colors or flower forms. They may be stockier or be significantly taller or shorter, and they may have enhanced disease-resistant qualities or tolerance to a wider range of growing conditions. Unfortunately, these special qualities are usually not passed along in seeds gathered from the plants. The only way the home gardener can acquire plants with the desired characteristics is to purchase them or to propagate them by division *(pages 80-85),* stem cuttings *(pages 86-87),* or root cuttings *(pages 88-89).*

How far apart should I plant my perennials?

Plant spacing depends on the mature height and spread of the individual plant, but as a rule, most perennials are planted 12 to 15 inches apart. However, a spacing of 18 to 24 inches allows better air circulation between plants and reduces the tendency of larger plants to shade smaller ones, thus promoting stockier growth, with less need to stake. For larger plants, such as daylilies and irises, consider a 24- to 30-inch spacing, whereas peonies do best with 36-inch spacing and hibiscus (giant mallow) with 4-foot spacing. If your garden looks a little bare, plant annuals to fill the gaps while your perennials mature.

I have a perennial border with lots of bold colors like red, orange, and yellow. These colors are compatible, but my garden seems to lack continuity. What can I do?

Tie your bold colors together by introducing perennials with blue flowers. Leadwort *(Ceratostigma)*, globe thistle *(Echinops)*, flax *(Linum)*, Siberian iris *(Iris sibirica)*, Russian sage *(Perovskia)*, false indigo *(Baptisia)*, and blue cultivars of moss phlox *(Phlox subulata)* are a few of the best. You may also try plants with silver or gray foliage such as lavender *(Lavandula angustifolia)*, lamb's ears *(Stachys byzantina)*, or *Artemisia* 'Silver Mound'. Repeat your selections along the length of the border, and remember to mass blue-flowered plants as much as possible because blue is a receding color.

How many perennials of each variety should I plant in a group?

If your garden is to be viewed close up, you may be able to make do with just one plant, but gardens that are to be viewed from a distance require masses of the same plant to catch the eye. One rule of thumb is to buy three plants of each variety if the garden is to be viewed from 25 feet away, and 15 plants if the distance is 75 feet. Each grouping should be planted in irregular patterns called drifts to promote a natural look.

I have tried unsuccessfully over the years to grow delphiniums in my garden. Plants that I purchase from nurseries will flourish for the summer and then fail to return the following year. Are delphiniums really perennials?

Most gardeners plant various forms of the Pacific Coast hybrids. Members of this strain do exceptionally well in climates where cold winters and cool summers prevail. But they do not do well in areas where winter temperatures fluctuate above and below freezing and where summer temperatures are hot. If you live in a less-than-perfect delphinium climate, you might try *Delphinium bellamosa*, *D. belladonna*, and *D. chinense* and their cultivars, which are more forgiving, before abandoning delphiniums altogether.

I'm having trouble establishing Oriental poppies despite my planting them the recommended 2 inches deep and in ideal growing conditions. Any suggestions?

Most Oriental poppies prefer the colder regions (Zones 5-7). Where winter temperatures fluctuate, poppies may break dormancy during warm periods, only to be struck down a few days later by a frost. Winter mulching can sometimes protect them, but don't mulch during the rest of the year lest you invite crown rot. Also, poppies hate wet feet during their late-summer dormant period, so don't water them in late spring when their foliage begins to brown.

With so many different kinds of irises and daylilies on the market, how do I know which are the best ones to buy?

Every year the American Iris Society and the American Hemerocallis Society select one iris and one daylily to be given the Dykes Medal and the Stout Medal, respectively. These award winners have withstood the scrutiny of many experts. You could also write to the national secretary of each organization and obtain a list of favorite cultivars. They can also provide you with regional lists that would be helpful in selecting cultivars that grow best in your area.

Should I plant evergreen or dormant daylilies in my garden? What is the difference between them?

Evergreen daylily hybrids were developed in the southern and southwestern states and have the landscape advantage of maintaining their foliage on a year-round basis. Many evergreen daylily cultivars are not winter-hardy in the North because they refuse to go dormant and freeze to death. Likewise, some dormant forms, which never show any foliage during the winter in the North, cannot tolerate scorching southern heat.

GARDEN MAINTENANCE

A lot of perennials in my garden need staking in the late summer. This requires a good bit of work on my part and the result looks rather artificial. Is there any way to avoid this tedious task?

First of all, if you know that a favorite plant is going to need support, put a protective hoop around it or make a frame of stakes and string *(pages 72-74)* as the plant is coming up; the developing foliage will soon hide the supports. Second, perennials require less staking if you select cultivars that are naturally more compact, if you space your plants far enough apart so that sunlight and circulating air reach all the foliage, and if you feed them a low-nitrogen organic fertilizer. Pinching back your unruly plants is another trick.

How late in the season can I pinch back my chrysanthemum plants?

Pinching back your mums will produce compact, bushy plants with lots of flowering stems, but every time you pinch back, you delay blooming time by 3 to 4 weeks. Be careful that your last pinching doesn't push flowering so late into the fall that your flower buds will be killed by frost. The farther south you go, the later you can pinch. A good cutoff date for Zone 7 is the second week of July; colder zones would have earlier dates.

When is the best time of day to water during the summer?

When you water is not critical as long as you don't water too often. Watering in the morning or during the day has the advantage of raising the humidity around your plants, which reduces water loss from transpiration and prevents wilting during the heat of the day. Many people refuse to water at night because they believe it promotes mildew and other fungal diseases, which may be possible, especially if the weather has been hot. Normally, though, an occasional night watering, like rain, serves to purge leaves of fungal spores.

Are there any garden perennials that don't thrive when mulched?

Yes. The crowns of tall bearded irises and delphiniums rot if they are mulched; Oriental poppies suffer from crown rot as well. When planting peonies, do not cover the buds—also called eyes—with mulch; the plants may flower poorly or not bloom at all.

SOILS, COMPOSTING, AND FERTILIZERS

How do I prepare soil in the different sections of my garden to accommodate various perennials I want to plant? It seems that some species like more acid soil and some like more alkaline soil.

Of the thousands of perennials to select from, only a few have pH requirements that fall outside the average range for most garden soils. Develop a pH between 6 and 7, and almost any perennial will do well. For those plants that require more alkalinity, dig dolomitic limestone into the soil at the planting location; it won't leach out into the surrounding soil. In the case of acid-loving plants, try adding peat moss to the planting locations.

My soil is a heavy clay. What amendments should I add to improve the structure of my soil?

Your first impulse might be to add sand, but while sand will loosen your heavy clay, it is not enough to transform it into a good garden soil. You will need to add lots of organic matter as well. Compost is an excellent choice; you can also use peat moss, leaf mold, bark chips or ground bark, sawdust, and well-rotted animal manures.

Is there any problem with composting perennial garden clippings, weeds, and other garden debris?

Generally, composting garden debris is fine—with some exceptions. You don't want weed seeds in your compost, and some plants may carry pests or diseases. Composting clippings and dead leaves from infected plants may only serve to spread the disease throughout your garden. If you see that a plant is obviously sick, don't throw it into your compost.

Is it safe to use commercially processed sewage sludge on a perennial garden?

The practice is controversial and potentially dangerous. The main problem is that these products may contain high levels of heavy metals and non-biodegradable organics. It is best to stay away from them—and definitely avoid their use on vegetables and fruit trees.

What is the best fertilizer formula to use on flowering plants?

Any fertilizer used on flowering plants should be low in nitrogen, because high-nitrogen fertilizers stimulate leafy growth at the expense of flowers. Two fertilizers that work well are 5-20-5 and 3-18-18 (alfalfa fertilizer). Organic fertilizers are especially good because they contain micronutrients that promote healthy texture as well as good flower color.

LIGHT AND EXPOSURE

My perennial bed gets 6 hours of morning sun. Will my plants thrive with this amount of light?

Plant requirements for sun are determined by the intensity and duration of sunlight. For sun-loving perennials, 6 hours of sun is adequate only when it occurs at midday or in the afternoon. In other words, when picking plants for a garden with morning sun and afternoon shade, you should opt for shade plants. If, on the other hand, your garden is shaded all morning but has afternoon sun, pick plants that require full sun.

I'd like to grow perennials under a large Norway maple tree. What are some good choices?

Norway maples have a network of surface roots that can rob plants of moisture. Plants that can tolerate these dry shade conditions include violets *(Viola)*, woodland strawberries *(Fragaria)*, dead nettle *(Lamium)*, *Hosta*, *Epimedium*, and leadwort *(Ceratostigma)*.

PESTS AND DISEASES

Do you recommend using traps to catch insects like Japanese beetles?

Insect traps today are quite improved over the ones on the market a few years ago. Be sure not to place them directly in the flower garden, however, because you will only attract insects from outside areas to the very plants you are trying to protect.

What can I do to control aphids in my perennial garden without overdoing heavy-duty sprays?

The first thing you should do is keep a watchful eye and don't let your aphid populations get a head start. Spray your plants with a steady stream of water to knock the aphids off and discourage them from returning. If that doesn't work, try a diluted insecticidal soap solution or a recommended insecticide. Also, consider encouraging or introducing predatory insects, such as lacewings, ladybugs, and minute pirate bugs.

One of my perennials has yellow, stunted foliage. When I dug it up, it had nodules all over the roots. What is the problem?

More than likely your plant has root knot nematodes. You can control this pest by using a nontoxic material made from ground crab shells that is available at better garden centers.

I have a bed of irises that is overrun with iris borer. What should I do?

First, establish a new iris bed in another location. Then dig up and divide irises from your infested bed in mid- to late summer, selecting only healthy, young rhizomes. Throw away all the old rhizomes and plant debris. Dip the transplants in a solution of one part chlorine bleach to nine parts water, and let them dry in the shade before planting. Keep the new bed clear of decaying foliage to discourage the adult moths from laying their eggs in the vicinity.

My peonies have petals that are brown all over, and they don't open properly. What is wrong and how can I correct it?

One of three things could be happening. First, your flower buds could be suffering from excessive heat—more than 85°F—at bloom time (called bullheading). Second, your peonies could have a fungal disease called botrytis blight *(page 100)*, or, third, the damage could be caused by tiny sucking insects called thrips *(page 99)*.

Troubleshooting Guide

Even the best-tended gardens can fall prey to pests and diseases. To keep them in check, regularly inspect your perennials for warning signs, remembering that lack of nutrients, improper pH levels, and other environmental conditions can cause symptoms like those typical of some diseases. If wilting or yellowing appears on neighboring plants, the source is probably environmental; pest and disease damage is usually more random.

This guide is intended to help you identify and solve most of your pest and disease problems. In general, good drainage and air circulation will help prevent infection, and the many insects, such as ladybugs and lacewings, that prey on pests should be encouraged. Natural solutions to garden problems are best, but if you must use chemicals, treat only the affected plant. Try to use horticultural oils, insecticidal soaps, and the botanical insecticide *neem;* these products are the least disruptive to beneficial insects and will not destroy the soil balance that is at the foundation of a healthy garden.

PESTS

PROBLEM: Leaves curl, are distorted, and may be sticky and have a black, sooty appearance. Buds and flowers are deformed, new growth is stunted, and leaves and flowers may drop.

CAUSE: Aphids are pear-shaped, semitransparent, wingless sucking insects, about ⅛ inch long and ranging in color from green to red, pink, black, or gray. Aphids suck plant sap, and through feeding may spread viral disease. Infestations are most severe in spring and early summer, when the pests cluster on new shoots, the undersides of leaves, and around flower buds. Winged forms appear when colonies become overcrowded. Aphids secrete a sticky substance known as honeydew onto leaves, which fosters the growth of a black fungus called sooty mold.

SOLUTION: Spray plants frequently with a steady stream of water from a garden hose to knock aphids off plants and discourage them from returning. In severe cases, prune off infested areas, and use a diluted insecticidal soap solution or a recommended insecticide. Ladybugs or lacewings, which eat aphids, may be introduced into the garden.
SUSCEPTIBLE PLANTS: MANY PERENNIALS, INCLUDING ASIATIC LILY, CHRYSANTHEMUM, COLUMBINE, DELPHINIUM, GLOBE THISTLE, HOLLYHOCK, IRIS, POPPY, PRIMROSE, SUNFLOWER.

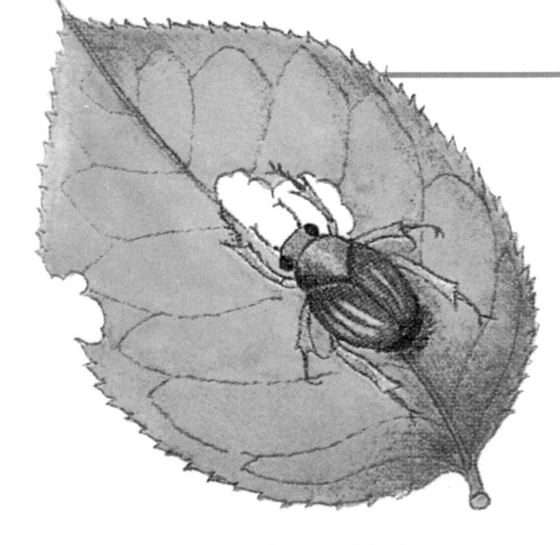

PROBLEM: Small, round holes are eaten into leaves, leaf edges, and flowers. Leaves may be reduced to skeletons with only veins remaining.

CAUSE: Japanese beetles, iridescent blue-green with bronze wing covers, are the most destructive of a large family of hard-shelled chewing insects ranging in size from ¼ to ¾ inch long. Other genera include Asiatic garden beetles (brown), northern masked chafers (brown with dark band on head), and Fuller rose beetles (gray), as well as blister beetles (metallic black, blue, purple, or brown) and flea beetles (shiny dark blue, brown, black, or bronze), which are noted for their jumping ability. Japanese and other adult beetles are voracious in the summer. Larvae, the white grubs, feed on roots of plants and are present from midsummer through the following spring, when they emerge as adults.

SOLUTION: Handpick small colonies *(Caution: Use gloves when picking blister beetles),* placing them in a can filled with soapy water. Japanese beetles can be caught in baited traps. Place traps in an area away from susceptible plants so as not to attract more beetles into the garden. The larval stage can be controlled with milky spore disease, which can be applied to the whole garden. For heavy infestations, contact your local Cooperative Extension Service for information on registered pesticides and the best times to apply them in your region.
SUSCEPTIBLE PLANTS: ASTILBE, FOXGLOVE, HOLLYHOCK, NEW YORK ASTER, PURPLE CONEFLOWER, ROSE MALLOW.

PROBLEM: Holes appear in leaves, buds, and flowers; stems may also be eaten.

CAUSE: Caterpillars, the wormlike larvae of moths, butterflies, and sawflies, come in a variety of shapes and colors and can be smooth, hairy, or spiny. These voracious pests are found in gardens during the spring.
SUSCEPTIBLE PLANTS: MANY PERENNIALS, ESPECIALLY TENDER NEW SHOOTS.

SOLUTION: Handpick to control small populations. The organic pesticide *Bacillus thuringiensis* (Bt) kills many types without harming plants. If caterpillars return to your garden every spring, spray Bt as a preventive measure. Identify the caterpillar species to determine the control options and timing of spray applications. Several species are susceptible to sprays of insecticidal soap, which must directly hit the caterpillar. Keep the garden clear of debris and cultivate frequently. Deep spading in early spring can destroy many species that pupate underground. Destroy all visible cocoons and nests.

PROBLEM: Stems of emerging young plants are cut off near the ground; seedlings may be completely eaten. Leaves of older plants show ragged edges and chewed holes.

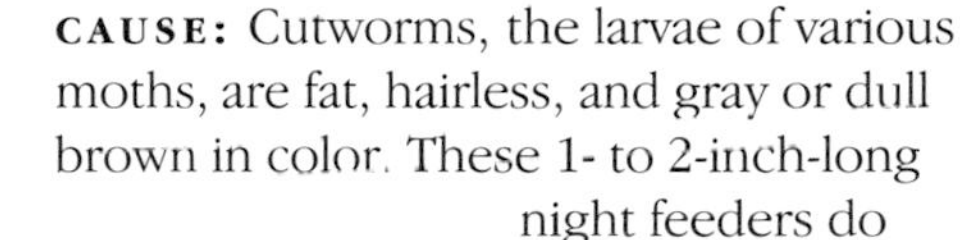

CAUSE: Cutworms, the larvae of various moths, are fat, hairless, and gray or dull brown in color. These 1- to 2-inch-long night feeders do the most damage in the spring. In the daytime, they curl up into a C shape and are found under debris or below the soil surface next to the plant stem.

SOLUTION: Place barriers called cutworm collars around the base of a plant. Force cutworms to the surface of the soil by flooding the area and then handpick them. To reduce hiding places, keep the area weeded and free of debris. Spade the soil in late summer and fall to expose and destroy cutworms. Apply *Bacillus thuringiensis* (Bt).
SUSCEPTIBLE PLANTS: YOUNG SEEDLINGS AND TRANSPLANTS.

PROBLEM: Iris leaves show irregular brown lines or tunnels, and leaf edges are ragged. Leaves wilt and discolor. Rhizomes may be rotten, foul smelling, and soft.

CAUSE: Iris borers, cream-colored chewing moth larvae, emerge in the spring from eggs laid the previous fall. They bore into new iris leaves and eat the soft interior tissue, migrating through leaves to flower stalks and buds. By late summer the larvae—1½ inches long, pink with brown heads—gradually work down into the rhizomes, where boring activity often results in foul-smelling bacterial soft rot.
SUSCEPTIBLE PLANTS: IRIS, ESPECIALLY BEARDED VARIETIES.

SOLUTION: After first frost, remove and destroy all damaged and dead foliage and stems to eliminate overwintering eggs. In spring, young borers are visible in the leaves and may be removed by hand. When new plant growth is 4 to 6 inches high, apply a labeled systemic insecticide—one that is intended for use on ornamental plants—to kill young larvae. In midsummer, apply beneficial nematodes in the soil at the base of stems to kill larvae. When irises are dug and divided in late summer, rhizomes that are heavily damaged should be destroyed.

PROBLEM: Leaves become stippled with white dots, then turn yellowish brown or have a burned look around the edges. Leaves and stems curl upward; young leaves become distorted. Plant growth may be stunted.

CAUSE: Leafhoppers are small (¼ inch long), yellow-green, cricketlike, wedge-shaped sucking insects that jump quickly into flight when disturbed. Most active in spring and summer, they feed on the undersides of leaves and, like aphids, secrete a sticky honeydew that fosters sooty mold.

SOLUTION: Spray with water to knock exposed leafhoppers off plants. Remove and destroy damaged foliage and heavily infested plants. Direct spraying with insecticidal soap will give short-term control, but leafhoppers migrate freely, so repeated applications may be necessary. A labeled systemic insecticide will provide the longest control.
SUSCEPTIBLE PLANTS: BABY'S-BREATH, CATMINT, CHRYSANTHEMUM, COREOPSIS, ITALIAN BUGLOSS.

PROBLEM: White or light green tunnels appear in leaves; older tunnels turn black. Leaves may lose color, dry up, and die. Seedlings may be stunted or die.

CAUSE: Leaf miners—minute (1⁄16 to ⅛ inch long), translucent, pale green larvae of certain flies, moths, or beetles—are hatched from eggs laid on the leaves of plants. During spring and summer, the larvae eat the tender interior below the surface of the leaf, leaving behind serpentine trails of blistered tissue known as mines.
SUSCEPTIBLE PLANTS: CHRYSANTHEMUM, COLUMBINE, DELPHINIUM, MONKSHOOD, PRIMROSE, SHASTA DAISY.

SOLUTION: Damage may be unsightly but is usually not lethal. Pick off and destroy infested leaves as they appear. In the fall, cut the plant to the ground and discard stalks. Remove and destroy leaves with egg clusters. Keep the garden well weeded since organic waste attracts maggots. Use a systemic insecticide, timing applications at proper intervals, before leaf mining becomes extensive.

PROBLEM: Leaves become stippled or flecked, then discolor, turning yellow or nearly white with brown edges. Often the entire leaf becomes yellowed or bronzed and curled; flowers and buds discolor or dry up, and webbing may be seen, particularly on the undersides of leaves. Growth is stunted. Leaves may drop.

CAUSE: Mites are pinhead-size, spiderlike sucking pests that can be reddish, pale green, or yellow. These insects can become a major problem, especially in hot, dry weather when several generations of mites may occur in a single season. Adults of some species hibernate over the winter in sod, in bark, and on weeds and plants that retain foliage.
SUSCEPTIBLE PLANTS: CANDYTUFT, CHRYSANTHEMUM, CLEMATIS, COLUMBINE, DAYLILY, DELPHINIUM, FOXGLOVE, HOLLYHOCK, IRIS, PHLOX, PRIMROSE, PURPLE CONEFLOWER, SHASTA DAISY.

SOLUTION: Damage is worst to plants in full sunlight and hot areas. Keep plants watered and mulched. Regularly spray the undersides of leaves, where mites feed and lay eggs, using water or a diluted soap solution. Horticultural oils can also be applied to the undersides. Insecticidal soaps control nymphs and adults but not eggs. Introduce predators such as green lacewing larvae.

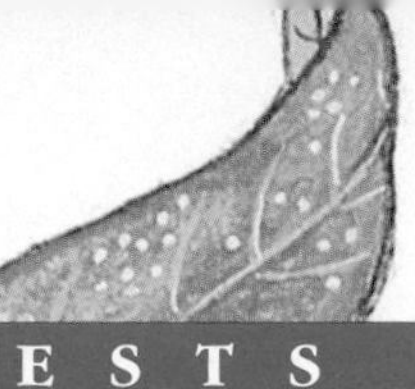

PROBLEM: Light-colored sunken brown spots appear on the upper surfaces of leaves. Foliage may wilt, discolor, and fall from the plant. Shoots may be distorted or blackened. Flower buds may be deformed.

CAUSE: Plant bugs include the four-lined plant bug, lygus bug, and tarnished plant bug. These ¼-inch-long sucking insects are brown, black, green, yellow, or brightly colored or patterned with antennae and wings, and are active from early spring to early summer.

SOLUTION: In most cases, plants recover from the feeding injury, and control is often unnecessary. But if infestation is severe, eliminate debris that could be breeding grounds. Spray plants with water or a diluted soap solution, or use an insecticidal soap to control nymphs. *SUSCEPTIBLE PLANTS: CLEMATIS, CORAL BELLS, PURPLE CONEFLOWER.*

PROBLEM: Ragged holes are eaten in leaves, especially those near the ground. New shoots and seedlings may disappear. Telltale silver streaks appear on leaves and garden paths.

CAUSE: Slugs or snails hide during the day, emerging at night or on overcast or rainy days to feed on low-hanging leaves. They prefer damp soil in a shady location and are most damaging in summer, especially in wet regions or during rainy years. *SUSCEPTIBLE PLANTS: VIRTUALLY ANY PLANT, ESPECIALLY THOSE WITH YOUNG OR TENDER FOLIAGE. HOSTA IS HIGHLY SUSCEPTIBLE.*

SOLUTION: Keep garden clean to minimize hiding places. Handpick, or trap them by placing saucers of beer near plants. Slugs will also collect under inverted grapefruit halves or melon rinds. Salt kills slugs and snails but may damage plants. Poison bait is available at garden centers. Because slugs and snails find it difficult to crawl over rough surfaces, barrier strips of coarse sand or cinders placed around beds will deter them. Spading in the spring destroys dormant slugs and eggs.

PROBLEM: Peony buds fail to open, or have brown petals. Other perennials have darkened buds and silvery speckling or streaks on leaves, which eventually wither and die. Flowers may be tattered, twisted, or deformed and have whitish flecks or streaks. Leaves and stems may be twisted, and growth of plants may be stunted. Daylilies have leaf spots and distorted flowers.

CAUSE: Thrips are quick-moving, sucking insects that are barely visible to the naked eye; they look like tiny slivers of yellow, black, or brown wood. Emerging in early spring, thrips are especially active in hot, dry weather. They are weak fliers but are easily dispersed by wind and therefore can travel great distances. Larvae are wingless and feed on stems, leaves, and flower buds.

SOLUTION: Control of thrips is difficult, especially during a migratory period in early summer. Systemic insecticides can provide some level of control. Lacewings, minute pirate bugs, and several predaceous mites feed on thrips. Late in the growing season such predators often check thrip populations. Remove and destroy damaged buds and foliage. Spray plants with an insecticidal soap or insecticide. *SUSCEPTIBLE PLANTS: ASIATIC LILY, CHRYSANTHEMUM, DAYLILY, DELPHINIUM, FOXGLOVE, GLADIOLUS, HOLLYHOCK, PEONY, SIBERIAN IRIS.*

PROBLEM: A sudsy white substance resembling foam appears in the area between the leaf and the stem.

CAUSE: Spittlebugs hatch from eggs in the spring, and young insects produce the foamy substance for protection while they feed on sap under tender leaves and stems.

SOLUTION: Although unsightly, spittlebugs and their residue are not serious. To control, wash off plants with water spray or a diluted soap solution. *SUSCEPTIBLE PLANTS: MANY PERENNIALS.*

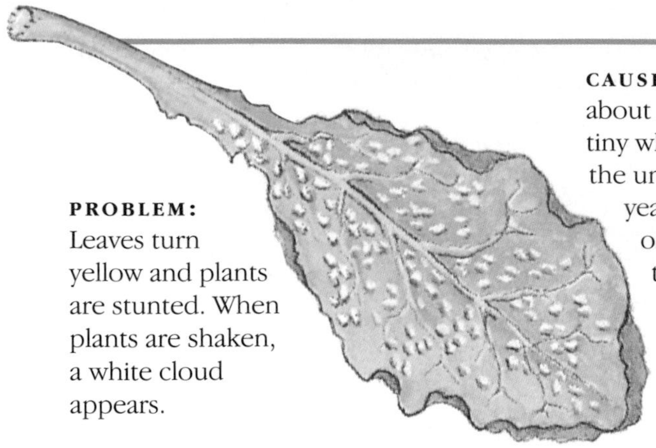

PROBLEM: Leaves turn yellow and plants are stunted. When plants are shaken, a white cloud appears.

CAUSE: Whiteflies, sucking insects about 1/16 of an inch long that look like tiny white moths, generally collect on the undersides of young leaves. Found year round in warmer climates but only in summer in colder climates, they like warm, still air. Whiteflies are often brought home with greenhouse plants and can carry virus and secrete honeydew, which promotes sooty mold.

SOLUTION: Keep the garden well weeded. Spray affected plants with a diluted soap solution or an insecticide. Whiteflies are attracted to the color yellow, so flypaper can be hung in the garden to help control the population.
SUSCEPTIBLE PLANTS: CHRYSANTHEMUM, COLUMBINE, LUPINE, PRIMROSE, ROSE MALLOW.

DISEASES

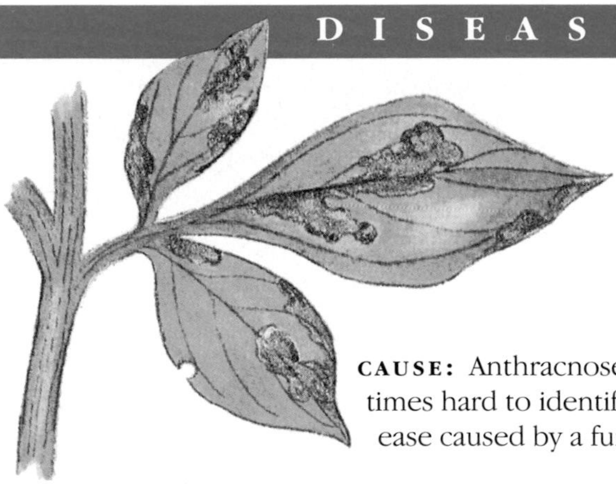

PROBLEM: Foliage develops irregular yellow to purplish brown spots that darken with age. These spots may also expand and join to cover the leaves. Purplish lesions form along the stem; plant growth is often stunted.

CAUSE: Anthracnose, sometimes hard to identify, is a disease caused by a fungus.

SOLUTION: Grow resistant plant varieties. Thin stems and tops to improve air circulation. Remove and destroy all shoots after first frost in the fall. If infection is severe, spray with a fungicide in early spring.
SUSCEPTIBLE PLANTS: PEONY.

PROBLEM: Foliage suddenly yellows. Flowers are small and immature and have a greenish color. New root, flower, and leaf growth is distorted, and leaves are stunted. Plants wilt and die.

CAUSE: Aster yellows, a viral disease that despite its name attacks many different kinds of plants, can appear throughout the growing season.

SOLUTION: Remove and destroy infected plants. Aster yellows overwinters in perennial weeds, so keep garden weeded and mow nearby weedy areas.
SUSCEPTIBLE PLANTS: BELLFLOWER, BLANKET-FLOWER, CHRYSANTHEMUM, COREOPSIS, DELPHINIUM, ENGLISH DAISY, PURPLE CONEFLOWER, SAGE.

PROBLEM: Flowers are streaked with white, gray, or tan fuzzy growth. Stalks weaken, flowers droop, shoots fall over. Buds may not open, or may wither and blacken. Discolored blotches appear on leaves, stems, flowers, and bulbs, and form fuzzy mold. Stem bases rot. Affected plant parts turn brown and dry.

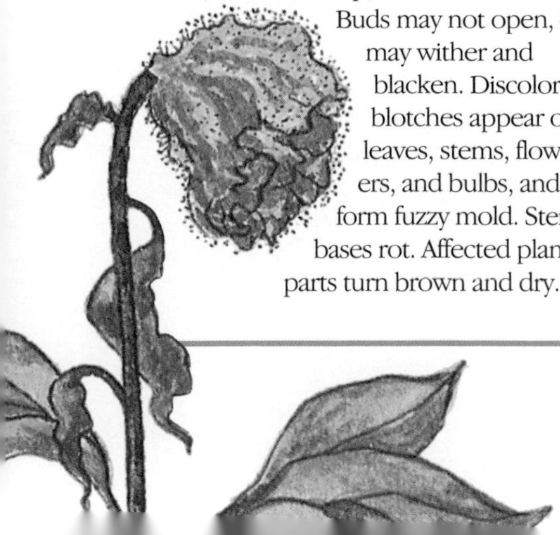

CAUSE: Botrytis blight, a disease caused by several species of fungi, produces microscopic spores that can be carried by the wind to spread infection. The blight survives the winter as hard, black lumps. The problem is most severe during damp, cool, cloudy weather.

SOLUTION: Avoid overwatering. Place plants in well-drained soil. Thin out plants so they get more light and air circulation, or transplant them to a dry, sunny location. Cut away, remove, and destroy diseased portions, and cut stalks to the ground in fall and destroy. As new growth starts in the spring, spray plants with a labeled systemic fungicide.
SUSCEPTIBLE PLANTS: CHRYSANTHEMUM, TRANSVAAL (GERBERA) DAISY, LILY, LUPINE, PEONY.

DISEASES

PROBLEM: Overnight, young seedlings suddenly topple over. Stems are rotted through at the soil line.

CAUSE: Damping-off is a disease caused by several fungi that form in the soil and attack seeds and roots of seedlings at ground level. The problem often occurs in wet, poorly drained soil with a high nitrogen content. *SUSCEPTIBLE PLANTS: SEEDLINGS OF MOST PERENNIALS.*

SOLUTION: Use fresh or treated seeds. Plant in a sterile medium topped with a thin layer of dry material (sand or perlite) to keep seedlings dry at the stem line. Plants in containers are more susceptible than those growing outdoors. Give them well-drained soil with plenty of light; avoid overcrowding. Do not overwater seed flats or seedbeds.

PROBLEM: Leaves turn yellow. Angular pale green or yellow blotches appear on the leaf's upper surface, with gray or tan fuzzy growths that resemble tufts of cotton forming on the underside. Leaves wilt, turn brown, and die.

CAUSE: Downy mildew, caused by a fungus, thrives in cool, wet weather, often in late summer and early fall. *SUSCEPTIBLE PLANTS: ASTER, CINQUEFOIL, CRANESBILL, GEUM, LUPINE, PURPLE CONEFLOWER, SPEEDWELL, WORMWOOD.*

SOLUTION: Grow resistant species and cultivars. Promote dry conditions by not watering plants overhead after morning. Space plants and thin stems to encourage air circulation. Remove and destroy blighted plant parts or the entire plant if the infection is severe.

PROBLEM: Yellow blotches that progress to brown may appear on leaves. Damaged areas are bound by large leaf veins. Eventually the leaf dies and becomes brittle. Young foliage curls and twists; growth is stunted. Symptoms appear first on older leaves, then move up the plant. Flowers and buds may also be affected.

CAUSE: Foliar nematodes, microscopic worms, feed on the outside of young foliage and the inside of mature foliage, spending most of their time inside a leaf. They thrive in warm, wet summers. Wet conditons help them migrate on films of water to infect plants and soil. *SUSCEPTIBLE PLANTS: ALUMROOT, BERGENIA, CHRYSANTHEMUM, HOSTA, IRIS, LILY, PEONY, PHLOX, SOLOMON'S-SEAL, WILD INDIGO, WINDFLOWER.*

SOLUTION: Remove and destroy infected plants. If plant is not severely infected, pull off affected leaves and their two closest healthy neighbors. In fall, cut plants to the ground and destroy stalks. Avoid watering foliage since splashing water can spread the disease.

PROBLEM: Leaves develop small yellow spots that gradually turn brown, frequently surrounded by a ring of yellow or brownish black tissue. Spots often join to produce large, irregular blotches. The leaf may turn yellow, wilt, and drop. Extensive defoliation can occur, weakening plant. The problem usually starts on lower leaves and moves up.

CAUSE: Leaf-spot diseases, caused by various fungi and bacteria, are spread by air currents and splashing water. Most prevalent from summer into fall, they thrive when humidity is high. *SUSCEPTIBLE PLANTS: ASTER, CARDINAL FLOWER, CHRYSANTHEMUM, CRANESBILL, DELPHINIUM, FOXGLOVE, IRIS, MONKSHOOD, PHLOX, POPPY, SEA LAVENDER.*

SOLUTION: Remove and destroy infected leaves as they appear; do not leave infected material in the garden over the winter. Water only in the morning. Thin plants to encourage good air circulation. A fungicide can protect healthy foliage but will not destroy fungus on infected leaves.

DISEASES

PROBLEM: Leaves become mottled with light green or yellow spots or streaks. New growth is spindly, and plant growth is often stunted.

CAUSE: Mosaic viruses, often spread by aphids, are a group of viruses that can occur at any time of the growing season. *SUSCEPTIBLE PLANTS: ASTER, BLANKET-FLOWER, CHRYSANTHEMUM, COLUMBINE, DELPHINIUM, PEONY.*

SOLUTION: Viral infections cannot be controlled. They are spread when a diseased plant touches a healthy one, and also via hands, tools, and insects moving from plant to plant. Remove and destroy infected plants, and keep the garden well weeded since viruses overwinter in perennial weeds.

PROBLEM: White or pale gray powdery growth appears on upper leaves, later causing leaf distortion, yellowing, withering, and leaf drop. Signs may also be seen on stems and buds.

CAUSE: Powdery mildew, a fungal disease, is especially noticeable in late summer and early fall when cool, humid nights follow warm days. More unsightly than harmful, it rarely kills the plant.

SOLUTION: Grow mildew-resistant varieties. Place susceptible plants in full sun with good air circulation. Water overhead only in the early morning. Cut infected plants to the ground in fall and discard. Fungicides may be used. Also effective are summer oil sprays and antitranspirants, which decrease the loss of water through the leaves. *SUSCEPTIBLE PLANTS: ASTER, BEE BALM, BOLTONIA, CLEMATIS, COREOPSIS, DELPHINIUM, MONKSHOOD, PHLOX, PURPLE CONEFLOWER.*

PROBLEM: Leaves turn yellow or brown or are stunted and wilted; the entire plant may wilt and die. Roots are discolored dark brown or black and may rot off.

CAUSE: Root rot, caused by a variety of fungi, is a common soil-borne disease found in moist soils during the growing season. *SUSCEPTIBLE PLANTS: ASTER, CHRYSANTHEMUM, DELPHINIUM.*

SOLUTION: Remove and destroy affected plants and surrounding soil. Plant in well-drained soil; do not overwater. Keep mulch away from base of plants. Avoid damaging roots when digging. A garden fungicide may be used in the soil.

PROBLEM: Upper leaf surfaces have pale yellow or white spots; undersides of leaves are covered with orange or yellow raised pustules. Leaves wilt and hang down along the stem. Pustules may become more numerous, destroying leaves and occasionally the entire plant. Plants may be stunted in severe cases.

CAUSE: Rust, a disease caused by a fungus, is a problem in the late summer and early fall, and is most prevalent when nights are cool and humid.

SOLUTION: Grow resistant varieties. Water early in the day; avoid wetting leaves. Remove and destroy infected leaves. In fall, cut infected plants to the ground and destroy stalks. Spray with sulfur or a garden fungicide. *SUSCEPTIBLE PLANTS: MANY PERENNIALS, INCLUDING ORNAMENTAL GRASSES, CLEMATIS, BEE BALM, CHRYSANTHEMUM, COLUMBINE, CONEFLOWER, COREOPSIS, DELPHINIUM, DIANTHUS, GAY-FEATHER, HOLLYHOCK, IRIS, LUPINE, PHLOX, SEA LAVENDER.*

DISEASES

PROBLEM: Plant is wilted, yellowed, or stunted, and it may die. Sometimes roots have knots or galls.

CAUSE: Soil nematodes—colorless, microscopic worms that live in the soil and feed on roots—inhibit a plant's intake of nitrogen. Damage is at its worst in warm, sunlit, sandy soils that are moist.

SOLUTION: Only a lab test can detect nematodes. Be wary of swollen or stunted roots. There are no chemical controls; dispose of infected plants and the surrounding soil, or solarize the soil by fixing a sheet of clear plastic over the ground and leaving it in place 1 to 2 months. Grow resistant varieties; rotate or interplant with plants that repel nematodes, such as marigolds. Add nitrogen fertilizer.
SUSCEPTIBLE PLANTS: MOST PERENNIALS, ESPECIALLY CHRYSANTHEMUM, CLEMATIS, CRANESBILL, DAYLILY, GLADIOLUS, IRIS, PHLOX, AND VIOLET.

PROBLEM: Leaves and stems turn yellow, wilt, rot, and die. Crowns may mold. Stems blacken and rot at base. White fibers and small tan lumps are visible at the base of the plant. Roots show signs of decay.

CAUSE: Southern blight, a disease caused by a fungus, enters the stems at soil level. It is most prevalent in hot weather.

SOLUTION: Remove and discard all infected plants and the soil that surrounds them. Thin out overcrowded plants, improve soil drainage, and avoid overwatering by letting soil dry out somewhat between waterings. Organic matter helps reduce disease.
SUSCEPTIBLE PLANTS: BALLOON FLOWER, BUGLEWEED, COLUMBINE, DELPHINIUM, HOSTA, IRIS, PURPLE CONEFLOWER, TORCH LILY.

PROBLEM: Entire plant becomes yellow, wilts, fails to grow, and eventually dies. Symptoms usually appear first on the lower and outer plant parts. A cut made across the stem near the base reveals dark streaks or other discoloration on the tissue inside.

CAUSE: Vascular wilt caused by fusarium and verticillium fungi in the soil display similar symptoms. Fusarium wilt is more prevalent in hot weather, and verticillium wilt is found in cool weather.

SOLUTION: Remove and destroy infected plants; substitute wilt-resistant varieties. Wash hands and disinfect tools. There are no effective chemical controls. Fungus stays in the soil a long time, so transplant susceptible plants away from infected area. Solarize the soil by fixing a sheet of clear plastic over the ground and leaving it in place 1 to 2 months.
SUSCEPTIBLE PLANTS: ASTER, BLEEDING HEART, CHRYSANTHEMUM, COREOPSIS, DELPHINIUM, MONKSHOOD, PINKS, POPPY.

Plant Selection Guide

Organized by flower color, this chart provides information needed to select species and varieties that will thrive in the particular conditions of your garden. For additional information on each plant, refer to the Encyclopedia of Perennials that begins on page 112.

		ZONES									SOIL					LIGHT		BLOOMING SEASON				PLANT HEIGHT			NOTED FOR			
		ZONE 3	ZONE 4	ZONE 5	ZONE 6	ZONE 7	ZONE 8	ZONE 9	ZONE 10	ZONE 11	SANDY	LOAM	DRY	WELL-DRAINED	MOIST	FULL SUN	SHADE	SPRING	SUMMER	FALL	WINTER	UNDER 2 FT.	2-3 FT.	OVER 3 FT.	LONG BLOOM SEASON	FRAGRANCE	DISTINCTIVE FOLIAGE	CUT FLOWERS
WHITE	ACONITUM NAPELLUS 'SNOW WHITE'	✔	✔	✔	✔	✔	✔					✔		✔	✔	✔	✔		✔	✔				✔	✔			
WHITE	AGAPANTHUS ORIENTALIS 'ALBIDUS'						✔	✔	✔			✔		✔	✔	✔			✔					✔				
WHITE	ANAPHALIS TRIPLINERVIS	✔	✔	✔	✔	✔	✔	✔				✔		✔	✔	✔	✔		✔	✔		✔						✔
WHITE	ANEMONE X HYBRIDA 'HONORINE JOBERT'			✔	✔	✔	✔					✔		✔		✔	✔		✔	✔			✔					
WHITE	ARABIS CAUCASICA 'SNOW CAP'	✔	✔	✔	✔	✔	✔				✔			✔		✔		✔				✔				✔		
WHITE	ARENARIA MONTANA			✔	✔	✔	✔	✔						✔	✔	✔	✔	✔				✔						
WHITE	ARTEMISIA LACTIFLORA			✔	✔	✔	✔						✔	✔		✔			✔	✔				✔			✔	
WHITE	ARUNCUS DIOICUS	✔	✔	✔	✔	✔	✔	✔				✔			✔		✔		✔					✔			✔	
WHITE	ASTILBE JAPONICA 'DEUTSCHLAND'		✔	✔	✔	✔	✔					✔			✔		✔		✔				✔				✔	
WHITE	BOLTONIA ASTEROIDES 'SNOWBANK'		✔	✔	✔	✔	✔							✔	✔	✔			✔	✔				✔				✔
WHITE	CAMPANULA PERSICIFOLIA 'ALBA'	✔	✔	✔	✔	✔						✔		✔		✔	✔		✔				✔					
WHITE	CHRYSANTHEMUM NIPPONICUM				✔	✔	✔	✔				✔		✔		✔	✔			✔		✔						✔
WHITE	CHRYSANTHEMUM X SUPERBUM 'ALASKA'		✔	✔	✔	✔	✔	✔				✔		✔		✔	✔		✔	✔			✔		✔			✔
WHITE	CIMICIFUGA RAMOSA	✔	✔	✔	✔	✔	✔					✔			✔		✔		✔	✔				✔	✔			
WHITE	CRAMBE CORDIFOLIA				✔	✔	✔	✔				✔		✔		✔			✔					✔			✔	
WHITE	DICENTRA EXIMIA 'ALBA'	✔	✔	✔	✔	✔	✔					✔		✔	✔		✔	✔	✔			✔					✔	
WHITE	FILIPENDULA ULMARIA	✔	✔	✔	✔	✔	✔	✔				✔			✔		✔		✔					✔			✔	✔
WHITE	GILLENIA TRIFOLIATA		✔	✔	✔	✔	✔					✔		✔	✔		✔	✔	✔				✔					
WHITE	GYPSOPHILA PANICULATA 'PERFECTA'		✔	✔	✔	✔	✔	✔				✔		✔	✔	✔			✔				✔					✔
WHITE	HELLEBORUS NIGER		✔	✔	✔	✔	✔					✔		✔	✔		✔	✔			✔	✔						
WHITE	HEUCHERA SANGUINEA 'SNOWFLAKES'		✔	✔	✔	✔	✔					✔		✔	✔	✔	✔		✔			✔					✔	
WHITE	HOSTA PLANTAGINEA	✔	✔	✔	✔	✔	✔	✔				✔			✔		✔		✔				✔			✔	✔	
WHITE	IBERIS SEMPERVIRENS 'LITTLE GEM'		✔	✔	✔	✔	✔					✔		✔	✔	✔	✔	✔				✔					✔	
WHITE	IRIS 'CINDY'		✔	✔	✔	✔	✔	✔				✔		✔		✔		✔						✔				✔
WHITE	IRIS SIBIRICA 'WHITE SWIRL'		✔	✔	✔	✔	✔	✔				✔		✔		✔		✔						✔				✔
WHITE	LIATRIS SCARIOSA 'WHITE SPIRES'	✔	✔	✔	✔	✔	✔	✔			✔			✔		✔	✔		✔	✔				✔				✔
WHITE	LUPINUS 'RUSSELL HYBRIDS' WHITE	✔	✔	✔	✔							✔		✔	✔	✔	✔		✔					✔			✔	
WHITE	LYSIMACHIA CLETHROIDES		✔	✔	✔	✔	✔					✔			✔	✔	✔		✔				✔				✔	

		ZONES									SOIL					LIGHT		BLOOMING SEASON				PLANT HEIGHT			NOTED FOR			
		ZONE 3	ZONE 4	ZONE 5	ZONE 6	ZONE 7	ZONE 8	ZONE 9	ZONE 10	ZONE 11	SANDY	LOAM	DRY	WELL-DRAINED	MOIST	FULL SUN	SHADE	SPRING	SUMMER	FALL	WINTER	UNDER 2 FT.	2-3 FT.	OVER 3 FT.	LONG BLOOM SEASON	FRAGRANCE	DISTINCTIVE FOLIAGE	CUT FLOWERS
WHITE	MACLEAYA CORDATA		✔	✔	✔	✔	✔	✔				✔		✔	✔	✔	✔		✔					✔			✔	✔
WHITE	PAEONIA LACTIFLORA ‘KRINKLED WHITE’	✔	✔	✔	✔	✔	✔					✔		✔		✔	✔	✔					✔			✔	✔	✔
WHITE	PENNISETUM CAUDATUM			✔	✔	✔	✔	✔				✔		✔		✔			✔	✔				✔			✔	
WHITE	PHLOX MACULATA ‘MISS LINGARD’		✔	✔	✔	✔	✔	✔				✔		✔	✔	✔			✔	✔			✔					
WHITE	RODGERSIA PODOPHYLLA			✔	✔	✔	✔					✔			✔	✔	✔	✔	✔				✔				✔	
WHITE	ROMNEYA COULTERI					✔	✔	✔	✔				✔			✔			✔					✔				✔
WHITE	SILENE ‘ROBIN'S WHITE BREAST’		✔	✔	✔	✔	✔				✔			✔		✔	✔		✔	✔		✔			✔		✔	
WHITE	SMILACINA RACEMOSA		✔	✔	✔	✔	✔					✔			✔		✔	✔					✔			✔	✔	
WHITE	TRICYRTIS HIRTA		✔	✔	✔	✔	✔	✔				✔			✔		✔		✔	✔			✔		✔			
WHITE	VERBASCUM CHAIXII ‘ALBUM’			✔	✔	✔	✔	✔			✔			✔		✔	✔		✔				✔				✔	
WHITE	VERONICA SPICATA ‘ICICLE’		✔	✔	✔	✔	✔					✔		✔		✔		✔	✔			✔			✔			✔
YELLOW	ACHILLEA FILIPENDULINA ‘CORONATION GOLD’		✔	✔	✔	✔	✔						✔	✔		✔		✔	✔				✔			✔		✔
YELLOW	ALCHEMILLA MOLLIS	✔	✔	✔	✔	✔	✔					✔		✔	✔	✔	✔	✔	✔			✔					✔	✔
YELLOW	ANTHEMIS TINCTORIA	✔	✔	✔	✔	✔	✔						✔	✔		✔			✔	✔			✔		✔	✔		✔
YELLOW	AQUILEGIA CHRYSANTHA	✔	✔	✔	✔	✔	✔					✔		✔	✔	✔	✔		✔					✔				
YELLOW	AURINIA SAXATILIS		✔	✔	✔	✔	✔	✔	✔		✔			✔		✔		✔	✔			✔					✔	
YELLOW	CENTAUREA MACROCEPHALA	✔	✔	✔	✔	✔	✔					✔		✔		✔		✔	✔					✔				✔
YELLOW	COREOPSIS GRANDIFLORA ‘SUNRAY’		✔	✔	✔	✔	✔	✔				✔		✔		✔		✔	✔			✔			✔			✔
YELLOW	COREOPSIS VERTICILLATA		✔	✔	✔	✔	✔	✔				✔		✔		✔		✔	✔				✔		✔			✔
YELLOW	DIGITALIS GRANDIFLORA		✔	✔	✔	✔	✔					✔		✔	✔		✔	✔	✔				✔					
YELLOW	DORONICUM ‘MISS MASON’		✔	✔	✔	✔	✔					✔			✔	✔	✔	✔				✔						✔
YELLOW	GAILLARDIA X GRANDIFLORA ‘YELLOW QUEEN’	✔	✔	✔	✔	✔	✔				✔			✔		✔			✔	✔			✔		✔			✔
YELLOW	HELENIUM AUTUMNALE ‘BUTTERPAT’	✔	✔	✔	✔	✔	✔					✔			✔	✔			✔	✔			✔		✔			✔
YELLOW	HELIANTHUS ANGUSTIFOLIUS				✔	✔	✔	✔				✔		✔	✔	✔				✔				✔				✔
YELLOW	HELIANTHUS X MULTIFLORUS ‘FLORE PENO’		✔	✔	✔	✔	✔	✔				✔		✔	✔	✔			✔	✔				✔				✔
YELLOW	HELIOPSIS HELIANTHOIDES VAR. SCABRA ‘KARAT’		✔	✔	✔	✔	✔	✔				✔		✔	✔	✔			✔	✔				✔				✔
YELLOW	HEMEROCALLIS ‘HYPERION’	✔	✔	✔	✔	✔	✔	✔	✔			✔		✔		✔	✔		✔	✔				✔		✔		
YELLOW	HEMEROCALLIS ‘STELLA DE ORO’	✔	✔	✔	✔	✔	✔	✔	✔			✔		✔		✔	✔		✔	✔		✔			✔			
YELLOW	INULA ENSIFOLIA		✔	✔	✔	✔	✔	✔						✔		✔	✔		✔			✔						
YELLOW	IRIS PSEUDACORUS			✔	✔	✔	✔	✔							✔	✔	✔	✔	✔					✔			✔	
YELLOW	LIGULARIA DENTATA ‘DESDEMONA’		✔	✔	✔	✔	✔								✔	✔	✔		✔					✔			✔	
YELLOW	LINUM FLAVUM			✔	✔	✔	✔	✔			✔			✔		✔	✔		✔			✔						

Color	Plant	Zones: Zone 3	Zone 4	Zone 5	Zone 6	Zone 7	Zone 8	Zone 9	Zone 10	Zone 11	Soil: Sandy	Loam	Dry	Well-Drained	Moist	Light: Full Sun	Shade	Blooming Season: Spring	Summer	Fall	Winter	Plant Height: Under 2 Ft.	2-3 Ft.	Over 3 Ft.	Noted For: Long Bloom Season	Fragrance	Distinctive Foliage	Cut Flowers
YELLOW	LYSIMACHIA PUNCTATA		✔	✔	✔	✔	✔					✔			✔	✔	✔	✔	✔				✔					
YELLOW	OENOTHERA FRUITICOSA		✔	✔	✔	✔	✔					✔		✔		✔			✔			✔				✔		
YELLOW	PAEONIA MLOKOSEWITSCHII				✔	✔	✔					✔		✔		✔	✔	✔				✔				✔	✔	✔
YELLOW	PRIMULA AURICULA	✔	✔	✔	✔	✔	✔					✔			✔		✔	✔				✔				✔		
YELLOW	RANUNCULUS REPENS		✔	✔	✔	✔	✔	✔				✔		✔	✔	✔	✔	✔				✔						
YELLOW	RUDBECKIA FULGIDA 'GOLDSTURM'		✔	✔	✔	✔	✔	✔				✔				✔	✔		✔	✔		✔			✔			✔
YELLOW	SEDUM AIZOON		✔	✔	✔	✔	✔	✔	✔					✔		✔	✔	✔	✔			✔					✔	
YELLOW	SOLIDAGO 'PETER PAN'	✔	✔	✔	✔	✔	✔	✔						✔		✔	✔		✔	✔			✔					✔
YELLOW	THALICTRUM MINUS			✔	✔	✔	✔	✔						✔	✔	✔	✔	✔	✔				✔				✔	
YELLOW	TROLLIUS EUROPAEUS		✔	✔	✔	✔	✔								✔	✔	✔	✔	✔			✔			✔			✔
YELLOW	VERBASCUM CHAIXII			✔	✔	✔	✔	✔			✔			✔		✔	✔		✔				✔					
ORANGE	ANTHEMIS SANCTI-JOHANNIS			✔	✔	✔	✔						✔	✔		✔			✔	✔			✔			✔		
ORANGE	ASCLEPIAS TUBEROSA	✔	✔	✔	✔	✔	✔	✔						✔		✔			✔				✔					✔
ORANGE	BELAMCANDA CHINENSIS			✔	✔	✔	✔	✔	✔					✔	✔	✔	✔		✔				✔					✔
ORANGE	CROCOSMIA MASONIORUM				✔	✔	✔	✔			✔			✔		✔		✔	✔				✔					✔
ORANGE	GEUM QUELLYON 'MRS. BRADSHAW'			✔	✔	✔	✔					✔		✔		✔	✔	✔	✔			✔						
ORANGE	HEMEROCALLIS FULVA	✔	✔	✔	✔	✔	✔	✔						✔		✔	✔		✔					✔			✔	
ORANGE	INULA ROYLEANA		✔	✔	✔	✔								✔		✔	✔		✔				✔					
ORANGE	LYCHNIS ARKWRIGHTII					✔	✔	✔				✔		✔		✔	✔		✔			✔						
ORANGE	PAPAVER ORIENTALE 'GLOWING EMBERS'	✔	✔	✔	✔	✔	✔	✔						✔		✔	✔	✔	✔				✔					
ORANGE	PHLOX PANICULATA		✔	✔	✔	✔	✔	✔						✔		✔			✔				✔					
ORANGE	POTENTILLA NEPALENSIS 'ROXANA'		✔	✔	✔	✔					✔			✔		✔	✔		✔			✔						
ORANGE	SEDUM KAMTSCHATICUM	✔	✔	✔	✔	✔	✔							✔		✔	✔		✔			✔					✔	
ORANGE	TROLLIUS LEDEBOURII 'GOLDEN QUEEN'		✔	✔	✔	✔	✔								✔	✔	✔	✔	✔				✔					✔
	ACHILLEA MILLEFOLIUM 'FIRE KING'		✔	✔	✔	✔	✔						✔	✔		✔			✔			✔						✔
	ARMERIA ALLIACEA 'BEE'S RUBY'	✔	✔	✔	✔	✔	✔				✔			✔		✔		✔	✔			✔						
	ASTILBE 'FANAL'		✔	✔	✔	✔	✔					✔			✔		✔		✔			✔					✔	
	CENTRANTHUS RUBER 'ATROCOCCINEUS'		✔	✔	✔	✔	✔	✔				✔		✔		✔			✔				✔					✔
	DIANTHUS DELTOIDES 'BRILLIANT'		✔	✔	✔	✔	✔							✔	✔	✔	✔	✔	✔			✔						
	EPIMEDIUM X RUBRUM			✔	✔	✔	✔							✔	✔		✔	✔				✔					✔	
	GAILLARDIA X GRANDIFLORA 'BURGUNDY'	✔	✔	✔	✔	✔	✔				✔			✔		✔			✔	✔		✔						✔
	HELENIUM AUTUMNALE 'CRIMSON BEAUTY'	✔	✔	✔	✔	✔	✔					✔			✔	✔			✔	✔			✔		✔			✔

		Zones									Soil					Light		Blooming Season				Plant Height			Noted For			
		Zone 3	Zone 4	Zone 5	Zone 6	Zone 7	Zone 8	Zone 9	Zone 10	Zone 11	Sandy	Loam	Dry	Well-Drained	Moist	Full Sun	Shade	Spring	Summer	Fall	Winter	Under 2 Ft.	2-3 Ft.	Over 3 Ft.	Long Bloom Season	Fragrance	Distinctive Foliage	Cut Flowers
RED	HEMEROCALLIS 'AUTUMN RED'	✔	✔	✔	✔	✔	✔	✔	✔					✔	✔	✔	✔		✔	✔			✔					
RED	HEUCHERA SANGUINEA 'RED SPANGLES'		✔	✔	✔	✔	✔					✔		✔	✔	✔	✔		✔			✔					✔	
RED	HIBISCUS 'LORD BALTIMORE'			✔	✔	✔	✔	✔				✔			✔	✔	✔		✔					✔	✔			
RED	IRIS 'ALREADY'		✔	✔	✔	✔	✔	✔				✔		✔		✔		✔				✔						
RED	LOBELIA CARDINALIS	✔	✔	✔	✔	✔	✔	✔				✔			✔		✔		✔				✔					
RED	LUPINUS RUSSELL HYBRID 'CARMINE'	✔	✔	✔	✔							✔		✔	✔	✔	✔		✔					✔			✔	
RED	MISCANTHUS SINENSIS 'GRACILLIMUS'			✔	✔	✔	✔	✔						✔		✔			✔	✔	✔			✔			✔	
RED	MONARDA DIDYMA 'CAMBRIDGE SCARLET'		✔	✔	✔	✔	✔	✔							✔	✔	✔		✔					✔		✔		
RED	PAEONIA TENUIFOLIA			✔	✔	✔	✔					✔		✔		✔	✔		✔			✔				✔	✔	
RED	PAPAVER ORIENTALE 'BEAUTY OF LIVERMORE'	✔	✔	✔	✔	✔	✔	✔						✔		✔	✔	✔	✔					✔				
RED	PENSTEMON BARBATUS 'PRAIRIE FIRE'		✔	✔	✔	✔	✔	✔						✔		✔	✔		✔					✔				✔
RED	PHORMIUM TENAX 'VARIEGATUM'							✔	✔			✔			✔	✔			✔					✔			✔	
RED	POTENTILLA ATROSANGUINEA			✔	✔	✔	✔				✔			✔		✔	✔	✔	✔			✔					✔	
RED	PRIMULA JAPONICA 'MILLER'S CRIMSON'				✔	✔	✔					✔			✔		✔	✔				✔						
RED	SEDUM MAXIMUM 'ATROPURPUREUM'		✔	✔	✔	✔	✔	✔	✔					✔		✔	✔		✔			✔					✔	
RED	SEDUM SPURIUM 'DRAGON'S BLOOD'	✔	✔	✔	✔	✔	✔							✔		✔	✔		✔			✔					✔	
RED	VERBENA PERUVIANA						✔	✔						✔		✔			✔	✔		✔			✔			
RED	VERONICA SPICATA 'RED FOX'		✔	✔	✔	✔	✔							✔		✔			✔			✔			✔			
PINK	ACANTHUS MOLLIS 'LATIFOLIUS'						✔	✔	✔					✔		✔	✔		✔					✔			✔	
PINK	ANEMONE X HYBRIDA 'SEPTEMBER CHARM'				✔	✔	✔					✔		✔		✔	✔		✔	✔			✔		✔			
PINK	ARMERIA MARITIMA 'LAUCHEANA'		✔	✔	✔	✔	✔				✔			✔		✔		✔				✔						
PINK	ASCLEPIAS INCARNATA	✔	✔	✔	✔	✔	✔				✔			✔		✔			✔	✔			✔			✔		
PINK	ASTILBE CHINENSIS 'PUMILA'			✔	✔	✔	✔					✔			✔		✔		✔			✔					✔	
PINK	ASTRANTIA MAJOR 'ROSEA'		✔	✔	✔	✔	✔	✔				✔		✔			✔	✔	✔				✔					✔
PINK	BEGONIA GRANDIS				✔	✔	✔	✔				✔			✔	✔	✔		✔	✔		✔					✔	
PINK	CALAMAGROSTIS ACUTIFLORA 'STRICTA'		✔	✔	✔	✔	✔							✔		✔			✔	✔	✔			✔			✔	
PINK	CENTAUREA DEALBATA		✔	✔	✔	✔	✔							✔		✔		✔	✔				✔					✔
PINK	CHRYSANTHEMUM MORIFOLIUM 'PINK DAISY'			✔	✔	✔	✔	✔	✔			✔		✔		✔	✔		✔	✔		✔						✔
PINK	COREOPSIS ROSEA		✔	✔	✔	✔	✔	✔						✔	✔	✔		✔	✔			✔						
PINK	DICENTRA EXIMIA	✔	✔	✔	✔	✔	✔							✔	✔		✔	✔	✔			✔			✔		✔	
PINK	DICENTRA SPECTABLIS	✔	✔	✔	✔	✔	✔							✔	✔		✔	✔	✔				✔				✔	
PINK	ECHINACEA PURPUREA 'THE KING'	✔	✔	✔	✔	✔	✔	✔						✔		✔	✔		✔					✔				✔

		ZONES									SOIL					LIGHT		BLOOMING SEASON				PLANT HEIGHT			NOTED FOR			
		ZONE 3	ZONE 4	ZONE 5	ZONE 6	ZONE 7	ZONE 8	ZONE 9	ZONE 10	ZONE 11	SANDY	LOAM	DRY	WELL-DRAINED	MOIST	FULL SUN	SHADE	SPRING	SUMMER	FALL	WINTER	UNDER 2 FT.	2-3 FT.	OVER 3 FT.	LONG BLOOM SEASON	FRAGRANCE	DISTINCTIVE FOLIAGE	CUT FLOWERS
PINK	ERIGERON SPECIOSUS 'FOERSTER'S LIEBLING'	✔	✔	✔	✔	✔	✔							✔		✔			✔			✔			✔			✔
PINK	EUPATORIUM FISTULOSUM	✔	✔	✔	✔	✔	✔	✔						✔	✔	✔	✔		✔	✔				✔				
PINK	FILIPENDULA RUBRA 'VENUSTA'	✔	✔	✔	✔	✔	✔	✔				✔			✔		✔		✔					✔				✔
PINK	GERANIUM CINEREUM			✔	✔	✔	✔							✔	✔	✔	✔		✔			✔			✔		✔	
PINK	GERANIUM DALMATICUM		✔	✔	✔	✔	✔							✔	✔	✔	✔	✔				✔						
PINK	HEMEROCALLIS 'COUNTRY CLUB'	✔	✔	✔	✔	✔	✔	✔	✔					✔	✔	✔	✔		✔			✔						
PINK	HEUCHERA SANGUINEA 'CHATTERBOX'		✔	✔	✔	✔	✔					✔		✔	✔	✔	✔		✔			✔			✔			
PINK	HIBISCUS 'LADY BALTIMORE'			✔	✔	✔	✔	✔				✔			✔	✔	✔		✔					✔				
PINK	IRIS ENSATA 'PINK LADY'			✔	✔	✔	✔	✔				✔			✔	✔	✔		✔				✔					✔
PINK	MALVA MOSCHATA 'ROSEA'		✔	✔	✔	✔	✔						✔	✔		✔	✔		✔	✔			✔		✔			
PINK	PAEONIA LACTIFLORA 'LOTUS BLOOM'	✔	✔	✔	✔	✔	✔					✔		✔		✔	✔	✔					✔			✔	✔	✔
PINK	PAPAVER ORIENTALE 'MRS. PERRY'	✔	✔	✔	✔	✔	✔	✔						✔		✔	✔	✔	✔				✔					
PINK	PHYSOSTEGIA VIRGINIANA 'VIVID'		✔	✔	✔	✔	✔						✔	✔	✔	✔	✔		✔	✔		✔						✔
PINK	PLATYCODON GRANDIFLORUS 'SHELL PINK'		✔	✔	✔	✔	✔	✔				✔		✔		✔	✔		✔				✔		✔			
PINK	POLYGONUM AFFINE		✔	✔	✔	✔						✔			✔	✔	✔		✔			✔					✔	
PINK	SAPONARIA OCYMOIDES		✔	✔	✔	✔	✔	✔						✔		✔		✔	✔			✔						
PINK	SEDUM 'AUTUMN JOY'	✔	✔	✔	✔	✔	✔	✔	✔					✔		✔	✔		✔	✔	✔	✔			✔		✔	
PINK	SIDALCEA MALVIFLORA 'ELSIE HEUGH'			✔	✔	✔	✔							✔	✔	✔	✔		✔				✔		✔			✔
PINK	VERONICASTRUM VIRGINICUM 'ROSEUM'		✔	✔	✔	✔	✔					✔		✔		✔	✔		✔					✔	✔			
PURPLE	AJUGA REPTANS	✔	✔	✔	✔	✔	✔	✔				✔		✔		✔	✔	✔				✔					✔	
PURPLE	ALLIUM CHRISTOPHII		✔	✔	✔	✔	✔					✔		✔		✔	✔		✔			✔						✔
PURPLE	ALLIUM GIGANTEUM			✔	✔	✔	✔					✔		✔		✔	✔		✔					✔				✔
PURPLE	ASTER NOVAE-ANGLIAE 'PURPLE DOME'		✔	✔	✔	✔	✔					✔		✔	✔	✔				✔		✔						✔
PURPLE	DELPHINIUM 'BLACK KNIGHT'	✔	✔	✔	✔	✔	✔					✔		✔	✔	✔			✔					✔				✔
PURPLE	DICTAMNUS ALBUS 'PURPUREUS'	✔	✔	✔	✔	✔	✔					✔		✔		✔	✔	✔	✔				✔			✔		
PURPLE	ERIGERON SPECIOSUS 'AZURE FAIRY'	✔	✔	✔	✔	✔	✔							✔		✔			✔				✔		✔			✔
PURPLE	EUPATORIUM COELESTINUM			✔	✔	✔	✔	✔						✔	✔	✔	✔		✔	✔		✔			✔			✔
PURPLE	IRIS ENSATA 'ROYAL BANNER'			✔	✔	✔	✔	✔				✔			✔	✔	✔		✔				✔					✔
PURPLE	IRIS SIBIRICA 'HARPSWELL HAZE'		✔	✔	✔	✔	✔	✔				✔			✔	✔		✔						✔				✔
PURPLE	LAVANDULA ANGUSTIFOLIA 'HIDCOTE'			✔	✔	✔	✔	✔						✔		✔			✔			✔				✔	✔	
PURPLE	LIATRIS SCARIOSA 'SEPTEMBER GLORY'		✔	✔	✔	✔	✔	✔			✔			✔		✔	✔		✔	✔				✔				✔
PURPLE	LIMONIUM LATIFOLIUM 'VIOLETTA'		✔	✔	✔	✔	✔	✔						✔		✔			✔				✔					✔

		ZONES									SOIL					LIGHT		BLOOMING SEASON				PLANT HEIGHT			NOTED FOR			
		ZONE 3	ZONE 4	ZONE 5	ZONE 6	ZONE 7	ZONE 8	ZONE 9	ZONE 10	ZONE 11	SANDY	LOAM	DRY	WELL-DRAINED	MOIST	FULL SUN	SHADE	SPRING	SUMMER	FALL	WINTER	UNDER 2 FT.	2-3 FT.	OVER 3 FT.	LONG BLOOM SEASON	FRAGRANCE	DISTINCTIVE FOLIAGE	CUT FLOWERS
PURPLE	SALVIA X SUPERBA			✔	✔	✔	✔	✔	✔			✔		✔		✔		✔	✔				✔					
PURPLE	STACHYS MACRANTHA		✔	✔	✔	✔	✔	✔						✔		✔	✔	✔	✔			✔						
PURPLE	THALICTRUM DELAVAYI			✔	✔	✔	✔	✔				✔		✔	✔	✔	✔		✔					✔				✔
PURPLE	THALICTRUM ROCHEBRUNIANUM				✔	✔	✔	✔				✔		✔	✔	✔	✔		✔					✔				
PURPLE	VERBENA BONARIENSIS						✔	✔						✔		✔			✔	✔				✔		✔		
PURPLE	VIOLA CORNUTA 'LORD NELSON'			✔	✔	✔	✔	✔				✔		✔	✔		✔	✔	✔	✔		✔			✔		✔	
BLUE	ACONITUM CARMICHAELII	✔	✔	✔	✔	✔	✔					✔		✔	✔	✔	✔		✔	✔				✔	✔			
BLUE	AGAPANTHUS AFRICANUS						✔	✔	✔			✔		✔	✔	✔			✔				✔					
BLUE	AMSONIA CILIATA					✔	✔	✔	✔					✔	✔	✔	✔	✔	✔				✔				✔	
BLUE	ANCHUSA AZUREA	✔	✔	✔	✔	✔	✔							✔		✔	✔	✔	✔					✔	✔			
BLUE	AQUILEGIA FLABELLATA	✔	✔	✔	✔	✔	✔							✔	✔	✔	✔		✔			✔					✔	
BLUE	ASTER X FRIKARTII				✔	✔	✔	✔				✔		✔	✔	✔			✔	✔			✔		✔			
BLUE	BAPTISIA AUSTRALIS	✔	✔	✔	✔	✔	✔	✔					✔	✔		✔		✔						✔			✔	✔
BLUE	BRUNNERA MACROPHYLLA		✔	✔	✔	✔	✔	✔				✔		✔	✔	✔	✔	✔				✔					✔	
BLUE	CAMPANULA CARPATICA 'BLAUE CLIPS'	✔	✔	✔	✔	✔	✔					✔		✔		✔	✔		✔	✔		✔			✔			
BLUE	CERATOSTIGMA PLUMBAGINOIDES			✔	✔	✔	✔	✔						✔		✔	✔		✔	✔		✔			✔		✔	
BLUE	CLEMATIS HERACLEIFOLIA 'DAVIDIANA'			✔	✔	✔	✔					✔		✔	✔	✔			✔				✔			✔		
BLUE	DELPHINIUM X BELLADONNA 'BELLAMOSUM'	✔	✔	✔	✔	✔	✔					✔		✔	✔	✔			✔					✔				✔
BLUE	ECHINOPS RITRO 'TAPLOW BLUE'	✔	✔	✔	✔	✔	✔	✔						✔		✔			✔					✔				✔
BLUE	ERYNGIUM ALPINUM			✔	✔	✔	✔	✔			✔		✔			✔			✔				✔					✔
BLUE	GERANIUM 'JOHNSON'S BLUE'		✔	✔	✔	✔	✔							✔	✔	✔	✔	✔	✔			✔			✔			
BLUE	LINUM PERENNE			✔	✔	✔	✔	✔			✔			✔		✔	✔	✔	✔			✔			✔			
BLUE	LOBELIA SIPHILITICA		✔	✔	✔	✔	✔					✔			✔		✔		✔				✔		✔			
BLUE	NEPETA X FAASSENII		✔	✔	✔	✔	✔							✔		✔			✔			✔				✔	✔	
BLUE	PEROVSKIA ATRIPLICIFOLIA			✔	✔	✔	✔	✔						✔		✔			✔					✔		✔	✔	
BLUE	PHLOX STOLONIFERA 'BLUE RIDGE'			✔	✔	✔	✔					✔		✔	✔	✔	✔	✔				✔					✔	
BLUE	PLATYCODON GRANDIFLORUS 'MARIESII'		✔	✔	✔	✔	✔	✔				✔		✔	✔	✔	✔		✔			✔			✔			
BLUE	PULMONARIA LONGIFOLIA 'ROY DAVIDSON'			✔	✔	✔	✔					✔			✔		✔	✔				✔					✔	
BLUE	SALVIA FARINACEA 'BLUE BEDDER'						✔	✔	✔			✔		✔		✔			✔	✔			✔		✔			
BLUE	SCABIOSA CAUCASICA 'FAMA'		✔	✔	✔	✔	✔	✔				✔		✔		✔			✔			✔			✔			✔
BLUE	STOKESIA LAEVIS 'BLUE DANUBE'			✔	✔	✔	✔	✔			✔			✔		✔			✔			✔			✔			
BLUE	VERONICA 'SUNNY BORDER BLUE'		✔	✔	✔	✔	✔					✔		✔		✔	✔		✔	✔		✔			✔			

A Zone Map of the United States

A plant's winter hardiness is critical in deciding whether it is suitable for your garden. The map below divides the United States into 11 climatic zones based on average minimum temperatures, as compiled by the United States Department of Agriculture. Find your zone and check the zone information in the Plant Selection Guide *(pages 104-109)* or the Encyclopedia entries *(pages 112-161)* to help you choose the plants most likely to flourish in your climate.

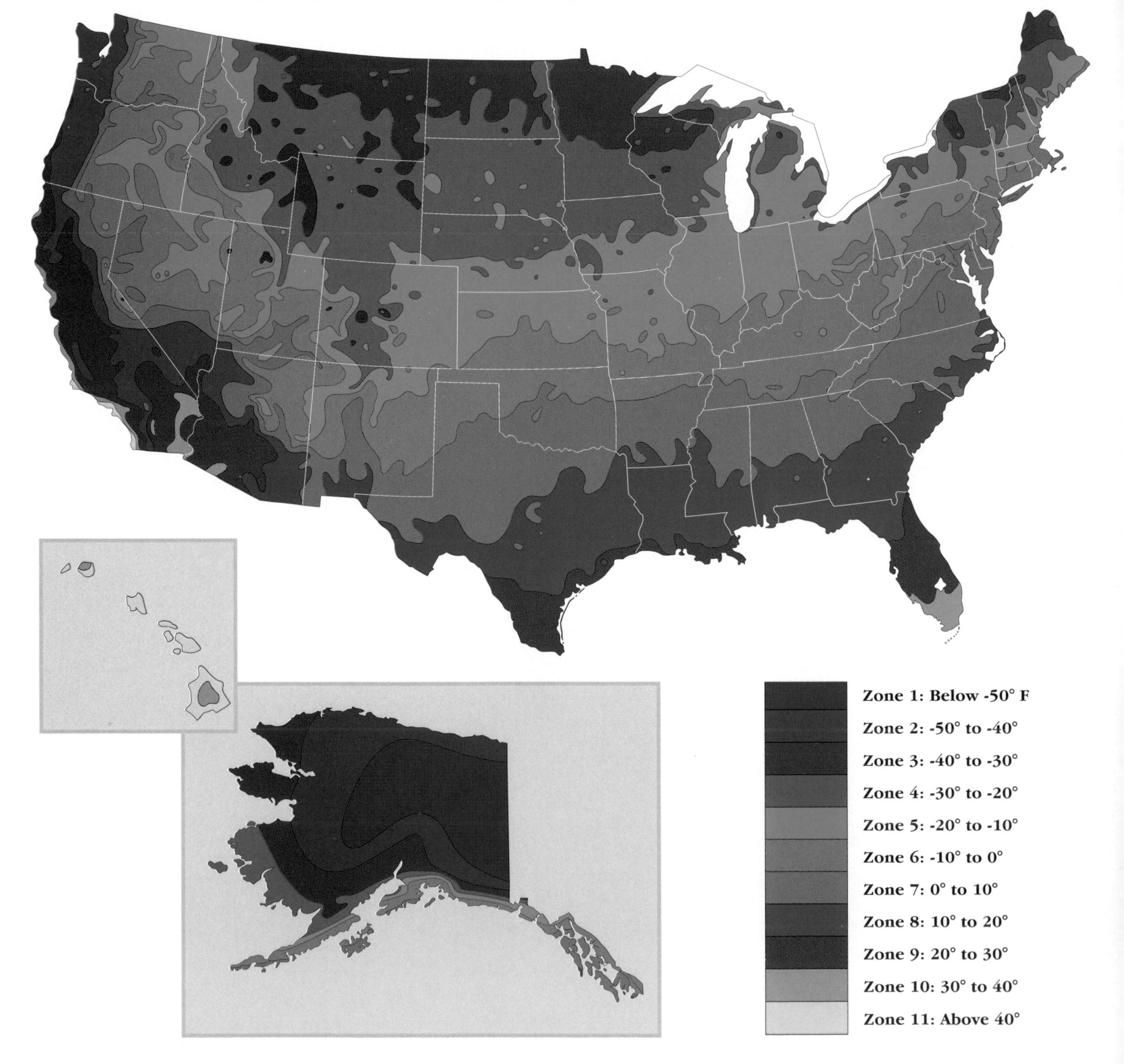

Cross-Reference Guide to Plant Names

African lily—*Agapanthus*
Alumroot—*Heuchera*
Avens—*Geum*
Baby's-breath—*Gypsophila*
Bachelor's-button—*Centaurea cyanus*
Balloon flower—*Platycodon*
Barrenwort—*Epimedium*
Basket-of-gold—*Aurinia*
Beardtongue—*Penstemon*
Bear's-breech—*Acanthus*
Bee balm—*Monarda*
Bee larkspur—*Delphinium elatum*
Bellflower—*Campanula*
Betony—*Stachys*
Bishop's hat—*Epimedium*
Blackberry lily—*Belamcanda*
Black-eyed Susan—*Rudbeckia hirta*
Black snakeroot—*Cimicifuga racemosa*
Blanket-flower—*Gaillardia*
Blazing star—*Liatris*
Bleeding heart—*Dicentra*
Bluestar—*Amsonia*
Boneset—*Eupatorium*
Bouncing Bet—*Saponaria officinalis*
Bowman's root—*Gillenia*
Bugbane—*Cimicifuga*
Bugleweed—*Ajuga*
Bugloss—*Anchusa*
Buttercup—*Ranunculus*
Butterfly bush—*Buddleia*
Butterfly weed—*Asclepias tuberosa*
California tree poppy—*Romneya*
Campion—*Lychnis*
Campion—*Silene*
Candytuft—*Iberis*
Cardinal flower—*Lobelia*
Carnation—*Dianthus*
Carpathian harebell—*Campanula carpatica*
Carpet bugle—*Ajuga*
Catchfly—*Lychnis*
Catchfly—*Silene*
Catmint—*Nepeta*
Chamomile—*Anthemis*
Checkerbloom—*Sidalcea malviflora*
Checkermallow—*Sidalcea*
Christmas rose—*Helleborus niger*
Cinquefoil—*Potentilla*
Colewort—*Crambe*
Columbine—*Aquilegia*
Coneflower—*Rudbeckia*
Coral bells—*Heuchera sanguinea*
Cornflower—*Centaurea montana*
Cranesbill—*Geranium*
Culver's root—*Veronicastrum*
Daylily—*Hemerocallis*
Dead nettle—*Lamium*
Dittany—*Dictamnus*
Dropwort—*Filipendula vulgaris*
Dusty-miller—*Artemisia stelleriana*
Dutchman's-breeches—*Dicentra cucullaria*
Eulalia—*Miscanthus*
Evening primrose—*Oenothera*
False dragonhead—*Physostegia*
False indigo—*Baptisia*
False Solomon's-seal—*Smilacina*
False spirea—*Astilbe*
False sunflower—*Heliopsis*
Five-finger—*Potentilla*
Flax—*Linum*
Fleabane—*Erigeron*
Flowering onion—*Allium*
Fountain grass—*Pennisetum*
Foxglove—*Digitalis*
Funkia—*Hosta*
Gas plant—*Dictamnus*
Gay-feather—*Liatris*
Globeflower—*Trollius*
Globe thistle—*Echinops*
Goatsbeard—*Aruncus*
Golden marguerite—*Anthemis tinctoria*
Golden-ray—*Ligularia*
Goldenrod—*Solidago*
Gooseneck loosestrife—*Lysimachia clethroides*
Hellebore—*Helleborus*
Himalayan fleeceflower—*Polygonum affine*
Italian bugloss—*Anchusa azurea*
Joe-Pye weed—*Eupatorium maculatum*
Jupiter's-beard—*Centranthus ruber*
Knapweed—*Centaurea*
Knotweed—*Polygonum*
Lady's-mantle—*Alchemilla*
Lamb's ears—*Stachys*
Lavender—*Lavandula*
Lavender cotton—*Santolina*
Leadwort—*Ceratostigma*
Lenten rose—*Helleborus orientalis*
Leopard's-bane—*Doronicum*
Lily-of-the-Nile—*Agapanthus*
Loosestrife—*Lysimachia*
Lungwort—*Pulmonaria*
Lupine—*Lupinus*
Mallow—*Malva*
Masterwort—*Astrantia*
Meadow rue—*Thalictrum*
Meadowsweet—*Filipendula*
Milkweed—*Asclepias*
Monkshood—*Aconitum*
Moss pink—*Phlox subulata*
Mullein—*Verbascum*
New Zealand flax—*Phormium*
Nippon daisy—*Chrysanthemum nipponicum*
Obedient plant—*Physostegia*
Ornamental onion—*Allium*
Oxeye—*Heliopsis*
Ozark sundrop—*Oenothera missouriensis*
Pearly everlasting—*Anaphalis*
Peony—*Paeonia*
Pincushion flower—*Scabiosa*
Pink—*Dianthus*
Plantain lily—*Hosta*
Plumbago—*Ceratostigma*
Plume poppy—*Macleaya*
Poppy—*Papaver*
Primrose—*Primula*
Purple coneflower—*Echinacea*
Queen-of-the-meadow—*Filipendula ulmaria*
Queen-of-the-prairie—*Filipendula rubra*
Red-hot poker—*Kniphofia uvaria*
Red valerian—*Centranthus*
Reed grass—*Calamagrostis*
Rock cress—*Arabis*
Rose mallow—*Hibiscus*
Rue—*Thalictrum*
Russian sage—*Perovskia*
Sage—*Salvia*
Sandwort—*Arenaria*
Sea holly—*Eryngium*
Sea lavender—*Limonium*
Sea pink—*Armeria*
Siberian bugloss—*Brunnera macrophylla*
Smartweed—*Polygonum*
Smokeweed—*Eupatorium maculatum*
Snakeweed—*Polygonum bistorta*
Sneezeweed—*Helenium*
Soapwort—*Saponaria*
Solomon's-seal—*Polygonatum*
Speedwell—*Veronica*
Statice—*Limonium*
Stokes' aster—*Stokesia*
Stonecrop—*Sedum*
Sundrop—*Oenothera*
Sunflower—*Helianthus*
Thrift—*Armeria*
Tickseed—*Coreopsis*
Toad lily—*Tricyrtis*
Torch lily—*Kniphofia*
Tritoma—*Kniphofia*
Vervain—*Verbena*
Violet—*Viola*
White sage—*Artemisia ludoviciana*
Wild indigo—*Baptisia*
Windflower—*Anemone*
Wolfsbane—*Aconitum*
Wormwood—*Artemisia*
Yarrow—*Achillea*

Encyclopedia of Perennials

Presented here and on the following pages is a selection of the most popular and most readily available perennials in the United States. The plants are listed alphabetically by their Latin botanical names; common names appear in bold type beneath the Latin. If you know a plant only by its common name, check the name against the cross-reference chart on page 111 or in the index.

A botanical name consists first of the genus name, such as Iris, which is usually printed in italics. Within a genus are one or more species, whose names are also in italics but are not capitalized, as in Iris ensata. Most species contain one or more varieties; those names appear in single quotation marks, as in Iris ensata 'Pink Lady.' An "x" in a name, such as Iris x 'Louisiana', indicates a hybrid. "Hardiness" refers to the U.S. Department of Agriculture Plant Hardiness Map (page 110). Plants grown outside recommended zones may do poorly or fail to survive.

Acanthus
(a-KAN-thus)
BEAR'S-BREECH

Acanthus spinosus

Hardiness: *Zones 7-9*
Flowering season: *summer*
Height: *3 to 4 feet*
Flower color: *white, rose, purple*
Soil: *well-drained, acid loam*
Light: *full sun to light shade*

Broad, deeply lobed, glossy evergreen leaves as much as 2 feet long make acanthus a stately foliage plant. Its dense, cylindrical spikes of tubular flowers unfold atop 3- to 4-foot stalks.

Selected species and varieties: *A. mollis* (soft-leaved acanthus)—white or purple flowers above lustrous, wavy, heart-shaped leaves; *A. mollis* 'Latifolius' is hardier and more robust than the species, with larger leaves and mauve to pink flowers; Zones 8-10. *A. spinosus* (spiny bear's-breech)—arching, deeply cut, spiky leaves and rose to mauve flowers; Zones 7-10.

Growing conditions and maintenance: Plant acanthus 3 feet apart. Propagate from seed or by division every 4 to 5 years. Acanthus is difficult to relocate, as fleshy root pieces inadvertently left behind quickly produce new plants at the original site.

Achillea
(ak-il-EE-a)
YARROW

Achillea 'Coronation Gold'

Hardiness: *Zones 4-8*
Flowering season: *summer*
Height: *6 inches to 4½ feet*
Flower color: *white, yellow, pink*
Soil: *well-drained, poor*
Light: *full sun*

Flat-topped flower clusters grown above green or gray-green fernlike foliage. Long-lasting when cut, the flowers also dry well.

Selected species and varieties: *A. filipendulina* (fernleaf yarrow)—yellow flower clusters up to 5 inches across; 'Gold Plate', 6-inch yellow flower heads on 4½-foot stems. *A.* 'Coronation Gold', a hybrid with 3-inch deep yellow flower clusters on 3-foot stems. *A.* x *lewisii* 'King Edward'—small yellow flowers on 4-inch stalks. *A. millefolium* (common yarrow)—2-inch white flowers with cultivars in shades from pink to red; 'Red Beauty' has broad crimson flower clusters.

Growing conditions and maintenance: Plant taller species 2 feet apart, dwarfs 1 foot apart. Propagate by division every 2 to 4 years in spring or fall or from midsummer stem cuttings.

Aconitum
(ak-o-NY-tum)
MONKSHOOD

Aconitum napellus 'Snow White'

Hardiness: *Zones 3-8*

Flowering season: *summer to early fall*

Height: *2 to 5 feet*

Flower color: *blue to purple*

Soil: *moist, well-drained, acid loam*

Light: *light shade to full sun*

Aconitum provides a long-lived bloom of 1- to 2-inch helmet-shaped flowers in spikes tipping dark green foliage. All parts of aconitum are poisonous.

Selected species and varieties: *A.* x *bicolor*—many quality selections, all 3 to 4 feet tall with violet or blue summer blooms, some with white edges; Zone 5. *A. carmichaelii* (azure monkshood)—blue blossoms on 3- to 4-foot stems, up to 6 feet tall. *A. napellus* (English monkshood)—blue flowers with visorlike extensions in midsummer.

Growing conditions and maintenance: Plant 1½ feet apart in fall to establish the root system before frost. Stake taller plants. Propagate from seed to flower in 2 to 3 years. Division is not recommended, since disturbing the roots injures aconitum.

Agapanthus
(ag-a-PAN-thus)
AFRICAN LILY

Agapanthus africanus

Hardiness: *Zones 8-10*

Flowering season: *summer*

Height: *3 to 5 feet*

Flower color: *blue, white*

Soil: *moist, well-drained, acid loam*

Light: *full sun*

Slender stems support loose clusters of 30 to 100 small, tubular flowers, which bloom for 2 months among narrow, glossy, dark green leaves. African lilies make good potted plants north of Zone 8; they are evergreen in warm winters.

Selected species and varieties: *A. africanus*—up to 30 eye-catching deep blue blossoms on 3-foot stems. *A. orientalis*—5 feet tall with up to 100 blue flowers in each cluster; 'Albidus' has white flowers.

Growing conditions and maintenance: Plant agapanthus 2 feet apart and water well during the growing season. Plants tolerate dryness while dormant. South-facing locations are preferable, as agapanthus leans toward light if not in full sun.

Ajuga
(a-JOO-ga)
BUGLEWEED

Ajuga reptans

Hardiness: *Zones 3-9*

Flowering season: *late spring to summer*

Height: *to 12 inches*

Flower color: *white, pink, violet, blue*

Soil: *well-drained, acid loam*

Light: *full sun to light shade*

An excellent ground cover, ajuga spreads into dense mats of attractive foliage that suppresses weeds; can be invasive. Growing in shades of green, deep purple, bronze, or creamy white mottled dark pink, the foliage is topped by whorled flowers.

Selected species and varieties: *A. genevensis* (Geneva bugleweed)—blue, pink, or white summer flowers on erect stems 6 to 12 inches tall; Zones 4-9. *A. pyramidalis* (upright bugleweed)—blue late-spring flowers on 4- to 6-inch spikes; less invasive than other species; Zones 3-9. *A. reptans* (common bugleweed)—violet flowers ¼ inch long in late spring on 3- to 6-inch prostrate stems; cultivars offer a wide choice of foliage colors; Zones 3-9.

Growing conditions and maintenance: Sow seeds in late summer or fall. Divide in spring or fall.

Alchemilla
(al-kem-ILL-a)
LADY'S-MANTLE

Alchemilla mollis

Hardiness: *Zones 3-8*

Flowering season: *late spring to early summer*

Height: *12 to 18 inches*

Flower color: *green, yellow-green*

Soil: *moist, well-drained loam*

Light: *full sun to light shade*

Lady's-mantle's sprays of tiny blossoms rise from low mats of attractive deeply lobed foliage that make it a good ground cover. The flowers are an excellent filler in arrangements and also dry well.

Selected species and varieties: *A. conjuncta*—pale green ⅛-inch flowers and star-shaped green leaves edged with silver; Zones 4-8. *A. mollis*—2- to 3-inch clusters of chartreuse blossoms above crinkled, velvety leaves; Zones 4-7.

Growing conditions and maintenance: Space lady's-mantle plants 1½ feet apart. In hot climates, select locations with partial shade. Propagate by digging up and replanting self-sown seedlings or by division in early spring or fall.

Allium
(AL-lee-um)
FLOWERING ONION

Allium sphaerocephalum

Hardiness: *Zones 3-9*

Flowering season: *late spring to early summer*

Height: *18 inches to 5 feet*

Flower color: *blue, purple, red, pink, white*

Soil: *well-drained, fertile loam*

Light: *full sun to partial shade*

Flowering onion bears unique globes of tiny blossoms on stiff stalks above leaf clumps that fade after bloom. They make excellent cut flowers.

Selected species and varieties: *A. aflatunense* (Persian onion)—4-inch lilac-purple flowers on 2- to 4-foot stems; Zones 3-8. *A. christophii* (stars-of-Persia)—10-inch violet spheres on 24-inch stems; Zones 4-8. *A. giganteum* (giant onion)—6-inch reddish purple flower clusters on 5-foot stalks; Zones 5-8. *A. sphaerocephalum* (drumstick chives)—green to purple flower clusters atop 2- to 3-foot stalks; Zones 4-8.

Growing conditions and maintenance: Plant bulbs in the fall. Propagate by seed and division.

Amsonia
(am-SO-nee-a)
BLUESTAR

Amsonia tabernaemontana

Hardiness: *Zones 3-10*

Flowering season: *late spring or summer*

Height: *1 to 3 feet*

Flower color: *pale blue*

Soil: *well-drained loam*

Light: *full sun to light shade*

Resilient, low-maintenance plants carry dense clusters of small star-shaped flowers above shrubby stems, with narrow, willowlike leaves that turn golden yellow in fall.

Selected species and varieties: *A. ciliata* (downy star flower)—blue flowers on stiff 3-foot stems; Zones 7-10. *A. tabernaemontana* (willow star flower)—drooping clusters of ½- to 1-inch pale blue flowers in early summer; Zones 3-9.

Growing conditions and maintenance: Space amsonia plants 1½ feet apart. Willow star flower grows well in damp soils near streams or pools. Cut plants back after flowering to promote bushier growth. Propagate from seed or by division in spring.

Anaphalis
(an-AFF-al-is)
PEARLY EVERLASTING

Anaphalis triplinervis

Hardiness: *Zones 3-9*

Flowering season: *late summer to early fall*

Height: *1 to 3 feet*

Flower color: *white*

Soil: *moist, well-drained loam*

Light: *full sun to light shade*

Anaphalis bears flat clusters of fluffy ¼-inch flower buttons atop erect stems lined with narrow silvery leaves. It provides a gray-white accent in borders and is excellent for drying.

Selected species and varieties: *A. margaritacea* (common pearly everlasting)—2½ feet tall with slender leaves that are green on top and woolly gray underneath. *A. triplinervis*—pearly flowers above silvery gray leaves that turn a soft gray-green toward the end of summer; 'Summer Snow' is more compact than the species, with clear white flowers.

Growing conditions and maintenance: Plant pearly everlasting 1 foot apart. *A. margaritacea* tolerates drought. Propagate by division in spring.

Anchusa
(an-KOO-sa)
BUGLOSS

Anchusa azurea

Hardiness: *Zones 3-8*

Flowering season: *late spring to midsummer*

Height: *3½ to 5 feet*

Flower color: *blue, pink, white*

Soil: *very well drained loam*

Light: *full sun to light shade*

Branching clusters of small trumpet-like flowers rise above hairy, tongue-shaped leaves. Blossoms persist a month or more, and a second bloom sequence is possible.

Selected species and varieties: *A. azurea* (Italian bugloss)—bright blue ¾-inch flowers bloom abundantly on 3- to 5-foot stems; 'Little John' is a dwarf cultivar growing to 18 inches with deep blue flowers; 'Loddon Royalist' grows 3 feet tall with royal blue flowers.

Growing conditions and maintenance: Plan anchusas 1½ to 3 feet apart. Tall varieties require staking. Cutting plants to the ground after flowers fade forces a second show of blossoms and prevents foliage from becoming lank. Provide good drainage, as standing moisture will rot roots in winter. Propagate by division every 2 to 3 years or from root cuttings.

Anemone
(a-NEM-o-ne)
WINDFLOWER

Anemone pulsatilla

Hardiness: *Zones 2-8*

Flowering season: *spring through fall*

Height: *3 inches to 2 feet*

Flower color: *white, cream, red, purple, blue*

Soil: *well-drained, fertile loam*

Light: *partial shade to full sun*

This diverse genus carries sprightly 1- to 3-inch-wide flowers with single or double rows of petals shaped like shallow cups on branched stems above mounds of handsome foliage. Many species brighten the garden during periods when few other plants with similar flowers are in bloom.

Selected species and varieties: *A.* x *hybrida* (Japanese anemone)—white or pink flowers with a silky sheen on their undersides above dark green foliage from late summer to midfall; Zones 6-8; 'Alba' cultivar grows 2 to 3 feet tall with large clear white flowers; 'Honorine Jobert' has white flowers with yellow centers on 3-foot stems; 'Prince Henry', deep rose flowers on 3-foot stems; 'Queen Charlotte', full, semidouble pink flowers; 'September Charm', single-petaled silvery pink flowers; 'September Sprite', single pink flowers on 15-inch stems. *A. magellanica*—cream-colored flowers bloom from late spring through summer atop 18-inch stems; Zones 2-8. *A. pulsatilla* [also classified as *Pulsatilla vulgaris*] (pasqueflower)—2-

inch-wide blue or purple bell-shaped spring flowers on 1-foot stems above hairy leaves; Zones 5-8. *A. sylvestris* 'Snowdrops' (snowdrops windflower)—1 to 1½ feet tall, with light green foliage topped by dainty, fragrant 2-inch spring flowers. *A. vitifolia* 'Robustissima' (grapeleaf anemone) —branching clusters of pink flowers from late summer to fall on 1- to 3-foot stalks; an invasive variety good for naturalizing; Zones 3-8.

Growing conditions and maintenance: Plant small anemones 1 foot apart, taller varieties 2 feet apart. The latter may require staking. Pasqueflowers need full sun and a neutral to alkaline soil in a cool location. Snowdrops windflowers prefer moist soil; grapeleaf anemones tolerate dry conditions. Protect all anemones from afternoon sun and do not allow to dry out completely. Propagate cultivars of Japanese anemone by root cuttings or division, others from seed. Divide Japanese and grapeleaf anemones in spring every 3 years to maintain robustness. Other species grow slowly and division is rarely needed.

Anemone sylvestris 'Snowdrops'

Anthemis
(AN-them-is)
CHAMOMILE

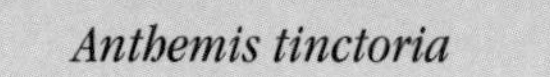

Anthemis tinctoria

Hardiness:	*Zones 3-8*
Flowering season:	*midsummer through early fall*
Height:	*2 to 3 feet*
Flower color:	*yellow, orange*
Soil:	*well-drained to dry, poor*
Light:	*full sun*

Anthemis has daisylike blossoms 2 to 3 inches across. They grow amid shrubby, aromatic, gray-green foliage and are excellent as cut flowers.

Selected species and varieties: *A. sancti-johannis* (St. John's chamomile)—bright orange flowers on evergreen shrubs; Zones 5-8. *A. tinctoria* (golden marguerite)—upturned gold-yellow flowers; 'Kelwayi' has bright yellow flowers; 'Moonlight', pale yellow; 'E.C. Buxton', creamy white; Zones 3-8.

Growing conditions and maintenance: Plant anthemis 1½ feet apart. Remove spent flowers for continuous bloom over several months. Propagate by division every 2 years or from stem cuttings in spring.

Aquilegia
(ak-wil-EE-jee-a)
COLUMBINE

Aquilegia 'McKana Hybrids'

Hardiness:	*Zones 3-8*
Flowering season:	*spring to early summer*
Height:	*1½ to 3 feet*
Flower color:	*white, yellow, pink, red, violet, blue*
Soil:	*well-drained, acid loam*
Light:	*full sun to light shade*

Columbine's graceful broad-lipped blossoms with backswept spurs bob atop delicate, ferny foliage.

Selected species and varieties: *A. caerulea* (Rocky Mountain columbine) —2- to 3-inch blue-and-white flowers. *A. canadensis* (Canadian columbine)—bicolored yellow-and-red flowers. *A. chrysantha* (golden columbine)—blooms in two tones of yellow. *A. flabellata* (fan columbine)—compact plants with lilac blue flowers; 'Nana Alba' dwarf variety has white flowers. *A.* x *hybrida* ('McKana Hybrids')—large blossoms in many pastel shades.

Growing conditions and maintenance: Plant columbines 1½ feet apart. Propagate from seed or by careful division in the spring.

Arabis

(AR-a-bis)

ROCK CRESS

Arabis caucasica

Hardiness: *Zones 3-7*

Flowering season: *spring*

Height: *6 to 12 inches*

Flower color: *pink, white*

Soil: *well-drained loam*

Light: *full sun*

Low-growing rock cress, with its flat-faced single- or double-petaled ½-inch flowers, makes an excellent creeping ground cover for the border or rock garden.

Selected species and varieties: *A. alpina*—'Flore Pleno' has white, fragrant double-petaled flowers. *A. caucasica* (wall rock cress)—'Rosabella' is a compact 5-inch plant with rosy pink flowers; 'Snow Cap' has pure white single flowers. *A. procurrens*—sprays of white flowers above mats of glossy evergreen leaves.

Growing conditions and maintenance: Rock cress is easily grown, but humid weather and standing water will cause rot. Prune after flowering to keep the plants compact. *A. procurrens* thrives in light shade as well as full sun. Propagate from seeds sown in spring or by division in fall.

Arenaria

(a-ren-AIR-ee-a)

SANDWORT

Arenaria montana

Hardiness: *Zones 5-9*

Flowering season: *spring*

Height: *2 to 8 inches*

Flower color: *white*

Soil: *moist but well-drained, sandy*

Light: *full sun to partial shade*

Sandwort forms mats of small, dainty evergreen foliage crowned with tiny white flowers. This low, spreading perennial is ideal in wall crevices and between pavers.

Selected species and varieties: *A. montana*—trailing stems up to 12 inches long topped by 1-inch white flowers with yellow centers. *A. verna caespitosa* [now formally listed as *Minuartia verna* ssp. *caespitosa*] (Irish moss)—narrow mosslike leaves and ⅜-inch star-shaped white flowers in dainty 2-inch clumps that withstand heavy foot traffic.

Growing conditions and maintenance: Plant sandwort 6 to 12 inches apart. Water well during dry spells in the growing season. Propagate by division in late summer or early fall.

Armeria

(ar-MEER-ee-a)

THRIFT, SEA PINK

Armeria maritima 'Laucheana'

Hardiness *Zones 3-8*

Flowering season: *spring or summer*

Height: *6 inches to 2 feet*

Flower color: *white, pink, rose*

Soil: *well-drained, sandy loam*

Light: *full sun*

Thrifts produce spherical clusters of flowers on stiff stems above tufts of grassy evergreen leaves.

Selected species and varieties: *A. alliacea* [also called *A. plantaginea*] (plantain thrift)—1¾-inch rosy pink or white flower clusters on 2-foot stems; 'Bee's Ruby' cultivar has intense ruby red flower clusters. *A. maritima* (common thrift)—white to deep pink flowers on 1-foot stems; 'Alba' is a dwarf cultivar with white flowers on 5-inch stems; 'Bloodstone' has brilliant bright red flowers on 9-inch stems; 'Laucheana', rose pink flowers on 6-inch stems.

Growing conditions and maintenance: Space thrifts 9 to 12 inches apart. Older clumps die out in the middle. Rejuvenate and propagate by division every 3 or 4 years.

Artemisia
(ar-tem-IS-ee-a)
WORMWOOD

Artemisia schmidtiana 'Silver Mound'

Hardiness: *Zones 3-9*

Flowering season: *summer through fall*

Height: *4 inches to 4 feet*

Flower color: *creamy white*

Soil: *well-drained to dry, and poor*

Light: *full sun*

Artemisia is primarily grown for its aromatic, silver gray feathery foliage, which provides an interesting accent or filler in the perennial garden. Most species have inconspicuous blooms.

Selected species and varieties: *A. abrotanum* (southernwood)—a 2- to 4-foot-tall semi-evergreen shrub with narrow, fragrant, gray-green leaves that give off a citrus- or camphorlike fragrance and are considered moth repellent; Zones 6-9. *A. absinthium* (common wormwood)—woody evergreen 2 to 4 feet tall with finely cut silvery leaves; long used as a medicinal plant and the source of absinthe, a liqueur alleged to induce bizarre behavior and cause mental deterioration; 'Lambrook Silver' is very drought tolerant, with extremely silvery, feathery foliage; Zones 4-9. *A. lactiflora* (white mugwort)—grows up to to 4 feet tall and is tipped with prominent feathery plumes of creamy white flowers; the only artemisia with undistinguished green foliage and the only one grown for its flowers. *A. ludoviciana* (white sage)—2- to 3-foot-tall erect, showy plants with 4-inch silver gray leaves; 'Silver King' is smaller than the species, with brilliant silver foliage; 'Silver Queen' is similar to 'Silver King' but has downier leaves; Zones 5-8. *A. schmidtiana* 'Silver Mound'—4- to 6-inch-high feathery mounds spread a foot wide; Zones 3-7. *A. stelleriana* (dusty-miller)—rapidly spreading, shrubby 2-foot-tall plant with grayish white, woolly, deeply divided leaves; a good choice for seaside gardens, thriving even in sand dunes; Zones 3-9. *A.* 'Powis Castle'—mounds of lacy, silvery green leaves 2 to 3 feet high and equally wide; Zones 5-8.

Growing conditions and maintenance: Space smaller artemisia plants 1 foot apart, taller ones 2 feet apart. *A. lactiflora* may need staking; *A. ludoviciana* can be invasive and may need regular division; prune back *A. abrotanum* in spring to prevent a weedy look later in the season. In fertile soil, artemisias become scraggly and floppy. Although white mugwort appreciates moisture, most artemisias rot in hot and humid conditions; dusty-miller is the most heat and humidity tolerant of all. Propagate *A. abrotanum* and *A. schmidtiana* by stem cuttings, *A. ludoviciana* and *A. stelleriana* by stem cuttings or division, other species by division in the spring or fall. 'Silver King' spreads quickly and needs annual division. 'Silver Mound' rarely needs dividing and should be left undisturbed.

Artemisia 'Powis Castle'

Aruncus
(a-RUNK-us)
GOATSBEARD

Aruncus dioicus

Hardiness: *Zones 3-9*

Flowering season: *early summer*

Height: *1 to 6 feet*

Flower color: *white*

Soil: *moist, rich loam*

Light: *partial shade*

Goatsbeard carries dramatic, long-lasting 6- to 10-inch plumes of tiny cream-colored blossoms on tall stalks of light green ferny foliage.

Selected species and varieties: *A. aethusifolius* (miniature goatsbeard)—dark green 12-inch foliage and long, creamy white flower spires lasting 6 weeks; Zones 3-8. *A. dioicus*—handsome shrubby foliage that grows up to 4 feet tall, with flower stalks up to 6 feet; 'Kneiffii' is more compact, with finely divided leaves to 3 feet tall; Zones 4-9.

Growing conditions and maintenance: Plant goatsbeard 4 to 5 feet apart, miniature goatsbeard 12 to 15 inches apart. Thrives in full sun where summers are cool. Propagate by division in spring or fall.

Asclepias
(as-KLEE-pee-as)
MILKWEED

Asclepias tuberosa

Hardiness: *Zones 3-9*	
Flowering season: *summer to fall*	
Height: *2 to 4 feet*	
Flower color: *rose, orange, yellow*	
Soil: *well-drained sandy, or moist and deep*	
Light: *full sun*	

Milkweed's flower stalks bear brilliantly colored flower clusters followed by canoe-shaped pods, which burst to release silky seeds. The flowers are excellent for cutting, and the decorative pods dry well.

Selected species and varieties: *A. incarnata* (swamp milkweed)—clusters of fragrant, pink to rose ¼-inch flowers on 2- to 4-foot stems. *A. tuberosa* (butterfly weed)—vibrant orange flower clusters on 2- to 3-foot stems; the leaves and stems are poisonous.

Growing conditions and maintenance: Plant asclepias 12 inches apart. Swamp milkweed prefers moist conditions; butterfly weed does best in dry soils, where its long taproot makes plants drought tolerant. Propagate from seed sown in spring to blossom in 2 years.

Aster
(AS-ter)
ASTER

Aster novae-angliae 'Harrington's Pink'

Hardiness: *Zones 3-9*	
Flowering season: *early summer to fall*	
Height: *6 inches to 8 feet*	
Flower color: *white, blue, purple, pink*	
Soil: *moist, well-drained, fertile*	
Light: *full sun*	

Asters are prized for their large, showy, daisylike flowers that appear over weeks and even months. Most varieties are subject to mildew.

Selected species and varieties: *A. alpinus*—a low-growing species forming 6- to 12-inch-high clumps topped by violet-blue 1- to 3-inch flowers with yellow centers; 'Dark Beauty' produces deep blue flowers; 'Goliath' grows a few inches taller than the species, with pale blue flowers; 'Happy End' has semidouble lavender flowers. *A.* x *frikartii* (Frikart's aster)—2- to 3-foot-tall plants topped by fragrant 2½-inch lavender-blue flowers with yellow centers blooming in summer and lasting 2 months or longer; 'Monch' has profuse blue-mauve flowers and is resistant to mildew. *A. novae-angliae* (New England aster)—3 to 5 feet tall with 4- to 5-inch leaves and 2-inch violet-purple flowers; less important than its many cultivars, most of which are quite tall and require staking; 'Alma Potschke' has vivid rose-colored blossoms from late summer to fall; 'Harrington's Pink' grows to 4 feet tall with large salmon pink flowers in fall; 'Purple Dome' is a dwarf variety, growing 18 inches tall and spreading 3 feet wide, with profuse deep purple fall flowers. *A. novi-belgii* (New York aster, Michaelmas daisy)—cultivars from 10 inches to 4 feet tall, blooming in white, pink, red, blue, and purple-violet from late summer through fall; 'Eventide' has violet-blue semidouble flowers on 3-foot stems; 'Professor Kippenburg' is compact and bushy, 12 to 15 inches tall with lavender-blue flowers; 'Royal Ruby' is a compact cultivar with large crimson fall flowers; 'Winston S. Churchill' grows violet-red flowers on 2-foot stems.

Growing conditions and maintenance: Choose sites for asters carefully to avoid mildew problems. Good air circulation is essential; well-drained soils deter rot. Space dwarf asters 1 foot apart, taller ones 2 to 3 feet apart, and thin out young plants to improve air circulation. Taller varieties may require staking. Prompt deadheading encourages a second

Aster novi-belgii 'Professor Kippenburg'

flowering in early summer bloomers. *A.* x *frikartii* in Zone 5 or colder must be mulched over the winter and should not be cut back or divided in fall; otherwise, divide asters in early spring or fall every 2 years or so when a plant's center begins to die out. Asters can also be propagated by stem cuttings in spring and early summer. Cultivars seldom grow true from seed.

Astilbe
(a-STIL-be)
ASTILBE, FALSE SPIREA

Astilbe rosea 'Peach Blossom'

Hardiness: *Zones 4-8*

Flowering season: *summer*

Height: *8 inches to 3½ feet*

Flower color: *white, pink, red, lavender*

Soil: *moist, rich*

Light: *light shade*

Astilbe's dramatic, feathery spikes stand on stiff stems above mounds of glossy, ferny foliage. Both graceful and rugged, astilbes are excellent as a border filler or massed in a shady spot as a ground cover.

Selected species and varieties: *A.* x *arendsii* (garden spirea)—hybrids producing 2- to 4-foot-tall flower spikes in white, pink, rose, red, coral, and lilac over clumps of foliage; 'Cattleya' has 36-inch rose flower spikes at midseason; 'Bridal Veil' blooms early, with elegant creamy white flower spikes to 30 inches; 'Erica' has pink midsummer blooms on 3-foot stems; 'Fire', coral red flowers on 30-inch stems; 'Fanal' is an early bloomer, 24 inches tall, with deep red flowers and bronze leaves. *A. chinensis* 'Pumila' (dwarf Chinese astilbe)—a drought-tolerant 12-inch-tall variety with dense, lilac-pink flower spires and deep green leaves 2 to 3 inches long; 'Finale' produces light pink blooms on stems to 18 inches tall; 'Veronica Klose', 30 inches tall, is dark pink. *A.* x *japonica* [also known as the Japonica Group Hybrids]—'Deutschland' is an early-blooming white on 2-foot stems; 'Montgomery' has bright red flowers on 20-inch stems; 'Washington', white flowers blooming in midsummer on 2-foot stems; 'Rheinland' is a 2-foot-tall early-blooming pink. *A.* x *rosea*—a hybrid of *A. chinensis* and *A. japonica* with several popular cultivars; 'Peach Blossom' is 3 to 4 feet tall with salmon pink blooms; 'Queen Alexandra' has darker pink flowers. *A. simplicifolia* [also known as the Simplicifolia Hybrid Group]—'Inshriach Pink' is a compact 12-inch-tall plant with pale pink flower spikes and crinkled foliage; 'Sprite' is a late-blooming variety with pale pink flowers on 12- to 18-inch stalks atop lacy foliage.

Growing conditions and maintenance: Plant astilbes 1½ to 2 feet apart and provide adequate moisture. Astilbes will grow in full sun with adequate water and mulching. Leave dried flower spikes on plants through the winter for ornamental effect. Propagate by division every 3 or 4 years in early spring or midsummer.

Astilbe chinensis

Astrantia
(as-TRAN-tee-a)
MASTERWORT

Astrantia major

Hardiness: *Zones 4-8*

Flowering season: *spring through summer*

Height: *2 to 3 feet*

Flower color: *white tinged with green, pink*

Soil: *well-drained, fertile loam*

Light: *partial shade*

Masterwort bears unique blossoms composed of a colorful collar of bracts supporting jagged petals.

Selected species and varieties: *A. major* (great masterwort)—unusual creamy white 2- to 3-inch blossoms tinged pink by the collar of purple bracts below the petals; 'Rosea' has rosy pink blooms suitable for drying and pressing; 'Sunningdale Variegated', stripes of cream and yellow on lobed green leaves.

Growing conditions and maintenance: Plant masterwort 18 inches apart. They will grow in full sun given adequate moisture. Propagate by division in spring or from seed sown in fall.

Aurinia
(o-RIN-ee-a)
BASKET-OF-GOLD

Aurinia saxatilis

Hardiness: *Zones 4-10*

Flowering season: *late spring to early summer*

Height: *6 to 12 inches*

Flower color: *yellow, gold*

Soil: *well-drained, sandy*

Light: *full sun*

Basket-of-gold's tiny flowers mass in frothy clusters on mats of silver gray foliage.

Selected species and varieties: *A. saxatilis* [formerly listed as *Alyssum saxatile*]—golden yellow flowers in open clusters; 'Citrina' has pale yellow flowers and gray-green, hairy foliage; 'Compacta' is slow spreading, with vivid yellow blossoms; 'Dudley Neville' grows light apricot blooms.

Growing conditions and maintenance: Space aurinia plants 9 to 12 inches apart. Plants become leggy if overfertilized. Cut plants back by a third after flowering. Remove and replace plants when they become woody after a few years. Propagate from seed sown in spring or fall or from cuttings.

Baptisia
(bap-TIZ-ee-a)
WILD INDIGO

Baptisia australis

Hardiness: *Zones 3-9*

Flowering season: *late spring*

Height: *3 to 6 feet*

Flower color: *blue, white*

Soil: *well-drained to dry, and sandy*

Light: *full sun*

Loose spires of butterfly-shaped flowers lift above blue-green to gray-green cloverlike foliage. The flowers are followed by fruit pods, which turn from green to black. Wild indigo is an excellent cut flower.

Selected species and varieties: *B. australis* (blue wild indigo)—intense blue flowers contrast with blue-green leaves on 5-foot gray-green stems. *B. pendula* (white wild indigo)—creamy white pendulous pea-like flowers on purplish 3-foot stems above pale green foliage.

Growing conditions and maintenance: Space wild indigo plants 2 to 3 feet apart. Wild indigo is slow growing, virtually indestructible, and will stay put for years. Propagate from seed or by division.

Begonia
(be-GO-nee-a)
HARDY BEGONIA

Begonia grandis

Hardiness: *Zones 6-9*

Flowering season: *early summer to frost*

Height: *2 feet*

Flower color: *pink*

Soil: *moist, rich loam*

Light: *full sun to partial shade*

Hardy begonia bears 1-inch flowers at the tips of reddish branched stems amid hairy leaves with red-tinted undersides and veins.

Selected species and varieties: *B. grandis*—sprays of pink flowers surrounded by heart-shaped leaves; 'Alba' has white flowers.

Growing conditions and maintenance: Plant hardy begonias 1½ feet apart. They tolerate full sun in cooler climates but require partial shade where summers are hot and dry. Propagate by digging and transplanting the sprouts that emerge from the small bulbils that form in leaf junctions, then fall to the ground to root.

Belamcanda
(bel-am-CAN-da)
BLACKBERRY LILY

Belamcanda chinensis

Hardiness: *Zones 5-10*	
Flowering season: *summer*	
Height: *2 to 4 feet*	
Flower color: *orange*	
Soil: *moist, well-drained loam*	
Light: *full sun to light shade*	

Belamcanda's spotted, lilylike flowers, which blossom for 2 weeks on branching stalks above straplike leaves, are followed by attractive seed pods that split to reveal shiny seeds resembling blackberries. The seed pods decorate the fall garden and can be used in fresh or dried arrangements.

Selected species and varieties: *B. chinensis*—loose sprays of 2-inch-wide orange-colored blossoms with red spots on 4-foot stems.

Growing conditions and maintenance: Blackberry lilies grow tallest in moist, fertile soils, shorter in dry soils. Mulch to protect from frost. Propagate by division or by transplanting the seedlings that surround the plant in the spring, for bloom in their second season.

Bergenia
(ber-JEN-ee-a)
BERGENIA

Bergenia cordifolia 'Purpurea'

Hardiness: *Zones 3-8*	
Flowering season: *spring*	
Height: *12 to 18 inches*	
Flower color: *white, pink, red, magenta*	
Soil: *moist, well-drained, poor*	
Light: *full sun to light shade*	

Bergenia bears flowers resembling tiny open trumpets in clusters 3 to 6 inches across held above handsome fleshy leaves that are evergreen in milder climates.

Selected species and varieties: *B. cordifolia* (heartleaf bergenia)—pink flower clusters; 'Purpurea' has magenta flowers above leaves that turn purplish in winter. *B. crassifolia* (leather bergenia)—reddish pink blossoms above leaves turning bronze in winter. *B.* hybrids—'Abendglut' ('Evening Glow') has magenta flowers on 1½-foot stems; 'Bressingham White', early-spring white flowers maturing to pale pink; 'Sunningdale', crimson flowers.

Growing conditions and maintenance: Plant bergenias 1 foot apart. Propagate by division after flowering.

Boltonia
(bowl-TO-nee-a)
BOLTONIA

Boltonia asteroides

Hardiness: *Zones 4-8*	
Flowering season: *late summer to fall*	
Height: *3 to 6 feet*	
Flower color: *white, pink, lilac*	
Soil: *moist, well-drained loam*	
Light: *full sun*	

Willowy stems burst with sprays of small daisylike blossoms for a month or longer; good for fall bouquets.

Selected species and varieties: *B. asteroides* (white boltonia)—abundant white or lilac to purple flowers up to 1 inch wide on branched stems to 6 feet tall; 'Pink Beauty' grows to 4 feet tall with pink blossoms; 'Snowbank', to 4 feet tall with graceful white flowers.

Growing conditions and maintenance: Plant in full sun for compact foliage; partial shade produces lanky growth. Tall boltonias may require staking. Propagate by division in spring or fall every 2 to 3 years.

Brunnera
(BRUN-er-a)
BRUNNERA

Brunnera macrophylla

Hardiness: *Zones 4-9*
Flowering season: *spring*
Height: *1 to 2 feet*
Flower color: *blue*
Soil: *moist, well-drained loam*
Light: *full sun to light shade*

Brunnera produces airy sprays of dainty azure blue flowers resembling forget-me-nots above dark green, heart-shaped foliage growing in loose, spreading mounds.

Selected species and varieties: *B. macrophylla* (Siberian bugloss)—boldly textured leaves up to 8 inches across and dainty bright blue flowers; 'Hadspen Cream' has light green leaves edged in cream; 'Langtrees', spots of silvery gray in the center of the leaves; 'Variegata', striking creamy white leaf variegations.

Growing conditions and maintenance: Plant brunneras 1 foot apart. Propagate from seed, by transplanting the self-sown seedlings, or by division in spring.

Calamagrostis
(kal-a-ma-GROS-tis)
REED GRASS

Calamagrostis acutiflora 'Stricta'

Hardiness: *Zones 6-9*
Flowering season: *summer*
Height: *5 to 7 feet*
Flower color: *purplish pink*
Soil: *well-drained loam*
Light: *full sun to light shade*

Plumy reed grass offers a vertical accent as a border backdrop or specimen planting. Flower spikes tip narrow, arching stems; the leaves, which turn golden tan in late fall, provide winter interest.

Selected species and varieties: *C. acutiflora* 'Stricta'—15-inch greenish pink plumes on stems to 7 feet tall, turning yellow in summer; 'Karl Foerster' is slightly shorter, with early purplish pink blossoms.

Growing conditions and maintenance: Plant calamagrostis 2 feet apart. Plants form noninvasive clumps. Cut overwintered stems to within 6 inches of the ground before new spring growth appears. Propagate by division in early spring.

Campanula
(cam-PAN-ew-la)
BELLFLOWER

Campanula glomerata

Hardiness: *Zones 3-9*
Flowering season: *early summer to late fall*
Height: *6 inches to 5 feet*
Flower color: *blue, violet, purple, white*
Soil: *well-drained loam*
Light: *full sun to light shade*

With spikes or clusters of showy, bell- or star-shaped flowers on stems rising from deep green foliage, bellflowers offer a long season of bloom. Dwarf and trailing varieties enhance a rock garden, wall, or border edge. Taller species form neat tufts or clumps in a perennial border or cutting garden.

Selected species and varieties: *C. carpatica* (Carpathian harebell)—2-inch-wide, bell-shaped, upturned blue flowers bloom on plants up to 1 foot tall; 'Blaue Clips' ('Blue Clips') has 3-inch-wide blue flowers on 6- to 8-inch stems; 'China Doll', lavender flowers on 8-inch stems; 'Wedgewood White' is compact, with white flowers; Zones 3-8. *C. glomerata* (clustered bellflower)—1- to 2-foot stems, with clusters of 1-inch white, blue, or purple flowers; 'Joan Elliott' grows deep violet blooms atop stems 18 inches tall; 'Schneekrone' ('Crown of Snow'), white flowers; 'Superba' grows to 2½ feet, with violet flowers; Zones 3-8. *C. latifolia* (great bellflower)—purplish blue flowers 1½ inches long on spikes, tipping 4- to 5-

foot stems; 'Alba' is similar to the species but with white flowers; 'Brantwood' has large violet-blue trumpet-shaped flowers; Zones 4-8. *C. persicifolia* (peachleaf bellflower)—spikes of 1½-inch blue or white cup-shaped blossoms on stems to 3 feet; 'Alba' has white flowers; 'Telham Beauty', 2- to 3-inch lavender-blue blooms lining the upper half of 4-foot flower stalks; Zones 3-7. *C. portenschlagiana* (Dalmatian bellflower)—a 6- to 8-inch dwarf species with blue flower clusters; Zones 5-7. *C. poscharskyana* (Serbian bellflower)—a mat-forming, creeping dwarf with abundant 1-inch lilac blossoms; Zones 3-8. *C. rotundifolia* (Scottish bluebell)—profuse, nodding, 1-inch-wide blue-violet blooms; 'Olympica' cultivar has bright blue flowers; Zones 3-7.

Growing conditions and maintenance: Plant small bellflowers 12 to 18 inches apart, larger ones 2 feet apart. Clip faded flowers to encourage further bloom. 'Superba' and Serbian bellflower are heat tolerant. Great bell-

Campanula carpatica 'Alba'

flower thrives in moist shade. Dalmatian and Serbian bellflowers do well in sandy or gritty soil. Dig up and divide every 3 or 4 years to maintain plant vigor. Propagate from seed or by division every 3 or 4 years.

Centaurea
(sen-TOR-ee-a)
KNAPWEED

Centaurea montana

Hardiness: *Zones 3-8*	
Flowering season: *spring to summer*	
Height: *1 to 3 feet*	
Flower color: *lavender, pink, blue, yellow*	
Soil: *well-drained loam*	
Light: *full sun*	

Centaurea's fringed, thistlelike flowers bloom at the tips of erect stems that are lined with distinctive gray-green foliage.

Selected species and varieties: *C. dealbata* (Persian centaurea)—feathery, lavender to pink 2-inch flowers on stems to 3 feet. *C. hypoleuca* 'John Coutts' (John Coutts' knapweed)—2- to 3-inch pink-and-white flowers on stems to 3 feet tall. *C. macrocephala* (globe centaurea)—yellow flowers up to 3 inches across on erect stems up to 4 feet tall. *C. montana* (mountain bluet, cornflower)—2-inch blue flowers on 1- to 2-foot stems.

Growing conditions and maintenance: Space centaureas 1 to 2 feet apart. Stake taller species. Propagate by transplanting self-sown seedlings, by division, or from seed.

Centranthus
(sen-TRAN-thus)
RED VALERIAN

Centranthus ruber

Hardiness: *Zones 4-9*	
Flowering season: *summer*	
Height: *1 to 3 feet*	
Flower color: *pink, red, white*	
Soil: *well-drained, neutral to slightly alkaline loam*	
Light: *full sun*	

Dense, round flower clusters that make excellent cut flowers tip each of red valerian's erect stems, which grow in vigorous clumps.

Selected species and varieties: *C. ruber* (Jupiter's-beard)—bushy plants to 3 feet tall with fragrant ½-inch spurred flowers in rounded terminal clusters above paired blue-green leaves; 'Atrococcineus' has deep red flowers; 'Coccineus', scarlet flowers; 'Albus', white flowers.

Growing conditions and maintenance: Plant red valerian 12 to 18 inches apart. It can thrive in sterile limestone soil. Propagate by transplanting self-sown seedlings, from seed, or by division in spring.

Ceratostigma

(ser-at-o-STIG-ma)

PLUMBAGO, LEADWORT

Ceratostigma plumbaginoides

Hardiness: *Zones 5-9*

Flowering season: *summer to fall*

Height: *8 to 12 inches*

Flower color: *dark blue*

Soil: *well-drained loam*

Light: *full sun to partial shade*

Brilliant blue flowers grow along plumbago's soft, spreading stems lined with lush foliage.

Selected species and varieties: *C. plumbaginoides*—gentian blue 3- to 4-inch flowers on plants growing 12 inches tall and spreading 24 inches across; its 1- to 3-inch leaves emerge dark green and then turn bronze-red in the fall in cooler zones.

Growing conditions and maintenance: Space plants 18 inches apart. Plumbago does not tolerate soggy soil or competition from tree roots. Its own roots can be invasive. Propagate by division in spring every 2 to 4 years.

Chrysanthemum

(kri-SAN-the-mum)

CHRYSANTHEMUM

Chrysanthemum morifolium 'Pink Daisy'

Hardiness: *Zones 4-10*

Flowering season: *spring to fall*

Height: *1 to 3 feet*

Flower color: *all colors but blue*

Soil: *well-drained, fertile loam*

Light: *full sun to partial shade*

Chrysanthemum flower forms vary widely but generally consist of tiny central disk flowers surrounded by petal-like ray flowers. Reliable performers in the garden, often blooming throughout summer, they are also valued as cut flowers.

Selected species and varieties: *C. coccineum* (painted daisy)—white, pink, lilac, crimson, and dark red single radiating flowers 2 to 4 inches wide, blooming from late spring to early summer on stems 2 to 3 feet tall; 'Eileen May Robinson' produces salmon pink flowers atop 30-inch stems; 'James Kelway', scarlet flowers with bright yellow centers on 18-inch stems; 'Robinson's Pink', 2-foot-tall plants with medium pink flowers; Zones 3-7. *C. frutescens* (marguerite)—single or double daisylike flowers in pink, white, or pale yellow colors throughout the summer on shrubby plants that grow up to 3 feet tall; perennial in Zones 9 and 10, annual elsewhere. *C. leucanthemum* (oxeye daisy)—solitary flowers 1½ inches across with white rays surrounding yellow disks on stems to 2 feet tall in spring and summer. *C. morifolium* (hardy chrysanthemum, florist's chrysanthemum)—rounded plants up to 3 feet tall with aromatic gray-green lobed leaves and 1- to 6-inch flowers in all colors but blue and in a wide range of forms; button chrysanthemums are usually under 18 inches tall with small double flowers less than an inch across; cushion mums usually grow less than 20 inches tall in rounded, compact mounds with numerous double blossoms; daisy chrysanthemums have pronounced yellow centers surrounded by a single row of ray flowers on 2-foot stems, the 'Pink Daisy' cultivar having 2-inch rose pink flowers; decorative chrysanthemums have semi-double or double 2- to 4-inch flowers

Chrysanthemum nipponicum

on loose, open plants to 3 feet tall; pompom chrysanthemums, ball-shaped flowers on 18-inch plants; spider chrysanthemums, rolled petals of irregular lengths; spoon chrysanthemums, petals rolled so that open tips resemble spoons. *C. nipponicum* (Nippon daisy)—solitary 1½- to 3½-inch blossoms with single white ray flowers and greenish yellow disk flowers in the fall on erect, branching stems to 2 feet tall over shrubby mounds. *C. parthenium* (feverfew)—pungently scented ¼-inch white flower buttons with yellow centers, growing from early summer through fall on plants 1 to 3 feet tall; 'Golden Ball' is a dwarf cultivar with yellow flowers; 'White Star', a dwarf with white flowers. *C.* x *super-*

bum (Shasta daisy)—white flowers with yellow centers up to 3 inches across from early summer to frost on 3-foot stems with narrow, toothed leaves up to a foot long; 'Alaska' cultivar has large single pure white flowers on 2- to 3-foot stems; 'Little Miss Muffet' is a 12-inch dwarf with semidouble white flowers.

Growing conditions and maintenance: Space chrysanthemums 1 to 2 feet apart. Their shallow root systems demand frequent watering and fertilizing. In cooler climates, apply winter mulch to prevent frost heaving. Divide *C. morifolium* and *C.* x *superbum* every 2 years to prevent overcrowding, which can lead to disease and fewer flowers. Cut back *C. morifolium* and Nippon daisies two or three times in spring and early summer to develop compact, bushy plants and abundant flowers. Feverfew and oxeye daisies self-sow. Shasta, feverfew, and oxeye daisies are easily propagated from seed. Propagate all chrysanthemums by division or from spring cuttings.

Chrysanthemum x superbum

Cimicifuga
(si-mi-SIFF-yew-ga)
BUGBANE

Cimicifuga ramosa 'Brunette'

Hardiness: *Zones 3-8*

Flowering season: *summer to fall*

Height: *3 to 8 feet*

Flower color: *white*

Soil: *moist, fertile loam*

Light: *full sun to partial shade*

Bugbane bears long spires of tiny flowers above mounds of lacy foliage.

Selected species and varieties: *C. racemosa* (black snakeroot, cohosh bugbane)—bottle-brush flowers on branched stems 4 to 8 feet tall in summer above mounds of dark green foliage. *C. ramosa* (branched bugbane)—creamy white flowers that bloom on 3- to 7-foot branched stems over a very long period in the fall; 'Atropurpurea' has dark purple leaves; 'Brunette' grows 3 to 4 feet tall and has deep bronze leaves. *C. simplex* (Kamchatka bugbane)—fall flowers on 3- to 4-foot stalks.

Growing conditions and maintenance: Space bugbane 2 feet apart in cooler areas of the garden with ample moisture and organic matter. Propagate by division in spring.

Clematis
(KLEM-a-tis)
CLEMATIS

Clematis integrifolia

Hardiness: *Zones 3-8*

Flowering season: *summer*

Height: *1½ to 5 feet*

Flower color: *blue, white, pink, purple*

Soil: *moist, well-drained, fertile loam*

Light: *full sun*

Clematis produces delicate summer flowers singly or in clusters, followed by feathery seed heads.

Selected species and varieties: *C. heracleifolia* 'Davidiana' (tube clematis)—fragrant blue flower bells in hyacinth-like clusters on 2- to 3-foot plants. *C. integrifolia* (solitary clematis)—solitary blue, urn-shaped flowers appear at the ends of 1½- to 2-foot stems. *C. recta* (ground clematis)—fragrant white flowers in clusters at the ends of 3- to 5-foot trailing stems; 'Purpurea' has purple foliage.

Growing conditions and maintenance: Space clematis 2 to 4 feet apart. Stake to grow erect border plants or allow to trail. Propagate from seed or from stem cuttings taken in summer.

Coreopsis

(ko-ree-OP-sis)

COREOPSIS, TICKSEED

Coreopsis grandiflora

Hardiness: *Zones 4-9*

Flowering season: *spring to summer*

Height: *6 inches to 3 feet*

Flower color: *yellow, orange, pink*

Soil: *well-drained loam*

Light: *full sun*

Coreopsis bears single- or double-petaled daisylike, predominantly yellow flowers on wiry, sometimes branching stems over a long season of bloom. The blossoms are excellent for indoor arrangements.

Selected species and varieties: *C. auriculata* (mouse-ear coreopsis)—bears 1- to 2-inch flowers in late spring and early summer above fuzzy leaves with lobed bases lining 1- to 2-foot stems; 'Nana' is a creeping variety 4 to 6 inches tall. *C. grandiflora*—yellow or orange single, semidouble, and double flowers 1 to 1½ inches across, blooming from early to late summer on 1- to 2-foot stems; 'Sunburst' grows to 2 feet tall, with large semidouble golden flowers; 'Sunray', 2 feet tall, with 2-inch double yellow flowers. *C. lanceolata* (lance coreopsis)—yellow flowers 1½ to 2½ inches across, with yellow or brown centers, blooming from late spring through summer on stems up to 3 feet tall; 'Brown Eyes' has maroon rings near the center of yellow flowers; 'Goldfink' is a 10- to 12-inch tall dwarf that blooms prolifically from summer to fall. *C. maritima* (sea dahlia)—1- to 3-foot stems with long yellow-green leaves and yellow flowers 2½ to 4 inches wide from early spring to summer; suited to the hot, dry summers of southern California. *C. rosea* (pink coreopsis)—delicate pink flowers with yellow centers on stems 15 to 24 inches tall lined with needlelike leaves; can be invasive. *C. verticillata* (threadleaf coreopsis)—yellow flowers 1 to 2 inches across from late spring to late summer grow atop stems that are 2 to 3 feet tall lined with finely cut, delicate leaves 2 to 3 inches long to form dense clumps about 2 feet wide; 'Zagreb' is a 12- to 18-inch tall dwarf with bright yellow flowers; 'Moonbeam' is a warm-climate variety that grows 18 to 24 inches tall with a prolific output of creamy yellow flowers; 'Golden Showers', 2 to 3 feet tall with 2½-inch-wide star-shaped flowers.

Coreopsis verticillata

Growing conditions and maintenance: Space coreopsis 12 to 18 inches apart. Remove spent flowers to extend bloom time. Transplant the self-sown seedlings of threadleaf coreopsis. Propagate *C. maritima* from seed, all other coreopsis from seed or by division in the spring.

Crambe

(KRAM-be)

CRAMBE, COLEWORT

Crambe cordifolia

Hardiness: *Zones 6-9*

Flowering season: *early summer*

Height: *4 to 6 feet*

Flower color: *white*

Soil: *well-drained, slightly alkaline loam*

Light: *full sun*

Huge, loose flower sprays bloom on tall stalks above crambe's fleshy, dramatic leaves.

Selected species and varieties: *C. cordifolia* (heartleaf crambe)—airy clusters 3 to 4 feet in diameter of fragrant white blossoms resembling baby's-breath and growing on stalks 4 to 6 feet tall above mounds of 2-foot-wide heart-shaped, blue-green, hairy leaves.

Growing conditions and maintenance: Space at least 4 feet apart to display the plant's unusual leaves. Crambe thrives in deep, fertile soil with even moisture. Plants may be short-lived. Propagate from seed to bloom in 3 years or from root cuttings.

Crocosmia
(kro-KOS-mee-a)
CROCOSMIA

Crocosmia x hybrida 'Lucifer'

Hardiness: *Zones 5-9*

Flowering season: *spring to summer*

Height: *1½ to 3½ feet*

Flower color: *orange to red*

Soil: *well-drained, acid loam*

Light: *full sun*

Tall, drooping clusters of lilylike flowers rise from crocosmia's clumps of sword-shaped leaves. Plants spread quickly into dense mats that repress weeds. Crocosmias are outstanding as cut flowers.

Selected species and varieties: *C. masoniorum*—orange to red-orange 1½-inch flowers on 3-foot arched stems; hardy to Zone 6. *C.* 'Lucifer' (a cross between *Crocosmia* and *Curtonus paniculatus*)—bright red flowers on 3- to 3½-foot stems.

Growing conditions and maintenance: Plant crocosmias in spring, spacing corms 6 to 12 inches apart. In colder zones, lift corms in fall and replant in spring. Overcrowding reduces flowering. Propagate by division in the spring or fall.

Delphinium
(del-FIN-ee-um)
DELPHINIUM

Delphinium Pacific hybrids 'Black Knight'

Hardiness: *Zones 3-8*

Flowering season: *summer*

Height: *2 to 6 feet*

Flower color: *blue, purple, red, pink, white, yellow*

Soil: *moist, well-drained, slightly alkaline loam*

Light: *full sun*

Delphiniums produce graceful, erect flower spikes heavy with spurred flowers, often with striking centers known as bees.

Selected species and varieties: *D.* x *belladonna*—grows 3 to 5 feet tall; 'Bellamosum' has dark blue flowers; 'Casa Blanca', white flowers. *D.* 'Connecticut Yankee'—wide color range on bushy plants to 30 inches tall. *D. elatum* (bee larkspur)—2-inch flowers in many colors on stalks up to 6 feet tall. *D.* Pacific hybrids—single and double flowers in spikes on stalks to 6 feet; 'Black Knight' has dark violet flowers with a black bee; 'King Arthur', purple flowers; 'Summer Skies', blue flowers with a white bee.

Growing conditions and maintenance: Space delphiniums 2 feet apart. Stake taller types. Propagate from seed or by division.

Dianthus
(dy-AN-thus)
PINK, CARNATION

Dianthus gratianopolitanus 'Karlik'

Hardiness: *Zones 4-8*

Flowering season: *spring to summer*

Height: *3 inches to 2 feet*

Flower color: *pink, red, white*

Soil: *moist, well-drained, slightly alkaline loam*

Light: *full sun to partial shade*

Pinks are old-fashioned perennials whose fragrant flowers with fringed petals are borne singly or in clusters above attractive grassy foliage that is evergreen in mild climates.

Selected species and varieties: *D.* x *allwoodii* (Allwood pink)—single or double flowers in a wide range of colors grow for 2 months above gray-green leaves in compact mounds 12 to 24 inches tall; 'Aqua' grows white double blooms atop 12-inch stems. *D.* x *a. alpinus* (Alpine pink)—dwarf varieties of Allwood pinks; 'Doris' grows very fragrant, double salmon-colored flowers with darker pink centers on 12-inch stems; 'Robin', coral red flowers. *D. barbatus* (sweet William)—a biennial species that self-seeds so reliably that it performs like a perennial; unlike other pinks, it produces flowers in flat clusters and without fragrance; 'Harlequin' grows ball-shaped pink-and-white flowers; 'Indian Carpet', single flowers in a mix of colors on 10-inch stems. *D. deltoides* (maiden pink)—¾-inch red or pink flowers on

12-inch stems above 6- to 12-inch high mats of small bright green leaves; 'Brilliant' has scarlet flowers; 'Flashing Light' ('Leuchtfunk'), ruby red flowers. *D. gratianopolitanus* (cheddar pink)—1-inch-wide flowers in shades of pink and rose on compact mounds of blue-green foliage 9 to 12 inches high; 'Karlik' has deep pink, fringed, fragrant flowers; 'Tiny Rubies', dark pink double blooms on plants just 4 inches tall. *D. plumarius* (cottage pink)—fragrant single or semidouble flowers 1½ inches across in shades of pink and white or bicolors above 12- to 18-inch-high mats of evergreen leaves; 'Essex Witch' produces fragrant salmon, pink, or white flowers.

Dianthus plumarius 'Essex Witch'

Growing conditions and maintenance: Space pinks 12 to 18 inches apart. Cut stems back after bloom and shear mat-forming types in the fall to promote dense growth. Maintain vigor by division every 2 to 3 years. Propagate from seed, from cuttings taken in early summer, by layering *(page 85)*, or by division in the spring.

Dicentra
(dy-SEN-tra)
BLEEDING HEART

Dicentra spectabilis

Hardiness: *Zones 3-8*

Flowering season: *spring to summer*

Height: *1 to 3 feet*

Flower color: *pink, white, purple*

Soil: *moist, well-drained loam*

Light: *partial shade*

Bleeding heart's unusual puffy, heart-shaped flowers dangle beneath arched stems above mounds of lacy leaves.

Selected species and varieties: *D. eximia* (fringed bleeding heart)—pink to purple flowers above 12-inch mounds of blue-green leaves; 'Alba' has white flowers. *D. formosa* (Pacific bleeding heart)—deep pink flowers on 12- to 18-inch stems; 'Luxuriant', cherry pink flowers; 'Sweetheart', white flowers on 12-inch stems. *D. spectabilis* (common bleeding heart)—pink, purple, or white flowers on arching 3-foot stems.

Growing conditions and maintenance: Space fringed and Pacific bleeding hearts 1 to 2 feet apart, common bleeding heart 2 to 3 feet. Propagate from seed or by division in the early spring.

Dictamnus
(dik-TAM-nus)
GAS PLANT, DITTANY

Dictamnus albus 'Purpureus'

Hardiness: *Zones 3-8*

Flowering season: *spring to summer*

Height: *2 to 3 feet*

Flower color: *pink to purple, white*

Soil: *moist, well-drained loam*

Light: *full sun to light shade*

Gas plant produces loose spikes of showy flowers followed by ornamental seed pods that are useful in dried arrangements. The common name refers to the flammable gas secreted by stems and roots, as well as by the leaves, which smell of lemon when crushed.

Selected species and varieties: *D. albus*—spikes of 1½- to 2-inch flowers on 3-foot-tall stems above mounds of shiny, leathery leaves spreading 2 to 3 feet wide; 'Purpureus' has pale purple flowers; 'Rubra', rose pink flowers.

Growing conditions and maintenance: Space gas plant 3 to 4 feet apart. Propagate from seed to bloom in 3 to 4 years. Division is not recommended because gas plant does not transplant well.

Digitalis
(di-ji-TAL-us)
FOXGLOVE

Digitalis x mertonensis

Hardiness: *Zones 4-8*
Flowering season: *spring to summer*
Height: *2 to 5 feet*
Flower color: *yellow, purple, pink, white*
Soil: *moist, well-drained, acid loam*
Light: *partial shade*

Bell-shaped flowers bloom densely in tall spires at the tips of foxglove's erect stems above clumps of hairy foliage.

Selected species and varieties: *D. grandiflora* (yellow foxglove)—2-inch yellow flowers with brown spots on stems up to 3 feet tall. *D. lutea* (straw foxglove)—white to pale yellow flowers on 2-foot stems. *D.* x *mertonensis* (strawberry foxglove)—strawberry red flowers with darker interior spots on 4-foot stems.

Growing conditions and maintenance: Space foxgloves 12 to 18 inches apart. They grow best in partial shade, but will tolerate full sun if sufficient moisture is supplied. Remove faded flower stems to encourage rebloom. Propagate from seed or by division in spring or fall.

Doronicum
(do-RON-i-kum)
LEOPARD'S-BANE

Doronicum cordatum

Hardiness: *Zones 4-8*
Flowering season: *spring*
Height: *1½ to 2 feet*
Flower color: *yellow*
Soil: *moist loam*
Light: *full sun to partial shade*

The daisylike flowers of leopard's-bane stand brightly above mounds of heart-shaped dark green leaves.

Selected species and varieties: *D. cordatum* (Caucasian leopard's-bane)—yellow flowers 2 to 3 inches across on 12- to 18-inch stems above mounds of leaves up to 24 inches across. *D.* 'Miss Mason'—compact 18-inch-tall plants with long-lasting foliage. *D.* 'Spring Beauty'—double-petaled yellow flowers.

Growing conditions and maintenance: Space leopard's-bane 1 to 2 feet apart in full sun but in cool locations where its shallow roots will receive constant moisture. Foliage dies out after flowers bloom. Propagate from seed or by division every 2 to 3 years.

Echinacea
(ek-i-NAY-see-a)
PURPLE CONEFLOWER

Echinacea purpurea

Hardiness: *Zones 3-9*
Flowering season: *summer*
Height: *2 to 4 feet*
Flower color: *pink, purple, white*
Soil: *well-drained loam*
Light: *full sun to light shade*

Drooping petals surrounding dark brown, cone-shaped centers bloom on purple coneflower's stiff stems over many weeks.

Selected species and varieties: *E. pallida* (pale coneflower)—rosy purple or creamy white flowers up to 3½ inches long on 3- to 4-foot stems. *E. purpurea*—pink, purple, or white flowers up to 3 inches in diameter on stems 2 to 4 feet tall; 'Bright Star' has rosy pink petals surrounding maroon centers; 'Robert Bloom', reddish purple blooms with orange centers on 2- to 3-foot stems; 'White Lustre', abundant white flowers with bronze centers.

Growing conditions and maintenance: Space plants 2 feet apart. Transplant self-sown seedlings or propagate from seeds or by division.

Echinops
(EK-in-ops)
GLOBE THISTLE

Echinops ritro

Hardiness: *Zones 3-9*
Flowering season: *summer*
Height: *3 to 4 feet*
Flower color: *blue*
Soil: *well-drained, acid loam*
Light: *full sun*

The round, spiny flowers of globe thistle are held well above coarse, bristly foliage on stiff, erect stems. Flowers are excellent for both cutting and drying.

Selected species and varieties: *E. exaltatus* (Russian globe thistle)—spiny flowers grow on stems up to 5 feet tall above deep green foliage. *E. ritro* (small globe thistle)—bright blue flower globes up to 2 inches across on stems 3 to 4 feet tall; 'Taplow Blue' has steel blue flowers 3 inches in diameter.

Growing conditions and maintenance: Space globe thistles 2 feet apart. Propagate from seed or by division in the spring.

Epimedium
(ep-i-MEE-dee-um)
BARRENWORT

Epimedium x versicolor 'Sulphureum'

Hardiness: *Zones 5-8*
Flowering season: *spring*
Height: *6 to 12 inches*
Flower color: *yellow, red, pink, white*
Soil: *moist, well-drained loam*
Light: *light to full shade*

Barrenwort's open clusters of dainty spring flowers hang above attractive heart-shaped leaves that provide a lovely ground cover. New spring leaves, tinted red, become deep green in the summer then turn bronze in the fall.

Selected species and varieties: *E. grandiflorum* 'Rose Queen'—deep pink flowers on 12-inch stalks in mid- to late spring. *E.* x *rubrum*—crimson midspring flowers with white spurs on 12-inch stems. *E.* x *versicolor* 'Sulphureum'—yellow early-spring flowers on 12-inch stems above leaves that are evergreen in warmer zones. *E.* x *youngianum* 'Niveum'—white flowers on 8-inch stems.

Growing conditions and maintenance: Space barrenwort 8 to 12 inches apart. Cut back the old foliage in spring before new growth begins. Propagate by division in spring or fall.

Erigeron
(e-RIJ-er-on)
FLEABANE

Erigeron speciosus 'Pink Jewel'

Hardiness: *Zones 3-8*
Flowering season: *summer*
Height: *1½ to 2 feet*
Flower color: *blue, lavender, pink*
Soil: *well-drained loam*
Light: *full sun*

Fleabane's asterlike blossoms grow singly or in branched clusters with a fringe of petal-like ray flowers surrounding a yellow center.

Selected species and varieties: *E. pulchellus* (Poor Robin's plantain)—pink, lavender, or white flowers 1½ inches across on plants up to 2 feet tall. *E. speciosus* (Oregon fleabane)—purple flowers 1 to 2 inches across on stems to 30 inches; 'Azure Fairy' has semidouble lavender flowers; 'Double Beauty', double blue-violet flowers; 'Foerster's Liebling', deep pink semidouble flowers; 'Pink Jewel', single lavender-pink flowers; 'Sincerity', single lavender flowers.

Growing conditions and maintenance: Plant fleabane 18 inches apart. Propagate by transplanting self-sown seedlings or by division in spring.

Eryngium
(e-RIN-jee-um)
SEA HOLLY

Eryngium bourgatii

Hardiness: *Zones 4-9*
Flowering season: *summer*
Height: *1 to 3 feet*
Flower color: *blue*
Soil: *dry, sandy loam*
Light: *full sun*

Sea holly's tiny flowers blossom in conical clusters surrounded by collars of spiny, petal-like bracts. The blooms, on stiff stems lined with leaves resembling those of holly, are unique accents in the garden and in arrangements.

Selected species and varieties: *E. alpinum* (bluetop sea holly)—frilly blue bracts surrounding blue conical centers on stems to 30 inches tall. *E. bourgatii* (Mediterranean sea holly)—blue flower heads surrounded by stiff gray-green bracts on 18- to 24-inch stems with white-veined leaves. *E. giganteum* (stout sea holly)—blue-green centers surrounded by silver bracts on stems to 3 feet tall.

Growing conditions and maintenance: Space sea hollies 12 to 18 inches apart. They tolerate salt and wind. Propagate from seed or from fall root cuttings.

Eupatorium
(yew-pa-TOR-ee-um)
BONESET

Eupatorium coelestinum

Hardiness: *Zones 3-9*
Flowering season: *summer to frost*
Height: *1 to 10 feet*
Flower color: *blue, mauve, purple*
Soil: *moist, well-drained loam*
Light: *full sun to partial shade*

Boneset bears broad, open clusters of tiny flowers on stiff stems lined with coarse, pointed leaves. Wild in many areas, it naturalizes easily; it makes an excellent cut flower.

Selected species and varieties: *E. coelestinum* (hardy ageratum)—flat clusters of fuzzy, blue to violet flowers on 1- to 2-foot stems. *E. fistulosum* (hollow Joe-Pye weed)—large clusters of mauve-pink flowers on stems 6 feet or taller. *E. maculatum* (Joe-Pye weed, smokeweed)—large flattened clusters of reddish purple or white flowers on 6- to 10-foot stems.

Growing conditions and maintenance: Space plants 18 to 24 inches apart; allow 3 feet between taller species. Propagate from seed or by division.

Filipendula
(fil-i-PEN-dew-la)
MEADOWSWEET

Filipendula rubra 'Venusta'

Hardiness: *Zones 3-9*
Flowering season: *spring to summer*
Height: *1 to 7 feet*
Flower color: *white, pink*
Soil: *moist loam*
Light: *partial shade*

Meadowsweet's long-lasting, feathery flower plumes bloom above loose mounds of fine-textured foliage.

Selected species and varieties: *F. rubra* (queen-of-the-prairie)—fluffy pink summer flower clusters on 4- to 7-foot stems that require no staking; 'Venusta' has deep pink flowers. *F. ulmaria* (queen-of-the-meadow)—feathery, creamy white summer flowers on 3- to 4-foot stems. *F. vulgaris* (dropwort)—white flowers in spring and early summer, sometimes tinged with red, in loose clusters on 1- to 3-foot stems; 'Flore Pleno' grows to 15 inches tall with double flowers; 'Grandiflora' has fragrant, yellow-tinted flowers.

Growing conditions and maintenance: Space meadowsweet 2 feet apart in sites with moist, even soggy, soils. Dropwort self-sows. Propagate from seed or by division.

Gaillardia

(gay-LAR-dee-a)

BLANKET-FLOWER

Gaillardia x grandiflora 'Goblin'

Hardiness:	*Zones 3-8*
Flowering season:	*summer through fall*
Height:	*1 to 3 feet*
Flower color:	*yellow, red, maroon*
Soil:	*well-drained loam*
Light:	*full sun*

Gaillardia produces cheerful daisylike flowers in bright color combinations above attractive mounds of hairy leaves. The flowers are excellent for cutting.

Selected species and varieties: *G.* x *grandiflora*—yellow flowers 3 to 4 inches across with yellow or reddish purple centers on stems up to 3 feet tall; 'Burgundy' has wine red flowers; 'Kobold' ('Goblin'), yellow-tipped red flowers on 2-foot stems; 'Yellow Queen', golden yellow flowers on stems up to 30 inches.

Growing conditions and maintenance: Space gaillardias 18 inches apart. They tolerate hot, dry locations, poor soil, and seaside conditions. Stake to prevent sprawl. Propagate from seed or by division.

Geranium

(jer-AY-nee-um)

CRANESBILL

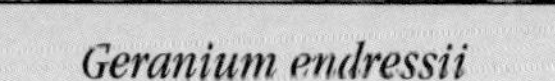

Geranium endressii

Hardiness:	*Zones 4-8*
Flowering season:	*spring to summer*
Height:	*4 inches to 4 feet*
Flower color:	*pink, purple, blue, white*
Soil:	*moist, well-drained loam*
Light:	*full sun to partial shade*

Cranesbill is valued for both its dainty flat, five-petaled flowers and its neat mounds of lobed or toothed leaves. The plants are sometimes called hardy geraniums to distinguish them from annual geraniums, which belong to the genus *Pelargonium*.

Selected species and varieties: *G. cinereum* (grayleaf cranesbill)—summer-long pink flowers with reddish veins above 6- to 12-inch-high mounds of deeply lobed, dark green leaves with a whitish cast. *G. dalmaticum* (Dalmatian cranesbill)—clusters of rosy pink inch-wide spring flowers on 4- to 6-inch trailing stems. *G. endressii* (Pyrenean cranesbill)—pink flowers ½ inch across in spring and summer above spreading 12- to 18-inch-high mounds of sometimes evergreen leaves; 'A.T. Johnson' has silver-pink flowers; 'Wargrave Pink', deep pink flowers. *G.* 'Johnson's Blue'—1½- to 2-inch blue flowers from spring to summer on plants up to 18 inches tall. *G. macrorrhizum* (bigroot cranesbill)—clusters of magenta or pink flowers with prominent stamens in spring and summer on spreading mounds of aromatic leaves turning red and yellow in fall. *G. maculatum* (wild geranium)—loose clusters of rose-purple or lavender-pink flowers in spring on 1- to 2-foot stems. *G. psilostemon* (Armenian cranesbill)—vivid purplish red flowers up to 2 inches across with darker centers on plants 2 to 4 feet tall and equally wide. *G. sanguineum* (bloody cranesbill)—solitary magenta flowers 1 to 1½ inches across in spring and summer on 9- to 12-inch-high spreading mounds of leaves turning deep red in fall; 'Album' has white flowers; *G. sanguineum* var. *striatum* [also listed as var. *lancastriense*], with red veins tracing light pink flowers.

Growing conditions and maintenance: Space Dalmatian cranesbill 12 inches apart, Armenian cranesbill 3 to 4 feet apart, and other species 1½ to 2 feet apart. Cranesbill grows in full sun to partial shade in cool areas but needs partial shade in warmer zones. Taller species may need staking. Propagate from seed, summer cuttings, or by division.

Geranium psilostemon

Geum

(JEE-um)

GEUM, AVENS

Geum triflorum 'Prairie Smoke'

Hardiness: *Zones 5-8*	
Flowering season: *spring to summer*	
Height: *8 to 30 inches*	
Flower color: *red, orange, yellow*	
Soil: *well-drained, fertile loam*	
Light: *full sun to light shade*	

Geums produce flat-faced flowers resembling wild roses with ruffled petals surrounding frilly centers and growing singly on slender stems. They make excellent cut flowers. The bright green, hairy leaves, which are lobed and frilled at their edges, form attractive mounds of foliage ideal for the front of a border or rock garden.

Selected species and varieties: *G. coccineum* [also called *G. borisii,* which is different from *G.* x *borisii,* below]—early-summer-blooming ½-inch bright orange flowers ride above bright green toothed leaves on 12-inch-tall stems; 'Red Wings' has semidouble scarlet flowers atop 2-foot stems. *G. quellyon* (Chilean avens)—scarlet flowers 1 to 1½ inches wide on plants 18 to 24 inches tall; 'Fire Opal' grows reddish bronze flowers up to 3 inches across; 'Mrs. Bradshaw' bears semidouble red-orange blossoms; 'Lady Stratheden' has semidouble deep yellow flowers; 'Princess Juliana', semidouble orange-bronze blooms; 'Starker's Magnificent', double-petaled deep orange flowers. *G. reptans* (creeping avens)—yellow or orange flowers on plants 6 to 9 inches tall that spread by runners; Zones 4-7. *G. rivale* (water avens)—tiny bell-shaped pink flowers on 12-inch stems above low clumps of dark green, hairy leaves; 'Leonard's Variety' produces copper-rose flowers on slightly taller stems than the species; Zones 3-8. *G. triflorum* 'Prairie Smoke'—nodding purple to straw-colored flowers on 6- to 18-inch-tall plants; Zones 5-10. *G.* x *borisii*—orange-scarlet flowers on 12-inch plants. *G.* 'Georgenberg'—drooping orange flowers on 10- to 12-inch stems.

Growing conditions and maintenance: Space geums 12 to 18 inches apart in soil enriched with organic matter. They grow best in moist but well-drained sites in cooler climates and will not survive wet winter soil. They may be kept robust by dividing annually. *G. reptans* requires full sun and alkaline soil. Propagate by division in late summer for plants that will be ready to flower the following year, or from seed.

Geum x borisii

Gillenia

(gil-LEE-nee-a)

BOWMAN'S ROOT

Gillenia trifoliata

Hardiness: *Zones 4-8*	
Flowering season: *spring to summer*	
Height: *2 to 4 feet*	
Flower color: *white*	
Soil: *moist, well-drained loam*	
Light: *light to moderate shade*	

Gillenia is a tall, delicate perennial with white, star-shaped flowers, often blushed with pink. The flowers emerge from wine-colored sepals, which remain as ornament after the petals drop.

Selected species and varieties: *G. trifoliata* [formerly *Porteranthus trifoliata*]—five-petaled flowers 1 inch wide, growing in loose, airy clusters on wiry, branching stems 2 to 4 feet tall above lacy leaves with toothed edges.

Growing conditions and maintenance: Space gillenia 2 to 3 feet apart in sites with abundant moisture. Incorporate organic matter into soil to help retain water. Plants often require staking. Propagate from seed or by division in spring or fall.

Gypsophila
(jip-SOFF-il-a)
BABY'S-BREATH

Gypsophila repens 'Rosea'

Hardiness: *Zones 4-9*
Flowering season: *summer*
Height: *3 to 4 feet*
Flower color: *white, pink*
Soil: *moist, well-drained, alkaline loam*
Light: *full sun*

Clouds of tiny flowers on widely branching stems rise above fine-textured foliage.

Selected species and varieties: *G. paniculata* (perennial baby's-breath)—airy clusters on stems to 4 feet tall; 'Bristol Fairy' has double white flowers; 'Perfecta' is similar to 'Bristol Fairy', with larger flowers; 'Pink Fairy' has pink double flowers on 18-inch stems. *G. repens* (creeping baby's-breath)—trailing stems 6 to 8 inches long; 'Alba' has white flowers; 'Rosea', pink flowers; 'Dorothy Teacher', dark pink flowers.

Growing conditions and maintenance: Space perennial baby's-breath plants 3 feet apart and stake; space creeping baby's-breath 18 inches apart. Established plants are difficult to divide or transplant. Propagate from seed.

Helenium
(he-LEE-nee-um)
SNEEZEWEED

Helenium autumnale

Hardiness: *Zones 3-8*
Flowering season: *summer to frost*
Height: *2½ to 6 feet*
Flower color: *yellow, orange, bronze, burgundy*
Soil: *moist loam*
Light: *full sun*

Sneezeweed's flower heads consist of fan-shaped petals that droop slightly from a darker, prominent center. Borne in clusters on branching stems over an 8- to 10-week period, they make good cut flowers.

Selected species and varieties: *H. autumnale* (common sneezeweed)—daisylike 2-inch flowers on stems up to 6 feet tall; 'Brilliant' has yellow, orange, and mahogany flowers; 'Butterpat', clear yellow flowers; 'Crimson Beauty', brick red to mahogany flowers.

Growing conditions and maintenance: Space sneezeweed 18 to 24 inches apart. Pinch stems in spring before bloom to promote bushiness; stake taller plants. Divide every 3 to 4 years to propagate and prevent crowding.

Helianthus
(hee-li-AN-thus)
SUNFLOWER

Helianthus x multiflorus 'Flore Pleno'

Hardiness: *Zones 4-9*
Flowering season: *summer to fall*
Height: *3 to 7 feet*
Flower color: *yellow*
Soil: *moist, well-drained loam*
Light: *full sun*

Sunflowers bear large bright yellow blossoms, some with single rows of petals, others with rows overlapping, on erect stems with coarse-textured leaves. The flowers are excellent for cutting.

Selected species and varieties: *H. angustifolius* (swamp sunflower)—flowers 2 to 3 inches across with dark brown to purple centers on stems to 7 feet tall. *H.* x *multiflorus* (many-flowered sunflower)—grows blooms 3 to 5 inches wide, often with overlapping petals; 'Flore Pleno' has double flowers on 4-foot stems; 'Lodden Gold', deep yellow double flowers on 5-foot stems; 'Morning Sun', golden yellow flowers on 5- to 6-foot stems.

Growing conditions and maintenance: Space sunflowers 2 to 3 feet apart. Propagate by division in spring.

Heliopsis
(hee-li-OP-sis)
FALSE SUNFLOWER

Heliopsis helianthoides

Hardiness: *Zones 4-9*

Flowering season: *summer to fall*

Height: *3 to 5 feet*

Flower color: *yellow, orange*

Soil: *moist, well-drained loam*

Light: *full sun*

False sunflower bears bright flowers in shades of yellow and gold with single or double rows of petals surrounding prominent centers on bushy plants. They make excellent cut flowers.

Selected species and varieties: *H. helianthoides* var. *scabra*—single, semidouble, or double flowers 2 to 3 inches across on plants 3 to 5 feet tall; 'Golden Plume' grows double yellow flowers; 'Incomparabilis', semidouble yellow flowers with dark centers; 'Summer Sun', semidouble golden yellow flowers; 'Karat', large single yellow flowers.

Growing conditions and maintenance: Space false sunflowers 2 feet apart and stake taller plants. Propagate from seed or by division.

Helleborus
(hell-e-BOR-us)
HELLEBORE

Helleborus orientalis

Hardiness: *Zones 3-8*

Flowering season: *winter to spring*

Height: *1 to 3 feet*

Flower color: *white, green, purple, pink*

Soil: *moist, well-drained loam*

Light: *partial shade*

Very early in the blooming season, hellebores produce cup- or bell-shaped flowers above clumps of usually evergreen leaves that are shaped like hands.

Selected species and varieties: *H. argutifolius* (Corsican hellebore)—light green flowers on 2- to 3-foot plants; hardy to Zone 8. *H. foetidus* (stinking hellebore)—light green flowers on plants to 24 inches tall; hardy to Zone 6. *H. niger* (Christmas rose)—white flowers with a pink blush on plants to 15 inches tall; hardy to Zone 4. *H. orientalis* (Lenten rose)—cream, maroon, or pink flowers on 18-inch plants; hardy to Zone 5.

Growing conditions and maintenance: Space smaller species 1 foot apart, larger ones up to 2 feet apart. Propagate from seed or by division.

Hemerocallis
(hem-er-o-KAL-lis)
DAYLILY

Hemerocallis 'Stella de Oro'

Hardiness: *Zones 3-10*

Flowering season: *summer to fall*

Height: *1 to 4 feet*

Flower color: *all shades but blue*

Soil: *moist, well-drained loam*

Light: *full sun to partial shade*

Daylilies produce dainty to bold flower trumpets with petals resembling those of true lilies. Their colors span the rainbow with the exception of blue and pure white, and blooms are often bi- or tricolored. Sometimes with ruffled edges or double or even triple rows of petals, and occasionally fragrant, the flowers rise above mounds of grasslike, arching leaves on branched stems called scapes. Each flower lasts only one day, but each scape supports many buds that continue to open in succession for weeks, even months. Daylilies have been extensively hybridized, offering a wide choice of plant sizes, flower colors and styles, and periods of bloom. In some hybrids, the normal number of chromosomes has been doubled, giving rise to tetraploid daylilies with larger, more substantial flowers on more robust plants. Miniature varieties with smaller flowers on shortened scapes have also been bred.

Selected species and varieties: *H. fulva* (tawny daylily)—the common orange daylily found along roadsides; 6 to 12 orange flower trumpets per scape on vigorous, robust plants in large clumps; 'Kwanso Variegata' is a larger plant than the species and produces double blooms; 'Rosea' has rose-colored flowers. *H. lilio-asphodelus* (lemon daylily) [also known as *H. flava*]—lemon yellow 4-inch flowers on 2- to 3-foot scapes over clumps of slender dark green leaves up to 2 feet long; spreads rapidly by rhizomatous roots; 'Major' grows taller than the species and produces larger, deep yellow flowers. *H.* hybrids—yellow-gold hybrids include 'Golden Chimes', a miniature variety with gold-yellow flowers; 'Stella de Oro', another yellow-gold miniature that blooms from late spring until frost; 'Happy Returns', a hybrid offspring of 'Stella de Oro' with abundant, ruffled lemon yellow blooms and a similarly long flowering season; 'Little Cherub', 3½-inch light yellow flowers on 22-inch scapes over evergreen foliage; 'Alice in Wonderland',

Hemerocallis 'Grapeade'

with 5½-inch ruffled lemon yellow flowers on 3-foot scapes and beautiful deep green foliage; 'Bountiful Valley', with 6-inch yellow blooms sporting lime green throats; 'Hyperion', an older variety still popular for its fragrant, late-blooming yellow flowers on 4-foot scapes; 'Fall Glow', a shorter alternative with late, golden orange blooms.

Among red hybrids are 'Artist's Dream', a midseason tetraploid bearing saturn red blooms with yellow midribs above a yellow-green throat; 'Anzac', true red blooms with yellow-green throats, 6 inches wide on 28-inch scapes; 'Cherry Cheeks', with cherry red petals lined by white midribs; 'Pardon Me', prolific producer of cerise flowers 2¾ inches across with green throats on 18-inch scapes; 'Autumn Red', sporting late-season red flowers with yellow-green throats.

Pink to purple hybrids include 'Country Club' and 'Peach Fairy', pink-peach-flowered varieties; 'Joyful Occasion', 6-inch medium pink flowers with green throats and ruf-

Hemerocallis 'Artist's Dream'

fled petals over evergreen foliage, 'Flower Basket', with coral pink double flowers; 'Catherine Woodbury', with pale lilac-pink flowers; and 'Grapeade', with green-throated purple blossoms.

Growing conditions and maintenance: Daylilies are among the least demanding of perennials, providing spectacular results with minimal care. Planted in groups, they spread to create a rugged ground cover that will suppress most weeds. Plant daylilies in spring or fall, spacing miniature varieties 18 to 24 inches apart, taller varieties 2 to 3 feet apart. Daylilies prefer sunny locations but adapt well to light shade. Light-colored flowers that fade in bright sun often show up better with some shade. Fertilize with an organic blend, if necessary, but do not overfeed, as this will cause rank growth and reduce flowering. Propagate by dividing clumps every 3 to 6 years.

Heuchera

(HEW-ker-a)

ALUMROOT

Heuchera sanguinea

Hardiness: *Zones 4-8*

Flowering season: *spring to summer*

Height: *12 to 24 inches*

Flower color: *white, pink, red*

Soil: *moist, well-drained, rich loam*

Light: *partial shade to full sun*

The delicate, bell-shaped flowers of alumroot line slender stalks held above neat mounds of lobed leaves.

Selected species and varieties: *H. micrantha* (small-flowered alumroot)—white flowers above gray-green heart-shaped leaves; 'Palace Purple' has dramatic, deep bronze leaves. *H. sanguinea* (coral bells)—red flowers persisting 4 to 8 weeks; 'Red Spangles' grows scarlet flowers on short stems; 'Chatterbox', rose pink flowers; 'Snowflakes', white flowers.

Growing conditions and maintenance: Space heuchera 1 to 1½ feet apart. Water well during dry spells. Plants tolerate full sun in cooler climates but prefer partial shade in warmer zones. Propagate from seed or by division every 3 years.

Hibiscus
(hy-BIS-kus)
ROSE MALLOW

Hibiscus coccineus

Hardiness: *Zones 5-9*

Flowering season: *summer*

Height: *3 to 8 feet*

Flower color: *red, white, pink, bicolors*

Soil: *moist loam*

Light: *full sun to light shade*

Hibiscus's large bell-shaped flowers add a colorful splash at the back of a flower bed or the edge of a pond from summer until frost.

Selected species and varieties: *H. coccineus* (scarlet rose mallow)—brilliant scarlet blossoms 5 to 6 inches wide on 6- to 8-foot flower stalks; *H.* 'Lord Baltimore' produces deep crimson flowers; 'Lady Baltimore', pink blossoms with crimson eyes. *H. moscheutos* (swamp mallow)—multistemmed shrub 3 to 8 feet tall with red, white, pink, or bicolored flowers 6 to 12 inches wide.

Growing conditions and maintenance: Set rose mallow plants 2 to 3 feet apart in moist locations with full sun. Propagate from seed, from cuttings, or, if desired, by division every 3 to 10 years, in spring or fall.

Hosta
(HOS-ta)
PLANTAIN LILY, FUNKIA

Hosta fortunei 'Gold Standard'

Hardiness: *Zones 3-9*

Flowering season: *summer*

Height: *8 inches to 3 feet*

Flower color: *white, lavender, violet*

Soil: *moist, rich, acid loam*

Light: *partial to dense shade*

Hostas are grown primarily for their clumps of attractive foliage, which may be dark green, yellow-green, blue-green, gold, or variegated with white or yellow, often with interesting textures. Tall, graceful spires of pale lilylike flowers appear above the clumps.

Selected species and varieties: *H. fortunei* (Fortune's hosta)—gray-green 5-inch leaves; 'Gold Standard' has light gold leaves edged in green; 'Aureo-marginata', green leaves with narrow yellow margins; 'Gloriosa', green oval-shaped leaves with white margins. *H.* 'Krossa Regal'—3-foot-wide mounds of arching blue-green leaves with lilac flowers on 5-foot stalks. *H. lancifolia* (narrow plantain lily)—narrow, dark green leaves with deep lilac-colored flowers. *H. plantaginea* (fragrant plantain lily)—2-foot-wide clumps of bright green, heart-shaped leaves and fragrant white 4-inch flowers on 2½-foot stems; 'Aphrodite' produces double white flowers on 2-foot stems above large, glossy, heart-shaped green leaves; 'Honeybells', fragrant lavender flowers and light green foliage; 'Royal Standard', deeply veined green leaves and fragrant white blooms on 2- to 3-foot stems. *H. sieboldiana* (Siebold plantain lily)—blue-green leaves, often 15 inches long and nearly round, in clumps 2 feet tall and 4 feet wide; 'Frances Williams' has gold leaves; 'Elegans', lavender flowers on 3-foot stems over steel blue foliage. *H. undulata* (wavy-leaf plantain lily)—undulating leaves 6 inches long and striped with white or cream; leaves of 'Albo-marginata' have broad white edges; 'Variegata' forms 10-inch-high mounds of leaves streaked with white in the center and edged in green. *H. ventricosa* (blue hosta)—4-foot-high mounds of broad, glossy,

Hosta sieboldiana 'Frances Williams'

dark green leaves and purple flowers with darker purple stripes; 'Aureo-marginata' has yellow-edged leaves. *H. venusta* (dwarf plantain lily)—a quick-spreading variety with oval, 1-inch leaves.

Growing conditions and maintenance: Plant smaller hostas 1 foot apart, larger species 2 to 3 feet apart, in a moist but well-drained soil; wet soil in winter often damages plants. Hostas prefer shade, but will adapt to full sun given sufficient water. Remove flowers to encourage more leaf growth. Propagate by division in spring or fall.

Iberis
(eye-BEER-is)
CANDYTUFT

Iberis sempervirens

Hardiness: *Zones 4-8*
Flowering season: *spring*
Height: *6 to 12 inches*
Flower color: *white*
Soil: *moist, well-drained loam*
Light: *full sun*

Clusters of flowers bloom atop candytuft's low-growing mounds of woody stems lined with narrow, dark, evergreen leaves.

Selected species and varieties: *I. sempervirens* (evergreen or edging candytuft)—a low-growing, semiwoody evergreen plant spreading 2 feet wide; 'Little Gem' is a free-flowering variety only 5 to 8 inches tall; 'Snow Mantle' grows in compact mounds 8 inches high; 'Snowflake' grows slightly higher, with large 2- to 3-inch flower clusters.

Growing conditions and maintenance: Space candytuft plants 12 to 15 inches apart. Cut back at least 2 inches after they flower to maintain vigorous foliage growth. Some protection of the leaves may be necessary where winters are severe to prevent sunscald. Propagate from stem cuttings taken after flowering or by division in spring or fall.

Inula
(IN-yew-la)
INULA

Inula ensifolia

Hardiness *Zones 4-9*
Flowering season: *summer*
Height: *12 inches*
Flower color: *yellow*
Soil: *well-drained, average fertility*
Light: *full sun to partial shade*

Inula produces cheerful, bright yellow, daisylike flowers at the tips of wiry stems that form mounds.

Selected species and varieties: *I. ensifolia* (swordleaf inula)—dense clumps, 12 inches tall and wide, of wiry, erect stems lined with narrow, pointed 4-inch leaves and tipped with 1- to 2-inch flowers. The blooms last 2 to 3 weeks in warmer zones, up to 6 weeks in cooler areas.

Growing conditions and maintenance: Space inulas 1 foot apart in massed plantings. Propagate from seed or by division in spring or fall.

Iris
(I-ris)
IRIS

Iris 'Best Bet'

Hardiness: *Zones 4-9*
Flowering season: *spring to fall*
Height: *6 inches to 5 feet*
Flower color: *many shades, bicolors, blends*
Soil: *moist, well-drained loam*
Light: *full sun to light shade*

Irises bloom in a rainbow of colors on zigzag stems rising from sword-shaped leaves that remain attractive even when plants are not in bloom. Iris flowers are so distinctive that special terms are used to describe their parts. Each flower is composed of three drooping petal-like sepals called falls, three usually erect petals called standards, and three narrow, petal-like styles. The falls may be bearded with a hairy tuft, crested with a raised ridge down the center, or beardless without a crest. With over 200 species and thousands of varieties, irises vary widely in many respects, including cultural requirements, height, flower size, type, color, and season.

Selected species and varieties: Bearded iris hybrids are classified according to plant height as dwarf, intermediate, and tall, and are then further subdivided by flower size and season.

Dwarf bearded iris hybrids derive many of their characteristics from the parent species, *I. pumila* and *I. chamaeiris.* Miniature dwarf bearded iris—less than 10 inches tall with 1½- to 2½-inch flowers in midspring; 'Already' has wine red flowers; 'Angel Eyes', white flowers with blue spots on falls; 'Banberry Ruffles', purple blossoms; 'Blue Frost', light blue flowers on 6-inch stems; 'Sky Baby', ruffled blue blooms. Standard dwarf bearded iris—10 to 15 inches tall with 1½- to 2½-inch blossoms that appear a week later than those of miniatures; 'Baby Snowflake' has white flowers; 'Bingo', velvety purple flowers; 'Early Sunshine', yellow flowers; 'Red Dandy', wine red flowers.

Intermediate and border bearded iris—2- to 4-inch flowers on plants 15 to 28 inches tall, with intermediates blooming in midspring, borders in late spring to early summer; 'Little Angel' has white flowers; 'Lemonade', white falls on yellow blossoms; 'Sweet Allegro', pink flowers.

Iris cristata

Tall bearded iris—plants that grow upwards of 28 inches tall with flowers to 8 inches across in late spring to summer; 'Cindy' has red-bearded white flowers; 'Charade', ruffled medium blue flowers; 'May Magic', light pink blossoms; 'Best Bet', ruffled lavender flowers.

Reblooming bearded iris—many heights and flower sizes, blossoming in spring and again any time from midsummer to fall; 'Lady Emma' has yellow blossoms; 'Autumn Bugler', violet flowers with dark purple falls.

I. cristata (crested iris)—blue or white flowers with yellow or white crested ridges on 6- to 9-inch plants in early to midspring; 'Shenandoah Sky' grows pale blue flowers; 'Summer Storm', deep blue; 'Alba', yellow-crested pure white flowers. *I. ensata* [sometimes listed as *I. kaempferi*] (Japanese iris)—beardless flowers up to 10 inches across from early to midsummer on stems to 4 feet; 'Favorite' grows medium blue flowers; 'Great White Heron', white semidouble flowers; 'Pink Lady', light pink blooms; 'Royal Banner', dark purple. *I. laevigata* (rabbit-ear iris)—flattened blue flowers similar to Japanese iris on stems up to 24 inches tall; 'Alba' has white flowers; 'Regal', red-purple blooms; 'Variegata' has leaves variegated white. *I.* 'Louisiana' (Louisiana hybrids)—flowers 3 to 4 inches across in a broad range of colors and types on stems to 4 feet tall, blooming in mid- to late spring. *I. pseudacorus* (yellow flag)—2-inch light yellow flowers with a brown blotch on the falls, blooming in late spring to early summer on stalks to 5 feet tall; *I. p.* var. *bastardii* has creamy yellow flowers atop 4-foot stalks; 'Golden Queen', larger yellow blooms without the brown blotches; 'Variegata' has leaves variegated yellow in spring but changing to green by midsummer. *I. sibirica* (Siberian iris)—deep blue, violet, or white flowers 2 inches wide on stems to 4 feet tall in late spring; 'Caesar's Brother' has dark violet-blue flowers; 'Dreaming Spires', lavender-and-royal blue flowers on 30-inch stalks; 'Flight of Butterflies', blue petals and pale blue to white veined falls; 'Harpswell Haze', pale lavender with pale edges; 'Little White', white blooms atop 12- to 18-inch stalks; 'Tealwood', dark violet flowers on 3-foot stalks; 'White Swirl', white with a yellow throat. *I. tectorum* (roof iris)—lilac or white crested flowers up to 6 inches wide blooming in late spring on stems up to 18 inches tall.

Iris pseudacorus

Growing conditions and maintenance: Space dwarf bearded, crested, and roof irises 1 foot apart. Allow 1½ feet between taller types. Most irises grow best in full sun. Yellow flag, Japanese, and roof irises tolerate partial shade; crested iris performs best in partial shade. Bearded irises thrive in a well-drained, neutral loam; roof irises prefer slightly acid, sandy soil with low fertility. Siberian, Louisiana, and Japanese irises need constant moisture and benefit from a soil high in organic matter. Japanese irises require an acid soil. Yellow flag and rabbit-ear irises need wet soil and will even thrive with their roots submerged along stream banks and pond edges. Propagate irises by dividing the rhizomes or clumps after they have flowered. Divisions of bearded irises consist of one fan of leaves cut back to about 6 inches and several feeder roots, which should be planted 1 inch deep. Divide Japanese and Siberian irises only when clumps show signs of reduced flowering or decline.

Iris sibirica 'Harpswell Haze'

Kniphofia
(ny-FO-fee-a)
TORCH LILY, TRITOMA

Kniphofia uvaria 'Robin Hood'

Hardiness: *Zones 5-9*
Flowering season: *summer to fall*
Height: *2 to 4 feet*
Flower color: *red, orange, yellow, cream*
Soil: *well-drained, sandy loam*
Light: *full sun*

Torch lily's stiff clusters of tubular flowers on bare stems held above tufts of stiff, gray-green leaves are a bold accent in a mixed border and a favorite of hummingbirds.

Selected species and varieties: *K. uvaria* (red-hot poker)—individual 1- to 2-inch flowers clustered along the top several inches of stem like a bristly bottle brush open a bright red then turn yellow as they mature.

Growing conditions and maintenance: Plant torch lilies 1½ to 2 feet apart in locations protected from strong winds. Propagate from seed, by division in spring, or by removing and transplanting the small offsets that develop at the base of plants. Plants grown from seed require 2 or 3 years to flower.

Lamium
(LAY-mee-um)
DEAD NETTLE

Lamium maculatum 'Aureum'

Hardiness: *Zones 4-8*
Flowering season: *spring to summer*
Height: *8 to 12 inches*
Flower color *red, pink, purple, white*
Soil: *well-drained, average loam*
Light: *partial to full shade*

Dead nettle produces whorls of hooded flowers at the ends of spreading stems lined with attractive puckered leaves, often splotched with color.

Selected species and varieties: *L. maculatum* (spotted dead nettle)—pink to purple flowers and 1- to 2-inch leaves with white stripes or spots along the midrib; 'Beacon Silver' has pink flowers and extremely showy, silvery foliage with narrow green edges; 'White Nancy', white flowers amid similar foliage.

Growing conditions and maintenance: Plant dead nettles 1½ to 2 feet apart. Dead nettle spreads rapidly above ground and self-seeds aggressively. Cut stems back to control spread and to encourage more compact growth. Propagate from cuttings taken any time during the growing season or by division in spring.

Lavandula
(lav-AN-dew-la)
LAVENDER

Lavandula angustifolia 'Munstead'

Hardiness: *Zones 5-9*
Flowering season: *summer*
Height: *1 to 3 feet*
Flower color: *lavender, purple, pink*
Soil: *any well-drained loam*
Light: *full sun*

Lavender is a fragrant evergreen perennial whose subtle gray-green, woolly foliage tipped with delicate flower spikes contrasts well with more brightly colored plants.

Selected species and varieties: *L. angustifolia* (true or English lavender)—produces flowers in 3- to 4-inch whorls at the tips of stems lined with narrow, aromatic, 1- to 2-inch leaves; 'Hidcote' has deep purple blossoms and silvery foliage 15 to 20 inches tall; 'Munstead Dwarf', extremely fragrant, lavender-blue flowers on spreading plants 12 inches tall.

Growing conditions and maintenance: Plant lavender 12 to 18 inches apart. Soils too rich or too heavy may lead to soft growth and winter damage. Cut back in early spring to maintain dense form. Propagate by division in the spring.

Liatris

(ly-AY-tris)

GAY-FEATHER

Liatris spicata 'Kobold Rose'

Hardiness: *Zones 3-9*	
Flowering season: *summer to fall*	
Height: *18 inches to 5 feet*	
Flower color: *purple, pink, lavender, white*	
Soil: *well-drained, sandy loam*	
Light: *full sun to light shade*	

Gay-feather's erect stalks rising from clumps of sword-shaped leaves are tipped with dramatic spikes of puffy flowers. The top buds open first, and bloom progresses downward.

Selected species and varieties: *L. pycnostachya* (Kansas gay-feather)—bright purple flower spikes on 4- to 6-foot stems. *L. scariosa* (tall gay-feather)—purple flowers on 5-foot stalks; 'September Glory' has deep purple blooms on 3- to 4-foot stalks; 'White Spires', white flowers. *L. spicata* (spike gay-feather)—purple flowers on 6-foot stems; 'Kobold' is a dwarf variety 2 feet tall with bright purple blooms.

Growing conditions and maintenance: Space gay-feather plants 1 foot apart. Stake taller varieties. Propagate from seed or by division in spring.

Ligularia

(lig-yew-LAY-ree-a)

GOLDEN-RAY

Ligularia dentata 'Desdemona'

Hardiness: *Zones 4-8*	
Flowering season: *summer*	
Height: *3 to 6 feet*	
Flower color: *yellow, orange*	
Soil: *moist loam or bog*	
Light: *full sun to partial shade*	

These coarse-textured plants develop into showy clumps of attractive, often variegated leaves up to 4 feet tall and as wide. Several species are also prized for their eye-catching flowers, some on stalks up to 6 feet tall.

Selected species and varieties: *L. dentata* (bigleaf golden-ray)—leathery, kidney-shaped leaves 20 inches wide forming lush mounds 3 to 4 feet high with yellow daisylike flowers on branched stalks; 'Desdemona' is more compact than the species, with leaf stems and undersides a striking mahogany red; 'Othello' is similar in color but less compact. *L.* 'Gregynog Gold'—heart-shaped leaves and bright orange flowers in conical spikes on stalks up to 6 feet tall. *L. stenocephala* 'The Rocket' [often listed under *L. przewalskii* or as a hybrid of the two species] (rocket ligularia)—light green leaves 8 to 12 inches wide with coarse-toothed edges in soft mounds punctuated by 4- to 6-foot stalks tipped with bright yellow flower spikes. *L. tussilaginea*—leathery leaves on woolly white stalks growing in clumps 2 feet tall, with clusters of pale yellow flowers on branched stems; 'Argentea' has leaves mottled gray-green, dark green, and cream; 'Aureo-maculata', leaves spotted yellow; Zones 7-10.

Growing conditions and maintenance: Plant ligularia 2 to 3 feet apart in cool, sunny, moist locations, a microclimate often best achieved alongside a pond or stream. Full sun may wilt leaves, but too much shade causes flowers to lean toward the light.

Ligularia przewalskii

Propagate both species and varieties by division in spring or fall; species can also be propagated from seed.

Limonium
(ly-MO-nee-um)
SEA LAVENDER

Limonium latifolium

Hardiness: *Zones 4-9*

Flowering season: *summer*

Height: *18 to 30 inches*

Flower color: *lavender-blue to violet*

Soil: *well-drained, slightly acid loam*

Light: *full sun*

Small, lacy flowers of sea lavender spread over the top of the plant like a cloud and persist for several weeks. The long-lasting flowers are outstanding in either fresh or dried arrangements.

Selected species and varieties: *L. latifolium*—branching flower stems carry an airy, rounded crown of lavender-blue blossoms above a tuft of leathery, oblong evergreen leaves; 'Blue Cloud' produces soft, light blue flowers; 'Violetta', deep violet.

Growing conditions and maintenance: Space plants 18 inches apart. Sea lavender tolerates seaside conditions. Extremely fertile soils produce weak branches that require staking. Propagate from seed or by division in the spring.

Linum
(LY-num)
FLAX

Linum perenne

Hardiness: *Zones 5-9*

Flowering season: *spring to summer*

Height: *12 to 24 inches*

Flower color: *blue, white, yellow*

Soil: *well-drained, sandy loam*

Light: *full sun to light shade*

Delicate flax blooms prolifically with inch-wide, cup-shaped flowers held aloft on soft stems. Though blossoms last only a day, new buds open continuously for 6 weeks or more.

Selected species and varieties: *L. flavum* (golden flax)—bright yellow flowers on stems 1 to 1½ feet tall. *L. perenne* (perennial flax)—sky blue, saucer-shaped flowers on stems up to 2 feet tall; 'Diamant White' has abundant white blossoms on 12- to 18-inch stems.

Growing conditions and maintenance: Space flax plants 18 inches apart in groups of 6 or more for an effective display. Flax is a short-lived perennial but often reseeds itself. Propagate from seed or from stem cuttings taken in late spring or summer, after new growth hardens.

Lobelia
(lo-BEE-lee-a)
CARDINAL FLOWER

Lobelia cardinalis

Hardiness: *Zones 3-9*

Flowering season: *summer*

Height: *2 to 4 feet*

Flower color: *red, pink, white, blue*

Soil: *moist, fertile loam*

Light: *light shade*

Cardinal flower bears spires of intensely colored blossoms with drooping lips on stiff stems rising from rosettes of dark green leaves.

Selected species and varieties: *L. cardinalis* (red lobelia)—1½-inch scarlet blossoms on 3-foot-tall flower stalks; pink and white varieties available. *L. siphilitica* (great blue lobelia)—1-inch-long blue flowers persist a month or more.

Growing conditions and maintenance: Plant lobelia 12 inches apart in locations with adequate moisture and in soil with ample organic matter. Lobelia will grow in full sun with sufficient moisture. Though short-lived, it self-sows freely. It can also be propagated by division in the fall.

Lupinus

(loo-PY-nus)

LUPINE

Lupinus 'Russell Hybrids'

Hardiness: *Zones 3-6*

Flowering season: *summer*

Height: *3 to 4 feet*

Flower color: *many shades*

Soil: *moist, well-drained, acid loam*

Light: *full sun to partial shade*

Dramatic lupines bear pea-like flowers packed tightly in heavy spikes held above palm-shaped leaves.

Selected species and varieties: *L.* 'Russell Hybrids'—dense white, pink, purple, red, blue, yellow, and bicolored flower clusters 12 to 24 inches long held well above the foliage.

Growing conditions and maintenance: Space lupines 2 feet apart. The plants may require staking. Lupines need cool night temperatures to perform well; in warmer areas, they are best planted in the fall and treated as annuals. Propagate from seed or from cuttings taken in the spring with a piece of the crown or of the root attached.

Lychnis

(LIK-nis)

CATCHFLY, CAMPION

Lychnis chalcedonica

Hardiness: *Zones 4-9*

Flowering season: *summer*

Height: *1 to 3 feet*

Flower color: *red, pink, purple, white*

Soil: *moist, well-drained, fertile loam*

Light: *full sun to partial shade*

Lychnis bears intensely colored flowers singly or in clusters on slender stems with airy foliage.

Selected species and varieties: *L.* x *arkwrightii* (Arkwright campion)—orange-red flowers contrast with bronze foliage. *L. chalcedonica* (Maltese cross)—4-inch clusters of scarlet flowers on 3- to 4-foot stems. *L. coronaria* (rose campion)—cerise flowers amid woolly gray-green leaves. *L. viscaria* (German catchfly)—magenta flowers on sticky 12-inch stems above tufts of grasslike leaves; 'Flore Pleno' grows deep pink to magenta double flowers; 'Splendens Plena', double rose pink flowers; 'Zulu', red blooms.

Growing conditions and maintenance: Plant lychnis 1 to 1½ feet apart. Rose campion self-sows. Other lychnises can be propagated from seed or by division.

Lysimachia

(ly-sim-MAK-ee-a)

LOOSESTRIFE

Lysimachia clethroides

Hardiness: *Zones 4-8*

Flowering season: *spring to summer*

Height: *2 inches to 3 feet*

Flower color: *white, yellow*

Soil: *moist, fertile loam*

Light: *full sun to partial shade*

Loosestrife varies in habit from low-growing ground covers to medium-tall, erect clumps. Flowers bloom singly or in small spikes amid attractive foliage. [NOTE: Most species are quite invasive and should be contained when planted *(page 49)*.]

Selected species and varieties: *L. clethroides* (gooseneck loosestrife)—white, arched flower spikes on 3-foot stems. *L. nummularia* (moneywort, creeping Jenny)—2- to 4-inch-tall creeper with ¾-inch yellow flowers amid small round leaves; 'Aurea' has yellow leaves. *L. punctata* (yellow loosestrife)—clusters of bright yellow ¾-inch flowers in the leaf axils along 18- to 30-inch stems.

Growing conditions and maintenance: Plant 2 feet apart. Loosestrife naturalizes easily, particularly alongside streams or in swampy areas. Propagate from seed or by division.

Macleaya
(mak-LAY-a)
PLUME POPPY

Macleaya cordata

Hardiness: *Zones 4-9*

Flowering season: *summer*

Height: *6 to 8 feet*

Flower color: *white*

Soil: *moist, well-drained loam*

Light: *full sun to partial shade*

Dramatic plume poppies bear loose spikes of tiny, fluffy blooms above clumps of attractive, deeply lobed leaves. The flowers are useful in fresh or dried arrangements, and the softly colored leaves provide an effective foil for other flowers.

Selected species and varieties: *M. cordata*—white flowers in 12-inch plumes at the tips of stiff stems above deeply lobed, 1-foot-wide leaves with gray-white undersides. *M. microcarpa* 'Kelway's Coral Plume'—coral pink flowers.

Growing conditions and maintenance: Plant plume poppies 3 to 4 feet apart. Plants can be quite invasive, especially in rich soil or in shade. Though quite tall, the sturdy stems do not require staking. Propagate from seed, from root cuttings, or by division every 3 to 4 years.

Malva
(MAL-va)
MALLOW

Malva moschata

Hardiness: *Zones 4-8*

Flowering season: *summer to fall*

Height: *1 to 4 feet*

Flower color: *pink, white*

Soil: *dry to moist, well-drained loam*

Light: *full sun to partial shade*

Mallows produce a profusion of satiny flowers with notched petals, growing throughout the summer and often into the fall above finely cut, bushy foliage.

Selected species and varieties: *M. alcea* 'Fastigiata' (hollyhock mallow)—2-inch pink blossoms on 3- to 4-foot stems. *M. moschata* (musk mallow)—white or rose flowers on plants 1 to 3 feet tall; 'Alba' has white blossoms; 'Rosea', mauve-pink.

Growing conditions and maintenance: Plant mallows 2 feet apart. Although these drought-tolerant plants are short-lived, they often self-sow. Propagate by division in spring or fall.

Miscanthus
(mis-KAN-thus)
EULALIA

Miscanthus sinensis

Hardiness: *Zones 5-9*

Flowering season: *summer*

Height: *6 to 8 feet*

Flower color: *pink, red, silver*

Soil: *well-drained loam*

Light: *full sun*

Eulalia produces feathery flower fans on tall stems above graceful clumps of arching leaves an inch wide.

Selected species and varieties: *M. sinensis*—varieties offer a selection of colors and blooming periods; 'Condensatus' has purple flowers; 'Gracillimus' (maiden grass), fall flowers above compact clumps of fine-textured leaves; 'Purpurascens', silvery pink summer flowers above red-tinted foliage; 'Strictus' (porcupine grass), upright leaves striped with horizontal yellow bands; 'Zebrinus' (zebra grass) is similarly striped with a more arching form.

Growing conditions and maintenance: Space clumps of miscanthus 3 feet apart. Cut plants back to 6 inches in late winter before new growth begins. Propagate by division in spring.

Monarda
(mo-NAR-da)
BEE BALM

Monarda didyma

Hardiness: *Zones 4-9*
Flowering season: *summer*
Height: *2 to 4 feet*
Flower color: *red, purple, pink, white*
Soil: *moist or dry loam*
Light: *full sun to light shade*

Bee balm has fragrant leaves and shaggy clusters of tiny tubular flowers attractive to bees, butterflies, and hummingbirds.

Selected species and varieties: *M. didyma*—scarlet flowers on 3- to 4-foot stems; 'Cambridge Scarlet', wine red flowers; 'Croftway Pink', rose pink; 'Mahogany', dark red; 'Blue Stocking', violet-blue; 'Snow Queen', white. *M. fistulosa* (wild bergamot)—lilac to pink flower clusters on plants up to 4 feet tall. *M. punctata* (spotted bee balm)—yellow blossoms with purple spots.

Growing conditions and maintenance: Plant monarda 1½ to 2 feet apart. It thrives in moist areas, although wild bergamot and spotted bee balm tolerate dry conditions. Propagate from seed, from cuttings, or by division in the spring.

Nepeta
(NEP-e-ta)
CATMINT

Nepeta mussinii

Hardiness: *Zones 4-8*
Flowering season: *summer*
Height: *1 to 3 feet*
Flower color: *lavender-blue, white*
Soil: *average, well-drained loam*
Light: *full sun*

Catmint's aromatic gray-green leaves and blue flowers provide fragrance and color, meandering through a rock garden, edging a walk, or filling in between bolder perennials in a border. The tiny flowers appear in whorls between heart-shaped leaves on square stems.

Selected species and varieties: *N.* x *faassenii* (blue catmint)—mounds 18 to 24 inches high with an equal or greater spread; 'Six Hills Giant' grows up to 3 feet tall. *N. mussinii* (Persian nepeta)—low-growing plants 12 inches high.

Growing conditions and maintenance: Plant catmint 1 to 1½ feet apart. Shearing plants after bloom encourages a second flowering. Propagate blue catmint from cuttings or by division, Persian nepeta from seed or by division.

Oenothera
(ee-no-THEE-ra)
SUNDROP

Oenothera fruticosa

Hardiness: *Zones 4-8*
Flowering season: *summer*
Height: *6 to 24 inches*
Flower color: *yellow, pink, white*
Soil: *well-drained loam*
Light: *full sun*

Showy, four-petaled, saucer-shaped flowers bloom on sundrops during the day and on evening primroses (night-blooming oenothera) at night.

Selected species and varieties: *O. fruticosa* (common sundrop)—prolific clusters of 1- to 2-inch bright yellow flowers at the tips of 18- to 24-inch stems. *O. missouriensis* (Ozark sundrop)—large 5-inch yellow flowers on 6- to 12-inch plants. *O. speciosa* (showy evening primrose)—white or pink blossoms on spreading stems that grow 6 to 18 inches tall. *O. tetragona*—yellow flowers similar to those of *O. fruticosa* but with young buds and stems tinted red.

Growing conditions and maintenance: Plant Ozark sundrops 2 feet apart, other species 12 to 18 inches apart. Propagate Ozark sundrops from seed, other species either from seed or by division.

Paeonia
(pee-O-nee-a)
PEONY

Paeonia lactiflora

Hardiness: *Zones 3-8*

Flowering season: *spring to summer*

Height: *18 to 36 inches*

Flower color: *white, pink, red*

Soil: *well-drained, fertile loam*

Light: *full sun to light shade*

Peonies are long-lived perennials beloved for their large, showy flowers and attractive foliage. Dramatic in the garden, they are stunning in bouquets. Peony flowers are classified by their form. Single-flower peonies have a single row of five or more petals surrounding a center of bright yellow stamens. Japanese and anemone peonies have a single row of petals surrounding modified stamens that resemble finely cut petals. Semidouble peonies have several rows of petals surrounding conspicuous stamens. Double-flowered peonies have multiple rows of petals crowded into ruffly hemispheres.

Selected species and varieties: *P. lactiflora* (garden or Chinese peony)—white, pink, or red flowers on 3-foot stems. *P. mlokosewitschii* (Caucasian peony)—very early blooming, 2-inch single lemon yellow flowers on 2-foot-tall stems with soft gray-green foliage. *P. officinalis* (common peony)—hundreds of varieties with 3- to 6-inch blooms in various forms and colors from red to light pink to white on 2-foot stems. *P. tenuifolia* (fern-leaf peony)—single deep red flowers and finely divided, fernlike leaves on 18- to 24-inch stems; 'Flore Pleno' has double flowers.

Hundreds of peony hybrids are available. 'Lobata' (red-pink), 'Lotus Bloom' (pink), and 'Krinkled White' are outstanding singles. 'Isani-Gidui' (white) and 'Nippon Beauty' (dark red) are lovely Japanese types. 'Gay Paree' (pink with white-blush center) grows anemone-type blossoms. Semidouble varieties include 'Ludovica' (salmon pink) and 'Lowell Thomas' (deep red). Among the double-flowered varieties, 'Festiva Maxima' (white with red marking), 'Red Charm' (deep true red, early blooming), 'Mons. Jules Elie' (early, pink), 'Karl Rosenfeld' (deep red), and 'Nick Shaylor' (blush pink) are all exceptional.

Paeonia mlokosewitschii

Growing conditions and maintenance: Plant peonies 3 feet apart in soil containing some organic matter. Set the buds (eyes) 2 inches below the soil surface; setting them deeper delays flowering. Propagate by dividing clumps in late summer-early fall into sections containing three to five eyes each.

Papaver
(pap-AY-ver)
POPPY

Papaver orientale

Hardiness: *Zones 3-9*

Flowering season: *spring to summer*

Height: *12 inches to 4 feet*

Flower color: *red, pink, orange, yellow, white*

Soil: *well-drained loam*

Light: *full sun to partial shade*

Poppies bear large, brilliantly colored, silky-textured blossoms on wiry stems above finely cut leaves.

Selected species and varieties: *P. nudicaule* (Iceland poppy)—fragrant flowers up to 3 inches across on 12- to 24-inch stems. *P. orientale* (Oriental poppy)—blossoms up to 8 inches across composed of tissue-thin petals on wiry stems rising from mounds of coarse, hairy leaves; 'Glowing Embers' has orange-red ruffled petals; 'Mrs. Perry', clear pink flowers; 'Beauty of Livermore', deep red petals spotted black at the base.

Growing conditions and maintenance: Space poppies 1½ feet apart. Propagate Oriental poppies from seed or from root cuttings. Grow Iceland poppies from seed to flower in their first year.

Pennisetum

(pen-i-SEE-tum)

FOUNTAIN GRASS

Pennisetum alopecuroides

Hardiness: *Zones 5-9*

Flowering season: *summer*

Height: *2 to 5 feet*

Flower color: *silvery mauve, white*

Soil: *well-drained loam*

Light: *full sun*

Fountain grass forms lovely clumps of slender arching leaves with bristly flower spikes that resemble bottle brushes. Their pleasing texture and soft color are effective from early summer through fall.

Selected species and varieties: *P. alopecuroides* (Chinese pennisetum, perennial fountain grass)—silvery mauve blooms above a mound of arching 3- to 4-foot leaves; 'Hameln' (dwarf fountain grass) grows only 2 feet tall. *P. caudatum* (white flowering fountain grass)—silvery white bloom spikes 4 to 5 feet tall.

Growing conditions and maintenance: Space plants 2 to 3 feet apart. Cut back to 6 inches before growth begins in the spring. Propagate the species from seed or by division, varieties by division.

Penstemon

(pen-STEE-mon)

BEARDTONGUE

Penstemon barbatus 'Prairie Fire'

Hardiness: *Zones 3-9*

Flowering season: *spring to fall*

Height: *18 to 36 inches*

Flower color: *red, pink, lavender, white*

Soil: *well-drained loam*

Light: *full sun to light shade*

Clusters of tubular flowers with fine hairs covering their lower lips nod above shrubby foliage over a long season of bloom. Low-growing varieties are well suited to rock gardens, dry walls, and the edges of beds. Taller types mix well with other perennials in the middle or back of a border or in a wildflower garden. The flowers are outstanding in arrangements.

Selected species and varieties: *P. barbatus* (beardlip penstemon)—pink or red blossoms on 3-foot flower stems above a tuft of dark green basal leaves; 'Alba' has white flowers; 'Bashful' stands only 12 inches high with salmon-colored flowers; 'Elfin Pink' grows clear pink flowers atop 12-inch stems; 'Hyacinth Mix' produces flowers in a mix of such colors as red, pink, violet, and blue; 'Nana Rondo' also produces a color mix, but on compact plants 12 to 14 inches tall; 'Prairie Dusk', rose-purple blooms atop 2-foot stems; 'Prairie Fire', scarlet flowers on 24-inch stems; 'Rose Elf', prolific rose pink flowers on 18-inch stems. *P. digitalis* (smooth white beardtongue)—white flowers with purple throats blooming late spring to midsummer; 'Huskers Red' grows pink-tinged white flower bells that contrast handsomely with bronze-purple leaves. *P. gloxinioides* (gloxinia penstemon)—showy 2-inch-wide red flowers, perennial only in Zones 9 and 10, annual in colder regions; 'Firebird' has scarlet flowers on 2-foot stems; 'Holly's White', white blooms with a pink blush; 'Lady Alice Hindley', mauve-and-white flowers; 'Midnight', deep purple flowers; 'Sour Grapes', indigo blue flowers. *P. heterophyllus*—purple to blue flowers on 2-foot stems above evergreen foliage; 'Blue Spring' produces blue flowers. *P. pinifolius* (pine-leaf penstemon)—bright red flowers amid 12-inch-tall green needle-shaped foliage; 'Mersea Yellow' grows true yellow blooms.

Growing conditions and maintenance: Space lower-growing penstemons 1 foot apart, taller species 2 feet apart. Penstemons tolerate drought and are useful in dry areas of average fertility. They are subject to rot if the soil remains damp, but do not require a highly fertile soil. Although most penstemons are short-lived, they are easily grown from seed to flower their first year. They can also be propagated from cuttings in midsummer or by division in spring.

Perovskia

(per-OV-skee-a)

RUSSIAN SAGE

Perovskia atriplicifolia

Hardiness: *Zones 5-9*

Flowering season: *summer*

Height: *3 to 4 feet*

Flower color: *lavender-blue*

Soil: *well-drained loam*

Light: *full sun*

The silvery gray leaves and long-lasting, fragrant, soft blue flowers of Russian sage provide a delicate filler in a sunny mixed border, where they combine particularly well with ornamental grasses. Planted in a mass, Russian sage develops into a summer hedge, and the stems remain attractive through the winter.

Selected species and varieties: *P. atriplicifolia* (Russian sage, azure sage)—tubular, two-lipped flowers growing in whorls along stems held above toothed, soft gray aromatic leaves.

Growing conditions and maintenance: Plant Russian sage 2 to 3 feet apart in full sun; shade causes floppy, sprawling growth. Cut the woody stems back to the ground before growth begins in the spring to promote flowers and bushiness. Propagate from seed or from summer cuttings.

Phlox

(flox)

PHLOX

Phlox divaricata 'Fuller's White'

Hardiness: *Zones 3-9*

Flowering season: *spring, summer, or fall*

Height: *3 inches to 4 feet*

Flower color: *pink, purple, red, blue, white*

Soil: *sandy and dry to moist, fertile loam*

Light: *full sun to full shade*

Versatile phlox produces flat, five-petaled flowers, either singly or in clusters, many with a conspicuous eye at the center. There is a species suitable for nearly every combination of soil and light, as well as for nearly any landscape use, from 3-inch creepers to upright border plants growing 4 feet tall.

Selected species and varieties: *P. divaricata* (wild blue phlox)—blue blossoms on 12-inch-tall creepers; 'Fuller's White' has creamy white flowers. *P. maculata* (wild sweet William)—elegant, cylindrical flower heads in shades of pink to white on 3-foot plants; 'Miss Lingard' [sometimes listed as a variety of *P. carolina*] has 6-inch trusses of pure white blossoms; 'Omega', white petals surrounding a lilac-colored eye; 'Alpha', rose pink petals around a darker pink eye. *P. paniculata* (summer phlox, garden phlox)—magnificent pyramidal clusters of white, pink, red, lavender, or purple flowers on 2- to 4-foot stems; 'Fujiyama' has white flower heads 12 to 15 inches long; 'Bright Eyes', pale pink petals surrounding a crimson eye; 'Orange Perfection', salmon orange blossoms; 'Starfire', cherry red. *P. stolonifera* (creeping phlox)—blue, white, or pink flowers on creeping 6- to 12-inch stems with evergreen leaves that form a dense ground cover; 'Blue Ridge' produces clear blue flowers. *P. subulata* (moss phlox, moss pink)—white, pink, blue, lavender, or red flowers above dense clumps of evergreen foliage 3 to 6 inches tall and 2 feet wide.

Growing conditions and maintenance: Space lower-growing phlox 1 to 1½ feet apart, taller species up to 2 feet apart. Wild blue phlox grows well in shady, moist sites; moss phlox thrives in sunny, dry spots. Creeping phlox grows in sun or shade. Wild sweet William and summer phlox thrive in full sun, provided they receive ample moisture during the growing season. Space summer phlox for good air circulation to avoid powdery mildew. Propagate phlox by division.

Phlox subulata

Phormium

(FOR-mee-um)

NEW ZEALAND FLAX

Phormium tenax

Hardiness: *Zones 9-10*

Flowering season: *summer*

Height: *8 to 15 feet*

Flower color: *red, yellow*

Soil: *moist loam*

Light: *full sun*

New Zealand flax produces clusters of flowers on zigzag stalks rising from the center of massive, fan-shaped clumps of stiff, swordlike leaves. The large plants are a unique specimen or bold garden accent in sunny, warm climates.

Selected species and varieties: *P. tenax*—dull red or yellow flowers 1 to 2 inches long with wine red, bronze-purple, gray-green, or variegated leaves; 'Variegatum' has leaves striped green and yellow.

Growing conditions and maintenance: Space plants 6 feet apart. New Zealand flax is tolerant of wind, heat, and seaside conditions. Divide every 4 or 5 years.

Physostegia

(fy-so-STEE-gee-a)

FALSE DRAGONHEAD

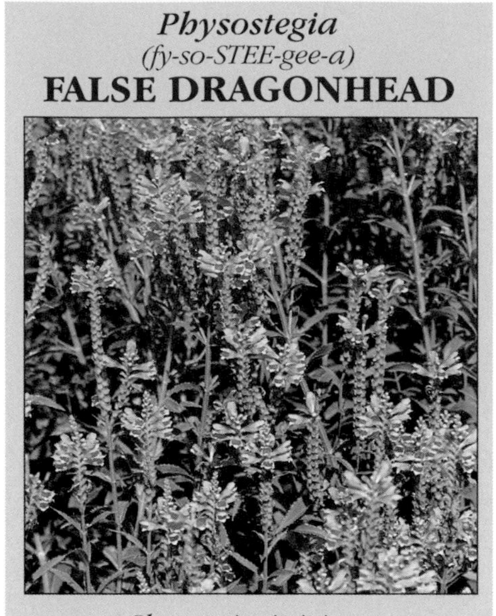

Physostegia virginiana

Hardiness: *Zones 4-8*

Flowering season: *late summer to fall*

Height: *2 to 4 feet*

Flower color: *pink, purple, white*

Soil: *moist or dry acid loam*

Light: *full sun to partial shade*

False dragonhead produces unusual 8- to 10-inch flower spikes with four evenly spaced vertical rows of blossoms resembling snapdragons.

Selected species and varieties: *P. virginiana*—pink flowers tipping each stem in clumps of 4-foot stalks; 'Variegata' has pink flowers above green-and-white variegated leaves; 'Vivid', rosy pink blossoms on compact plants only 20 inches tall; 'Summer Snow', early-blooming white flowers.

Growing conditions and maintenance: Plant false dragonhead 1½ to 2 feet apart. It is so tolerant of varying growing conditions that it can become invasive. Propagate from seed or by division every 2 years.

Platycodon

(plat-i-KO-don)

BALLOON FLOWER

Platycodon grandiflorus

Hardiness *Zones 4-9*

Flowering season: *summer*

Height: *10 to 36 inches*

Flower color: *blue, white, pink*

Soil: *well-drained, acid loam*

Light: *full sun to partial shade*

The balloon flower derives its common name from the fat, inflated flower buds that pop open into cup-shaped 2- to 3-inch-wide blossoms with pointed petals as they mature.

Selected species and varieties: *P. grandiflorus*—deep blue flowers on slender stems above neat clumps of blue-green leaves; 'Album' has white flowers; 'Shell Pink', pale pink flowers; 'Mariesii' is a compact variety 18 inches tall with bright blue flowers.

Growing conditions and maintenance: Space balloon flowers 18 inches apart. Pink varieties develop the best color when grown in partial shade. Propagate from seed to flower the second year or by division.

Polygonatum
(po-lig-o-NAY-tum)
SOLOMON'S-SEAL

Polygonatum multiflorum

Hardiness: *Zones 3-9*

Flowering season: *spring*

Height: *2 to 3 feet*

Flower color: *yellowish green to white*

Soil: *moist, acid loam*

Light: *partial to full shade*

Small, nodding flowers dangle from the graceful, arching stems of Solomon's-seal. Pairs of broad leaves up to 4 inches long line the stems. Solomon's-seal combines well with spring-flowering bulbs or shade-loving shrubs, and the foliage can be used in arrangements.

Selected species and varieties: *P. multiflorum* (European Solomon's-seal)—handsome bright green leaves up to 6 inches long on stems up to 3 feet long. *P. odoratum thunbergii* 'Variegatum' (fragrant Solomon's-seal)—white flowers tipped with green and leaves edged in white.

Growing conditions and maintenance: Plant 1 foot apart in cool, moist, shady sites whose soil contains ample organic matter. Propagate from seed or by division in spring.

Polygonum
(po-LIG-o-num)
SMARTWEED, KNOTWEED

Polygonum bistorta 'Superbum'

Hardiness: *Zones 4-9*

Flowering season: *summer*

Height: *6 inches to 3 feet*

Flower color: *pink, white, red*

Soil: *moist loam*

Light: *full sun to light shade*

Although *Polygonum* contains many weeds familiar to gardeners, it also boasts a few highly ornamental species with colorful flower spikes held above neat mats of foliage.

Selected species and varieties: *P. affine* (Himalayan fleeceflower)—spikes of rose pink flowers 6 to 9 inches tall above dark green leaves turning bronze in fall; 'Superbum' produces crimson flowers. *P. bistorta* (snakeweed)—pink flowers like bottle brushes on 2-foot stems above striking clumps of 4- to 6-inch-long wavy green leaves with a white midrib; 'Superbum' grows to 3 feet.

Growing conditions and maintenance: Space polygonums 1 foot apart. Himalayan fleeceflower thrives in full sun; snakeweed prefers some shade. Propagate by division in spring.

Potentilla
(po-ten-TILL-a)
CINQUEFOIL

Potentilla nepalensis 'Miss Wilmott'

Hardiness: *Zones 5-8*

Flowering season: *spring to summer*

Height: *2 to 18 inches*

Flower color: *white, yellow, pink, red*

Soil: *well-drained, sandy loam*

Light: *full sun to light shade*

Cinquefoil's neat, compound leaves, with three to five leaflets arranged like fingers on a hand, grow in spreading clumps of foliage. The open-faced, five-petaled flowers held above the leaves resemble wild roses. Cinquefoils are effective creeping between stones in the rock garden and as a ground cover on dry slopes.

Selected species and varieties: *P. atrosanguinea* (Himalayan or ruby cinquefoil)—dark red 1-inch-wide flowers and five-fingered green leaves with silvery undersides on plants 12 to 18 inches tall; 'Fire Dance' flowers have a scarlet center and a yellow border on 15-inch stems; 'Gibson's Scarlet' has bright scarlet flowers on 15-inch stems; 'William Rollinson' grows to 18 inches with deep orange and yellow semidouble flowers; 'Yellow Queen' grows bright yellow flowers with a red center on 12-inch stems above silvery foliage. *P. nepalensis* (Nepal cinquefoil)—cup-shaped flowers in shades of salmon, rose, red, orange, and purple, often flowering throughout the summer;

'Miss Wilmott' is a dwarf variety 10 to 12 inches tall with cherry red flowers; 'Roxana' has coppery orange petals surrounding red centers on 15-inch stems. *P.* x *tonguei* (staghorn cinquefoil)—apricot-colored flowers with red centers on trailing stems 8 to 12 inches long above evergreen foliage. *P. tridentata* (wineleaf cinquefoil) [also classified as *Sibbaldiopsis tridentata*]—clusters of tiny white flowers blooming late spring to midsummer on 2- to 6-inch plants with shiny, leathery evergreen leaves that turn wine red in the fall; 'Minima' is a low-growing cultivar (3 inches high) that performs well as a ground cover. *P. verna* (spring cinquefoil)—a prostrate, fast-spreading plant that grows 2 to 3 inches high and produces golden yellow flowers ½ inch wide; 'Nana' has larger flowers than the species and grows slightly higher.

Growing conditions and maintenance: Plant smaller cinquefoils 1 foot apart, larger species 2 feet apart. Potentillas prefer a poor soil; they will produce excess leafy growth if raised in fertile soil. Wineleaf cinquefoil develops its best fall color in acid soils. Cinquefoils are generally short-lived perennials and grow best in areas with mild winters and summers. *P. verna* can be invasive; its stems may root, forming a broad mat. Propagate from seed or by division every 3 years in spring or fall.

Primula

(PRIM-yew-la)

PRIMROSE

Primula japonica 'Postford White'

Hardiness: *Zones 3-8*

Flowering season: *spring*

Height: *2 to 24 inches*

Flower color: *wide spectrum*

Soil: *moist loam*

Light: *partial shade*

Neat, colorful primroses produce clusters of five-petaled blossoms on leafless stems above rosettes of tongue-shaped leaves, which are evergreen in milder climates. More than 400 species of primroses in nearly every color of the rainbow offer a multitude of choices in height and hardiness.

Selected species and varieties: *P. auricula* (auricula primrose)—fragrant, bell-shaped flowers in yellow, white, or other hues on plants 2 to 8 inches tall; hardy to Zone 3. *P. denticulata* (Himalayan primrose)—globe-shaped clusters of purple flowers with a yellow eye on 8- to 12-inch stalks; varieties are available in strong red, pink, and white flower tones; to Zone 6. *P. helodoxa* (amber primrose)—soft yellow flowers on 24-inch stems; to Zone 6. *P. japonica* (Japanese primrose)—whorls of white, red, pink, or purple flowers on 2-foot stalks; 'Miller's Crimson' has deep red blossoms; 'Postford White', white flowers; to Zone 6. *P.* x *polyantha* (polyanthus primrose)—flowers singly or in clusters on 6- to 12-inch stems in a wide choice of colors; to Zone 4. *P. sieboldii* (Japanese star primrose)—nodding heads of pink, purple, or white flowers on 12-inch stalks. *P. vulgaris* (English primrose)—fragrant single flowers in yellow and other colors on 6- to 9-inch stems.

Growing conditions and maintenance: Space primroses 1 foot apart in moisture-retentive soil. Water deeply during dry periods. Himalayan, amber, and Japanese primroses require a boglike soil. English and polyanthus primroses tolerate drier conditions, while other species mentioned fall somewhere in between. Polyanthus primroses are short-lived and often treated as annuals. Japanese star primroses go dormant after flowering. Propagate primroses from seed or by division every 3 to 4 years in spring. Auricula and Japanese star primroses can also be propagated from stem cuttings, Himalayan primroses from root cuttings.

Primula x polyantha

Pulmonaria
(pul-mo-NAY-ree-a)
LUNGWORT

Pulmonaria angustifolia

Hardiness: *Zones 4-8*

Flowering season: *early spring*

Height: *8 to 12 inches*

Flower color: *blue, pink, white*

Soil: *moist loam*

Light: *full sun to partial shade*

Pulmonaria's tiny flower bells clustered at the ends of arching stems nod among attractive oval leaves.

Selected species and varieties: *P. angustifolia* (blue lungwort)—pink buds open into deep blue flowers. *P. longifolia* (longleaf lungwort)—deep true blue blossoms and tapered, dark green leaves spotted gray; 'Bertram Anderson' has violet-blue flowers and dark green leaves with silvery spots; 'Roy Davidson', soft blue flowers amid silver-spotted foliage. *P. saccharata* (Bethlehem sage)—leaves mottled white; 'Mrs. Moon' has pink flowers that turn blue as they mature; 'Sissinghurst White' has white blossoms.

Growing conditions and maintenance: Space plants 1 to 1½ feet apart in locations that have ample moisture and some shade. Propagate by division in the fall.

Ranunculus
(re-NUN-kew-lus)
BUTTERCUP

Ranunculus asiaticus

Hardiness: *Zones 4-9*

Flowering season: *spring to summer*

Height: *12 to 30 inches*

Flower color: *yellow, white, orange, pink, red*

Soil: *moist, well-drained loam*

Light: *full sun to light shade*

Buttercups display flowers composed of waxy petals in single or double rows on plants with deeply lobed, divided leaves.

Selected species and varieties: *R. asiaticus* 'Superbissima' (Persian buttercup)—double or semidouble peony-like blooms 1 to 4 inches across in a wide range of colors on 12-inch stems; to Zone 8. *R. repens* (creeping buttercup)—single yellow flowers on 18- to 24-inch stems above dense mats of leaves 6 inches high; 'Flore Pleno' produces double ¾-inch flowers.

Growing conditions and maintenance: Space Persian buttercups 12 inches apart and grow them as annuals in colder areas, digging up the tubers each fall. Allow 18 inches between creeping buttercups. Propagate all varieties by division in spring or fall.

Rodgersia
(ro-JER-see-a)
RODGERSIA

Rodgersia podophylla

Hardiness: *Zones 5-8*

Flowering season: *spring to summer*

Height: *2 to 6 feet*

Flower color: *creamy white to pink*

Soil: *boggy loam*

Light: *full sun to light shade*

Rodgersia produces feathery flowers above bold, coarse-textured compound leaves.

Selected species and varieties: *R. aesculifolia* (fingerleaf rodgersia)—bronze-tinted, hand-shaped leaves resembling those of the horse chestnut tree on stems up to 4 feet tall tipped with 18-inch creamy white to pink flower plumes. *R. podophylla* (bronzeleaf rodgersia)—cream-colored 1-foot flower plumes on plants 3 feet tall and equally wide with leaves emerging bronze and turning green then copper as season unfolds.

Growing conditions and maintenance: Space rodgersias 3 feet apart in sites that are constantly wet, such as the edges of streams and ponds. Propagate by division in spring.

Romneya
(ROM-ney-a)
CALIFORNIA TREE POPPY

Romneya coulteri

Hardiness: *Zones 7-10*

Flowering season: *summer*

Height: *4 to 8 feet*

Flower color: *white*

Soil: *dry, infertile loam*

Light: *full sun*

Romneyas bear fragrant 3- to 6-inch flowers with golden centers surrounded by 6 pure white, silky petals with ruffled edges. Though short-lived, the flowers are striking in arrangements; sear the ends of the flower stems with a flame to seal in their milky sap for a longer period of freshness.

Selected species and varieties: *R. coulteri*—white flowers throughout the summer on branching 8-foot stems with gray-green leaves in clumps 3 feet wide.

Growing conditions and maintenance: Space California tree poppies 3 to 4 feet apart in sites where their wide-spreading, invasive roots will not present a problem. They grow best in Zones 8 to 9 but will survive in Zone 7 given a heavy winter mulch. Cut stems back to 6 inches in the fall. Propagate from seed.

Rudbeckia
(rood-BEK-ee-a)
CONEFLOWER

Rudbeckia fulgida 'Goldsturm'

Hardiness: *Zones 4-9*

Flowering season: *summer to fall*

Height: *18 inches to 6 feet*

Flower color: *yellow, orange*

Soil: *average loam*

Light: *full sun to light shade*

Rudbeckia produces daisylike flowers with a fringe of narrow petals surrounding a prominent center. The flowers bloom prolifically on wiry stems above vigorous clumps of deeply cut foliage.

Selected species and varieties: *R. fulgida* 'Goldsturm'—bright yellow flowers with brown centers, growing from midsummer to frost on compact 2-foot plants. *R. nitida*—bright yellow petals surrounding extremely large 2-inch centers on 2- to 7-foot stems; 'Herbstsonne' has green flower centers on stems up to 7 feet tall.

Growing conditions and maintenance: Plant coneflowers 1½ to 2 feet apart. They tolerate heat and dry conditions, making them particularly good choices for southern gardens. 'Goldsturm' resists powdery mildew, a problem for other coneflowers. Propagate from seed or by division every 2 years in spring.

Salvia
(SAL-vee-a)
SAGE

Salvia x superba 'May Night'

Hardiness: *Zones 4-10*

Flowering season: *spring to fall*

Height: *1 to 6 feet*

Flower color: *blue, purple, white, red*

Soil: *well-drained loam*

Light: *full sun*

Fragrant sage produces spires of two-lipped, hooded flowers in whorls lining square stems. From rounded 12-inch-high clumps to erect 6-foot-tall shrubs, there are sages suitable for almost every hardiness zone.

Selected species and varieties: *S. azurea* ssp. *pitcheri* (Pitcher's salvia)—azure blue 1-inch-long flowers from late summer to fall on 3- to 4-foot stems. *S. farinacea* (mealy-cup sage)—violet-blue or white flowers from midsummer to frost on 2- to 3-foot stems; 'Blue Bedder' has deep blue flowers in 8-inch clusters on compact plants to 2 feet tall. *S. haematodes* (meadow sage)—airy sprays of lavender-blue flowers from early to midsummer on plants to 3 feet tall. *S. jurisicii* (Jurisici's sage)—dangling lilac or white flowers on stems 12 to 18 inches tall. *S. officinalis* (garden sage)—bluish purple or white flowers bloom in whorls from late spring to early summer above neat 2-foot-high mounds of short stems lined with wrinkled, gray-green leaves, which can be used as a culinary seasoning. *S.* x *superba* (perennial salvia)—violet-purple flowers in dense whorls around 4- to 8-inch spikes from late spring to early summer on rounded plants to 3 feet tall; 'Blue Queen' grows 18 to 24 inches tall; 'East Friesland' has deep purple blossoms on 18-inch plants; 'May Night' grows to 24 inches with intense violet-blue flowers.

Growing conditions and maintenance: Sage grows best in dry soils; its roots should not stay wet over winter. Because they vary in hardiness, particular care must be given to selection of species. Garden sage is hardy to Zone 4; Pitcher's salvia and perennial salvia, to Zone 5; meadow sage and Jurisici's sage, to Zone 6; mealy-cup sage, to Zone 8 and evergreen in Zone 9. Plant smaller species every 18 inches, larger forms 2 to 3 feet apart. Propagate by division in spring or fall, from cuttings, or, except for perennial salvia, from seed.

Salvia x superba 'Blue Queen'

Santolina

(san-to-LEE-na)

LAVENDER COTTON

Santolina chamaecyparissus

Hardiness: *Zones 6-8*

Flowering season: *summer*

Height: *18 to 24 inches*

Flower color: *yellow*

Soil: *well-drained to dry loam*

Light: *full sun*

Santolina produces tiny yellow flower buttons on slender stems above broad, spreading clumps of aromatic leaves. The foliage makes an attractive edging for a bed, or a low-growing specimen in a rock garden. It can be sheared into a dense, low hedge.

Selected species and varieties: *S. chamaecyparissus*—dense silvery gray, evergreen leaves in shrubby mounds 2 feet wide. *S. virens*—green toothedged leaves in dense 18-inch clumps.

Growing conditions and maintenance: Space santolina plants 18 to 24 inches apart. Promote dense growth by shearing them heavily in early spring or after flowering. Propagate from seed or from stem cuttings taken in early summer.

Saponaria

(sap-o-NAR-ee-a)

SOAPWORT

Saponaria ocymoides

Hardiness: *Zones 4-9*

Flowering season: *spring and summer*

Height: *6 inches to 3 feet*

Flower color: *pink*

Soil: *well-drained loam*

Light: *full sun*

Saponarias bear clusters of tiny pink flowers at the tips of either erect or trailing stems.

Selected species and varieties: *S. ocymoides* (rock soapwort)—loose sprays of deep pink ½-inch flowers on trailing 6- to 12-inch reddish stems with semi-evergreen leaves in broad mounds. *S. officinalis* (bouncing Bet)—clusters of pale pink or white 1-inch flowers on erect 3-foot stems.

Growing conditions and maintenance: Plant rock soapwort 1 foot apart, *S. officinalis* 2 to 3 feet apart. Propagate from seed or by division in spring or fall.

Scabiosa
(skab-i-O-sa)
PINCUSHION FLOWER

Scabiosa caucasica 'Clive Greaves'

Hardiness: *Zones 4-9*	
Flowering season: *summer*	
Height: *18 to 24 inches*	
Flower color: *blue, lavender, white*	
Soil: *well-drained, neutral loam*	
Light: *full sun*	

Pincushion flowers produce blooms up to 3 inches across with prominent stamens resembling a dome of pinheads surrounded by a ruffle of petals. Tipping slender stems above low tufts of leaves, the blossoms offer rare blue color in a summer border.

Selected species and varieties: *S. caucasica* (pincushion flower, Caucasian scabiosa)—3-inch flowers on long stems; 'Clive Greaves' has lavender-blue flowers; 'Fama', deep blue petals encircling silver centers on 18-inch stems. *S. columbaria* 'Butterfly Blue' is a prolific compact form with small flowers on 15-inch stems.

Growing conditions and maintenance: Space pincushion flowers 18 to 24 inches apart. Remove faded flowers for continuous bloom. Propagate from seed or by division in spring.

Sedum
(SEE-dum)
STONECROP

Sedum 'Autumn Joy'

Hardiness: *Zones 3-10*	
Flowering season: *spring to fall*	
Height: *3 inches to 2 feet*	
Flower color: *white, yellow, orange, red, pink*	
Soil: *well-drained loam*	
Light: *full sun to light shade*	

Stonecrops are valued for both their flowers and their foliage, which add color and rich texture to a garden over a long season. Their thick, succulent leaves vary in color from bright green to blue-green to reddish green. Individual flowers are small and star-shaped, with 5 petals. Generally borne in dense clusters that cover the plant, they attract butterflies to the garden. The blooming season varies among species from spring to fall, with some flowers even persisting into winter. Sedums are easy to grow and tolerate drought, making them well suited to rock gardens and dry borders. They can be used as individual specimens, in groupings of three or more, or massed as a succulent ground cover.

Selected species and varieties: *S. aizoon* (Aizoon stonecrop)—yellow flowers above bright green leaves on stems 12 to 18 inches tall, blooming from spring to summer; 'Auranticum' has deep yellow flowers and red-tinted stems. *S.* 'Autumn Joy'—rosy pink flower buds that form above gray-green leaves on 2-foot stems in mid-summer, turn red before opening bronze-red in fall, and turn golden brown if left in place for the winter. *S. kamtschaticum* (orange stonecrop)—6 to 9 inches tall with a wide-spreading habit, excellent for rock gardens, grows small orange-yellow flowers in summer; 'Variegatum' produces deep orange flowers and green leaves with a broad white margin blushed with pink. *S. maximum* (great stonecrop)—greenish yellow, star-shaped flowers in late summer above oval, gray-green leaves on stems up to 2 feet tall; 'Atropurpureum' has red flowers and maroon leaves. *S. rosea* (roseroot)—tiny yellow or purple flowers atop clumps of 12-inch stems with small toothed leaves; *S. r. integrifolium* has pink to red-purple flowers. *S.* 'Ruby Glow'—ruby red fall flowers above purple-gray foliage on compact plants 8 inches tall; a good choice for the front of a border. *S.*

Sedum kamtschaticum

sieboldii (Siebold stonecrop)—dense heads of pink flowers effective throughout fall above nearly triangular blue-gray leaves on 6- to 9-inch somewhat trailing stems. *S. spectabile* (showy stonecrop)—a heat-tolerant species with bright pink flowers that bloom from late summer till frost on 18-inch stems; 'Brilliant' has raspberry red flowers; 'Carmen', rose pink flowers; 'Variegatum', bright pink flowers atop leaves variegated yellow and green; 'Meteor', large wine red blooms; 'Stardust', white flowers that stand out against blue-green leaves; 'Variegatum', bright pink blooms above variegated foliage; Zones 3-10. *S. spurium* (two-row stonecrop)—pink, red, or white summer flowers on vigorously spreading evergreen stems 3 to 6 inches tall that make a tough evergreen ground cover; 'Bronze Carpet' has pink flowers and red-brown foliage; 'Coccineum' has scarlet blooms; 'Dragon's Blood' produces purple-bronze leaves and deep crimson star-shaped flowers; 'Red Carpet', bronze leaves and red flowers;

Sedum spurium

'Variegatum', green leaves with creamy pink margins. *S.* 'Vera Jameson'—a slightly larger hybrid of *S.* 'Ruby Glow' with bronze foliage and magenta flowers.

Growing conditions and maintenance: Stonecrops are tough plants that spread without becoming invasive. Space *S. sieboldii* 1 foot apart, other species 1½ to 2 feet apart. They tolerate almost any well-drained soil, even if it is dry and sterile. They can be left undivided for many years, but can be propagated by division in spring or from stem cuttings taken in summer.

Sidalcea
(sy-DAL-see-a)
CHECKERMALLOW

Sidalcea 'Elsie Heugh'

Hardiness: *Zones 5-8*

Flowering season: *summer*

Height: *2 to 4 feet*

Flower color: *pale to deep pink*

Soil: *moist, well-drained loam*

Light: *full sun to partial shade*

Erect, stately stems, lined with blossoms in all shades of pink, bloom above glossy green mounds of foliage that form a lush ground cover. Sidalceas make superb cut flowers.

Selected species and varieties: *S. malviflora* (checkerbloom)—flowers resembling miniature hollyhocks rising above deeply lobed leaves; 'Elsie Heugh' grows 24 to 36 inches tall, with pale pink flowers composed of delicately fringed petals; 'Loveliness' grows to 30 inches, bearing deep rose pink blossoms.

Growing conditions and maintenance: Space plants 18 to 24 inches apart. Taller varieties require staking. Remove dead blossoms and cut back stems to extend the flowering season. Propagate the species by seed, the varieties by division every 3 or 4 years.

Silene
(sy-LEE-ne)
CAMPION, CATCHFLY

Silene schafta

Hardiness: *Zones 4-8*

Flowering season: *summer to fall*

Height: *4 inches to 2 feet*

Flower color: *white, pink, red*

Soil: *well-drained, sandy loam*

Light: *full sun to light shade*

Campions produce star-shaped flowers on branching stems for several weeks above tufts of low-growing, sometimes spreading foliage.

Selected species and varieties: *S. schafta* (moss campion)—rose pink or purple flowers on 12-inch stems above 6-inch rosettes of hairy, light green leaves. *S.* 'Robin's White Breast' —white flower bells above dense 8-inch mounds of silvery gray leaves. *S. virginica* (fire-pink catchfly)—clusters of pink to red flowers on sticky 2-foot stems above flat rosettes of evergreen leaves.

Growing conditions and maintenance: Space campions 12 inches apart. Propagate from seed or by division in the spring.

Smilacina
(smy-la-SEE-na)
FALSE SOLOMON'S-SEAL

Smilacina racemosa

Hardiness: *Zones 4-8*
Flowering season: *spring*
Height: *2 to 3 feet*
Flower color: *creamy white*
Soil: *moist, acid loam*
Light: *partial to full shade*

Fragrant flower plumes tipping arched stems lined with bright green leaves are followed by showy red berries in fall. The stems and leaves are similar to those of Solomon's-seal (polygonatum), which has less conspicuous, dangling flowers.

Selected species and varieties: *S. racemosa*—feathery white flower plumes on stems 2 to 3 feet tall, growing in mounds 3 to 4 feet across.

Growing conditions and maintenance: Space false Solomon's-seal plants 3 feet apart in locations with abundant moisture. They can be left undisturbed indefinitely. Propagate by division in spring or fall.

Solidago
(sol-i-DAY-go)
GOLDENROD

Solidago 'Peter Pan'

Hardiness: *Zones 3-9*
Flowering season: *summer to fall*
Height: *1 to 6 feet*
Flower color: *yellow to gold*
Soil: *well-drained loam*
Light: *full sun to light shade*

Goldenrod produces tiny flowers in dense, feathery clusters at the tips of stems lined with narrow, toothed leaves. The blooms provide an extended period of bold yellow tones in an informal border. They are excellent for fresh or dried arrangements.

Selected species and varieties: *S.* hybrids—'Goldenmosa' has deep yellow late-summer flowers on 3-foot stems; 'Cloth of Gold', dark yellow blossoms on vigorous 18- to 24-inch dwarf plants; 'Golden Fleece', arching plumes of golden flowers on tidy 2-foot-high dwarf plants; 'Peter Pan', canary yellow flowers on 2- to 3-foot stems.

Growing conditions and maintenance: Space goldenrod 18 to 24 inches apart. Tall varieties may require staking. Propagate hybrids by division.

Stachys
(STA-kis)
LAMB'S EARS, BETONY

Stachys byzantina

Hardiness: *Zones 4-9*
Flowering season: *summer*
Height: *6 to 18 inches*
Flower color: *pink to purple*
Soil: *well-drained loam*
Light: *full sun to light shade*

Whorls of tubular flowers bloom amid lamb's ears' bold, textured leaves. The plants spread into dense mounds of foliage.

Selected species and varieties: *S. byzantina* (lamb's ears, woolly betony)—pinkish purple flowers on upright stems grow above spreading mounds of leaves covered with soft white hairs that give them a velvety texture and gray-green color; 'Silver Carpet' is a nonflowering type for gardeners seeking textured foliage. *S. macrantha* [also identified as *S. grandiflora*] (big betony)—whorls of purple flowers on 18-inch stems above wrinkled, dark green, heart-shaped leaves.

Growing conditions and maintenance: Space lamb's ears 12 to 18 inches apart. Remove old leaves before new growth begins in spring. Propagate by transplanting self-sown seedlings, from seed, or by division.

Stokesia

(sto-KEE-zi-a)

STOKES' ASTER

Stokesia laevis 'Blue Danube'

Hardiness: *Zones 5-9*

Flowering season: *summer*

Height: *12 to 18 inches*

Flower color: *lavender, blue, white*

Soil: *well-drained, sandy loam*

Light: *full sun*

The showy, fringed flowers of Stokes' aster bloom on stems rising from neat rosettes of narrow, straplike leathery leaves that are evergreen in warmer climates. Stokes' aster is excellent in bouquets.

Selected species and varieties: *S. laevis*—solitary flower heads 2 to 4 inches across, blooming over a 4-week season in summer; 'Blue Danube' has clear blue flowers; 'Blue Moon', lilac flowers; 'Silver Moon', white.

Growing conditions and maintenance: Space Stokes' asters 18 inches apart. Mulch over winter in colder climates. Propagate the species from seed, and the species and its hybrids by division in spring.

Thalictrum

(thal-IK-trum)

MEADOW RUE

Thalictrum aquilegifolium

Hardiness: *Zones 5-9*

Flowering season: *spring to summer*

Height: *1 to 7 feet*

Flower color: *lavender, pink, yellow, white*

Soil: *moist, well-drained loam*

Light: *full sun to partial shade*

Clusters of airy blossoms on branching stems bloom above meadow rue's lacy foliage over several weeks.

Selected species and varieties: *T. aquilegifolium* (columbine meadow rue)—mauve-pink blossoms on stems up to 3 feet tall. *T. delavayi* (Yunnan meadow rue)—lavender-blue flowers on stems to 7 feet. *T. minus* (low meadow rue)—yellow-green flowers on 1- to 3-foot plants. *T. rochebrunianum* (lavender mist meadow rue)—lavender flowers on stems to 6 feet. *T. speciosissimum* (dusty meadow rue)—lemon yellow flowers on plants to 5 feet.

Growing conditions and maintenance: Space smaller meadow rues 12 inches apart, larger ones 24 inches. Stake taller species. Propagate from seed or by division in spring.

Tricyrtis

(try-SER-tis)

TOAD LILY

Tricyrtis hirta

Hardiness: *Zones 4-9*

Flowering season: *summer to fall*

Height: *2 to 3 feet*

Flower color: *white, yellow, purple*

Soil: *moist, fertile, acid loam*

Light: *partial shade*

Tricyrtis produces clusters of uniquely spotted and splayed flower trumpets often lasting as long as 6 weeks on arching stems above clumps of shiny dark green leaves.

Selected species and varieties: *T. formosana* (Formosa toad lily)—1-inch-long white to light pink flowers with a yellow throat and dark purple spots. *T. hirta* (hairy toad lily)—1-inch-long bell-shaped creamy white flowers with purple spots above hairy leaves.

Growing conditions and maintenance: Space toad lilies 18 to 24 inches apart in moisture-retentive soil. Formosa toad lily spreads via underground stolons but is not invasive. Propagate from seed or by division in early spring while plants are dormant.

Trollius
(TROL-ee-us)
GLOBEFLOWER

Trollius ledebourii 'Golden Queen'

Hardiness: *Zones 4-8*	
Flowering season: *spring to summer*	
Height: *18 inches to 3 feet*	
Flower color: *yellow, orange*	
Soil: *continuously moist loam*	
Light: *full sun to partial shade*	

Globeflower's brightly colored 2- to 4-inch blossoms, consisting of waxy, curved petals in dense balls, bloom on erect stems above clumps of deeply lobed leaves.

Selected species and varieties: *T. europaeus* (common globeflower)—lemon yellow flowers on stems up to 24 inches tall; 'Superbus' has light yellow flowers in spring and often again in late summer or fall. *T. ledebourii* (Ledebour globeflower)—orange flowers on 3-foot stems; 'Golden Queen' has golden orange blossoms. *T.* x *cultorum* (hybrid globeflower)—yellow to orange flowers.

Growing conditions and maintenance: Space globeflowers 18 inches apart in soil containing generous amounts of organic matter. Propagate from seed or by division in fall.

Verbascum
(ver-BAS-cum)
MULLEIN

Verbascum chaixii

Hardiness: *Zones 5-9*	
Flowering season: *summer*	
Height: *3 feet*	
Flower color: *yellow-and-purple, white*	
Soil: *well-drained, sandy loam*	
Light: *full sun to partial shade*	

Branched spikes of small, flat-faced blossoms rise from mullein's rosettes of fuzzy gray leaves. Mullein offers a stately vertical form for a mixed border.

Selected species and varieties: *V. chaixii* (chaix mullein)—½- to 1-inch-wide yellow flowers with fuzzy purple stamens creating a prominent eye; 'Album' has white flowers complementing the gray foliage.

Growing conditions and maintenance: Space plants 18 to 24 inches apart. Propagate species from seed or from root cuttings taken in early spring. Propagate named varieties from root cuttings only.

Verbena
(ver-BEE-na)
VERBENA, VERVAIN

Verbena canadensis 'Rosea'

Hardiness: *Zones 6-8*	
Flowering season: *summer to fall*	
Height: *4 inches to 5 feet*	
Flower color: *pink, red, purple*	
Soil: *well-drained loam*	
Light: *full sun*	

Verbena's tiny flowers bloom in flat, dainty clusters on wiry stems.

Selected species and varieties: *V. bonariensis* (Brazilian verbena)—fragrant purple flowers on stems to 5 feet. *V. canadensis* (rose verbena)—rose pink blossoms in rounded clusters on dense mats of creeping stems 6 inches tall; 'Rosea' produces fragrant rose-purple flowers blooming almost continuously. *V. peruviana* (Peruvian verbena)—crimson flowers on trailing stems 4 inches high. *V. tenuisecta* (moss verbena)—lavender flower clusters on 1-foot stems.

Growing conditions and maintenance: Space Brazilian verbena plants 2 feet apart, smaller forms 1 foot apart. Rose verbena is hardy to Zone 6, other species to Zone 8. Propagate from seed or from cuttings taken in the late summer.

Veronica
(ve-RON-i-ka)
SPEEDWELL

Veronica 'Crater Lake Blue'

Hardiness: *Zones 4-8*

Flowering season: *spring to summer*

Height: *12 to 24 inches*

Flower color: *blue, pink, white*

Soil: *well-drained loam*

Light: *full sun to partial shade*

Speedwell's tiny flower blossoms are packed in dense spires held above the foliage on erect stems.

Selected species and varieties: *V. austriaca* ssp. *teucrium* [also listed as *V. latifolia* ssp. *teucrium*] (Hungarian speedwell)—blue, rose, or white flowers on 18-inch stems; 'Crater Lake Blue' is a compact variety with deep blue flowers. *V. spicata* (spike speedwell)—blue, white, or pink flowers on stems up to 24 inches tall; 'Blue Spires' produces deep blue flowers; 'Icicle', white blossoms; 'Red Fox', rosy red flowers on 10- to 15-inch stems. *V.* 'Sunny Border Blue'—clear blue flowers on stems up to 24 inches.

Growing conditions and maintenance: Space veronicas 12 to 24 inches apart. Remove spent flowers to extend bloom. Propagate by division in spring or fall.

Veronicastrum
(ve-ro-ni-KAS-trum)
CULVER'S ROOT

Veronicastrum virginicum

Hardiness: *Zones 4-8*

Flowering season: *summer*

Height: *3 to 6 feet*

Flower color: *white, pale lavender, pink*

Soil: *well-drained, acid loam*

Light: *full sun to partial shade*

Veronicastrum produces branched clusters of tiny flower spikes on tall, erect stems.

Selected species and varieties: *V. virginicum* (blackroot)—tiny tubular flowers packed densely along 6- to 9-inch flower spikes on stems 6 feet tall in clumps 18 to 24 inches wide; 'Roseum' grows pink flowers; 'Album', white flowers.

Growing conditions and maintenance: Space veronicastrum 18 to 24 inches apart. Plants that are grown in shade may require support. Propagate by division in the fall.

Viola
(vy-O-la)
VIOLET

Viola canadensis var. rugulosa

Hardiness: *Zones 3-9*

Flowering season: *spring and fall*

Height: *3 to 12 inches*

Flower color: *yellow, white, rose, violet*

Soil: *moist, well-drained loam*

Light: *partial shade*

Violets produce dainty five-petaled blossoms on thin stems among heart-shaped leaves.

Selected species and varieties: *V. canadensis* (Canada violet)—white flowers with a yellow eye; *V. canadensis* var. *rugulosa* has narrower, wrinkled leaves with hairy undersides. *V. cornuta* (horned violet)—pansylike flowers on plants with evergreen leaves; 'Lord Nelson' has deep violet flowers. *V. cucullata* (marsh blue violet)—white flowers with purple veins; 'Royal Robe' has deep blue flowers. *V. odorata* (sweet violet)—fragrant flowers in shades of violet, rose, and white; 'Alba' has white blossoms; 'Czar', deep violet flowers. *V. tricolor* (Johnny-jump-up)—tricolored violet-blue-and-yellow flowers.

Growing conditions and maintenance: Space violets 8 to 12 inches apart. Propagate from seed or by division.

Acknowledgments

The editors wish to thank the following individuals and institutions for their valuable assistance in the preparation of this volume:

Jackie Allen, Bork Garden Center, Onarga, Ill.; Elsa Bakalar, Ashfield, Mass.; James E. Brown, Pittsburgh, Pa.; Rose Marie Casale, Hasbrouck Heights, N.J.; Laura Cooper, Los Angeles; Cathy Coyle, Short Glade Farm, Mt. Solon, Va.; Arthur and Helen Dawson, La Jolla, Calif.; Carol Dickenson, San Diego; Ethel M. Dutky, Extension Plant Pathologist, Department of Botany, University of Maryland, College Park; Jon Emerson, Baton Rouge, La.; Stanton Gill, Central Maryland Research and Education Center, University of Maryland Cooperative Extension, Ellicott City; Katherine Greenberg, Lafayette, Calif.; Sara Groves, Oxford, Ga.; Laura Hall, Walters Gardens, Zeeland, Mich.; Cyrus Hyde, Well Sweet Herb Farm, Port Murray, N.J.; Ginger Kennedy, Atlanta; Kit Klehm, Klehm Nursery, Champaign, Ill.; Sheela Lampietti, Purcellville, Va.; Ron Lutsko, Lutsko Associates, San Francisco; Hazel T. McCoy, Goldthwaite, Tex.; Janet Macunovich, Perennial Favorites, Waterford, Mich.; Elliot and Alana Megdal, Beverly Hills, Calif.; S. V. Nelson, Lafayette, Calif.; The Ottesen Garden, Md.; Pat Penn, Atlanta; Hattie Purtell, Milwaukee; Leslie Rich, Santa Fe, N.M.; Dolly Rulon-Miller Buswell, Charlottesville, Va.; Carolyn Singer, Foothill Cottage Gardens, Grass Valley, Calif.; Nick Taggart, Los Angeles; Betsy Thomas, Baton Rouge, La.; Susan Turner and Scott Purdin, Baton Rouge, La.; Georgia Vance, Short Glade Farm, Mt. Solon, Va.; James van Sweden, Oehme, van Sweden and Associates, Washington, D.C.; Christine Wotruba, La Mesa, Calif.

Picture Credits

The sources for the illustrations that appear in this book are listed below. Credits from left to right are separated by semicolons; credits from top to bottom are separated by dashes.

Cover: Charles Mann/designed by Penny Vogel, Estacata, Ore. Back cover inset: Joanne Pavia —art by Nicholas Fasciano and Yin Yee—Leonard Phillips/ JoAnna Palmer, Garden Designer. End papers: Charles Mann, courtesy Filoli Center, Woodside, Calif. 2, 3: Jerry Pavia/designed by Jim and Peggy Jeffcoat, Blythewood, S.C. 4: Susanna Napierala-Cox; courtesy Steven Still; courtesy André Viette. 6, 7: Bernard Fallon/ Janice Tidwell, Landscape Designer. 9: Jerry Harpur, Chelmsford, Essex, U.K. 10: William T. Smith, Landscape Architect, ASLA, Atlanta. 11: Art by Fred Holz. 12: © Jane Grushow/Grant Heilman Photography, Lititz, Pa. 13: Jerry Pavia/designed by Louise G. Smith. 14, 15: Jerry Pavia—Jerry Pavia/William T. Smith, Landscape Architect, ASLA, Atlanta. 16: Jerry Pavia. 17: Charles Mann—Jerry Pavia. 18: Jerry Pavia. 19: Art by Allianora Rosse. 20, 21: Clive Nichols, Reading, Berkshire, U.K.—chart by John Drummond, Time-Life Books; Alan and Linda Detrick; Jerry Pavia. 22, 23: Jerry Pavia—Jerry Pavia/designed by Lutsko Associates, San Francisco. 24: © Richard Shiell. 25, 26: © James van Sweden/designed by Oehme, van Sweden and Associates, Inc. 27: Photo © John Neubauer/designed by Oehme, van Sweden and Associates, Inc. 28: Roger Hyam, Garden Picture Library, London. 30: Christine Douglas. 31: Art by Fred Holz. 32, 33: Roger Foley/designed by Sheela Lampietti—art by Fred Holz. 34, 35: Jerry Pavia/designed by Louise G. Smith. 36: Art by Nicholas Fasciano. 37: Jerry Pavia. 39: Jerry Pavia—Joanne Pavia. 40: Art by Fred Holz. 41, 42: Art by Nicholas Fasciano and Yin Yee. 42: Art by Nicholas Fasciano. 43: Art by Nicholas Fasciano and Yin Yee. 43: © Jane Grushow/Grant Heilman Photography, Lititz, Pa.—art by Nicholas Fasciano. 44, 45: Art by Fred Holz. 46: Art by Nicholas Fasciano (2)—art by Fred Holz—art by Nicholas Fasciano (2). 47: Lynn Karlin. 48: Jerry Pavia. 49: Art by Nicholas Fasciano; art by Fred Holz. 50, 51: Roger Foley/designed by Sheela and François Lampietti. 52, 53: Andy and Sally Wasowski; © Tony Casper/designed by Judith Stark, Landscape Architect. 54, 55: Leonard Phillips/ JoAnna Palmer, Garden Designer. 56, 57: Jerry Pavia/designed by Oasis Gardens Landscaping; Charles Mann/designed by Julia Berman, Eden & Wardwell. 58, 59: Bernard Fallon/Sandy Kennedy/Kennedy Landscape Design Associates, Woodland Hills, Calif. 60, 61: Jerry Pavia/ designed by Fay B. Ireland. 62: Roger Foley/designed by Sheela and François Lampietti (2)—Andy and Sally Wasowski (2). 63: © Tony Casper/designed by Judith Stark, Landscape Architect (2)—Leonard Phillips/JoAnna Palmer, Garden Designer (2). 64: Jerry Pavia (2)—Charles Mann (2). 65: Bernard Fallon/ Sandy Kennedy/Kennedy Landscape Design Associates, Woodland Hills, Calif. (2)—Jerry Pavia/ designed by Fay B. Ireland (2). 66, 67: Bernard Fallon/Laura Cooper, Landscape Designer. 68: Art by Fred Holz. 69: Joanne Pavia—art by Fred Holz. 70, 71: Art by Fred Holz—Jerry Pavia/designed by Jon Emerson, Baton Rouge, La. 72: Art by Nicholas Fasciano and Yin Yee. 73: Cynthia Woodyard —art by Fred Holz. 74: Steven Still. 75: Art by Fred Holz. 76: Carole Ottesen—Steven Still; Carole Ottesen. 77: André Viette—art by Nicholas Fasciano—© R. Todd Davis. 78, 79: Roger Foley/designed by Sheela Lampietti. 80: Jerry Pavia. 82-84: Art by Dan Sherbo. 85: Art by Nicholas Fasciano. 87, 88: Art by Dan Sherbo. 89: Joanne Pavia—art by Dan Sherbo; art by Nicholas Fasciano. 90: Joanne Pavia. 91: Art by Dan Sherbo; art by Nicholas Fasciano. 96: Art by Lorraine Mosley Epstein. 97: Art by Lorraine Mosley Epstein—art by Fred Holz (2). 98, 99: Art by Lorraine Mosley Epstein, except top left, art by Fred Holz. 100: Art by Lorraine Mosley Epstein. 101: Art by Lorraine Mosley Epstein—art by Fred Holz (2)—art by Lorraine Mosley Epstein. 102, 103: Art by Lorraine Mosley Epstein, except top right, art by

Fred Holz. 110: Map by John Drummond, Time-Life Books. 112: © R. Todd Davis; Jerry Pavia. 113: Steven Still; Jerry Pavia (2). 114: © R. Todd Davis; Jerry Pavia; Steven Still. 115: Steven Still (2); Joanne Pavia. 116: © Richard Shiell; Jerry Pavia; © Saxon Holt. 117: Steven Still; Jerry Pavia; Joanne Pavia. 118: Joanne Pavia; Jerry Pavia; Steven Still. 119: Joanne Pavia; Jerry Pavia; © Richard Shiell. 120: Steven Still; Jerry Pavia; Steven Still. 121: Jerry Pavia; © R. Todd Davis; Jerry Pavia. 122: © R. Todd Davis; Jerry Pavia; © R. Todd Davis. 123: Jerry Pavia; Joanne Pavia (2). 124: Thomas E. Eltzroth; Jerry Pavia; Steven Still. 125: André Viette; Jerry Pavia (2). 126: Jerry Pavia; Steven Still (2). 127: Joanne Pavia; Jerry Pavia; Steven Still. 128: Steven Still; © R. Todd Davis; Jerry Pavia. 129: Jerry Pavia (2); © Saxon Holt. 130: © R. Todd Davis; Jerry Pavia (2). 131: Steven Still; © Saxon Holt; Jerry Pavia. 132: Steven Still (2); André Viette. 133: © Richard Shiell; Jerry Pavia (2). 134: Steven Still; Jerry Pavia (2). 135: Steven Still (2); André Viette. 136: © R. Todd Davis; Jerry Pavia (2). 137: Jerry Pavia (2); Joanne Pavia. 138: Steven Still; Jerry Pavia (2). 139: Steven Still; Jerry Pavia; © R. Todd Davis. 140: Jerry Pavia. 141: Jerry Pavia; Steven Still; © R. Todd Davis. 142: Alan L. Detrick; André Viette; © R. Todd Davis. 143: Steven Still; Jerry Pavia; Joanne Pavia. 144: Joanne Pavia; © R. Todd Davis (2). 145: Steven Still (2); Jerry Pavia. 146: Joanne Pavia; Steven Still; Joanne Pavia. 147: Jerry Pavia (2); Joanne Pavia. 148: Jerry Pavia; Steven Still. 149: Steven Still; Joanne Pavia; Jerry Pavia. 150: © Richard Shiell; Jerry Pavia (2). 151: © R. Todd Davis; Jerry Pavia (2). 152: Jerry Pavia. 153: © R. Todd Davis; Joanne Pavia; Jerry Pavia. 154: © Richard Shiell; © R. Todd Davis; Steven Still. 155: © R. Todd Davis; Jerry Pavia; © Richard Shiell. 156: Steven Still; Jerry Pavia (2). 157: Joanne Pavia; Steven Still; Joanne Pavia. 158: Steven Still; © R. Todd Davis; Joanne Pavia. 159: Joanne Pavia; Steven Still; © Saxon Holt. 160: © R. Todd Davis; Steven Still; Jerry Pavia. 161: Steven Still (2); Jerry Pavia.

Bibliography

Books:

Armitage, Allan M.:
Allan Armitage on Perennials (Burpee Expert Gardener series). New York: Prentice Hall Gardening, 1993.
Herbaceous Perennial Plants. Athens, Ga.: Varsity Press, 1989.

Barash, Cathy Wilkinson. *Evening Gardens.* Shelburne, Vt.: Chapters Publishing, 1993.

Better Homes and Gardens® Step-by-Step Landscaping. Des Moines: Meredith, 1991.

The Big Book of Gardening Skills (Garden Way Publishing). Pownal, Vt.: Storey Communications, 1993.

Brennan, Georgeanne (text), and Faith Echtermeyer (photography). *Fragrant Flowers.* San Francisco: Chronicle Books, 1994.

Bush-Brown, James. *America's Garden Book.* New York: Charles Scribner's Sons, 1980.

Carr, Anna, et al. *Rodale's Chemical-Free Yard and Garden.* Emmaus, Pa.: Rodale Press, 1991.

Clausen, Ruth Rogers, and Nicholas H. Ekstrom. *Perennials for American Gardens.* New York: Random House, 1989.

Cox, Jeff, and Marilyn Cox. *The Perennial Garden.* Emmaus, Pa.: Rodale Press, 1992.

Cox, Jeff (text), and Jerry Pavia (photography). *Creating a Garden for the Senses.* New York: Abbeville Press, 1993.

Cresson, Charles O. *Charles Cresson on the American Flower Garden* (Burpee Expert Gardener series). New York: Prentice Hall Gardening, 1993.

Crockett, James Underwood, and the Editors of Time-Life Books. *Perennials* (Time-Life Encyclopedia of Gardening series). New York: Time-Life Books, 1972.

Damrosch, Barbara. *The Garden Primer.* New York: Workman Publishing, 1988.

de Verteuil, Anne, and Val Burton. *Planning Your Garden.* New York: E. P. Dutton, 1988.

Douglas, William Lake, et al. *Garden Design.* New York: Simon and Schuster, 1987.

Druse, Ken, with Margaret Roach. *The Natural Habitat Garden.* New York: Clarkson Potter, 1994.

Ellis, Barbara W., and Fern Marshall Bradley (Eds.). *The Organic Gardener's Handbook of Natural Insect and Disease Control.* Emmaus, Pa.: Rodale Press, 1992.

Foster, Maureen. *The Flower Arranger's Encyclopedia of Preserving and Drying.* London: Blandford Press, 1988.

Garden Design Ideas (The Best of *Fine Gardening* series). Newtown, Conn.: Taunton Press, 1994.

Gardening in Small Spaces (Time-Life Gardener's Guide series). Alexandria, Va.: Time-Life Books, 1989.

Garden Perennials and Water Plants. Edited by Anthony Huxley, text adapted by Alan R. Toogood. New York: Macmillan, 1970.

Garden Pests and Diseases. Menlo Park, Calif.: Sunset Publishing, 1993.

Halpin, Anne, and the Editors of Rodale Press. *Foolproof Planting.* Emmaus, Pa.: Rodale Press, 1990.

Halpin, Anne, and Betty Mackey. *Cutting Gardens.* New York: Simon and Schuster, 1993.

Harper, Pamela J.:
Color Echoes. New York: Macmillan, 1994.
Designing with Perennials. New York: Macmillan, 1991.

Harper, Pamela J., and Fred McGourty. *Perennials: How to Select, Grow, and Enjoy.* Los Angeles: HPBooks, 1982.

Hart, Rhonda Massingham. *Bugs, Slugs, and Other Thugs* (Garden Way Publishing). Pownal, Vt.: Storey Communications, 1991.

Hériteau, Jacqueline, and André Viette, with the American Horticultural Society Staff and Consultants. *The American Horticultural Society Flower Finder.* New York: Simon and Schuster, 1992.

Hill, Lewis. *Secrets of Plant Propagation* (Garden Way Publishing). Pownal, Vt.: Storey Communications, 1985.

Hill, Lewis, and Nancy Hill:
Daylilies: The Perfect Perennial (Garden Way Publishing). Pownal, Vt.: Storey Communications, 1991.
Successful Perennial Gardening: A Practical Guide (Garden Way Publishing). Pownal, Vt.: Storey Communications, 1988.

How to Attract Birds. San Ra-

mon, Calif.: Ortho Books, 1983.
Joyce, David. *The Complete Guide to Pruning and Training Plants.* New York: Simon and Schuster, 1992.
Kramer, Jack. *Grow Your Own Plants from Seeds, Cuttings, Division, Layering, and Grafting.* New York: Charles Scribner's Sons, 1973.
Liberty Hyde Bailey Hortorium. *Hortus Third: A Concise Dictionary of Plants Cultivated in the United States and Canada.* Initially compiled by Liberty Hyde Bailey and Ethel Zoe Bailey. New York: Macmillan, 1976.
Lovejoy, Ann. *The American Mixed Border.* New York: Macmillan, 1993.
McClure, Susan, and C. Colston Burrell. *Perennials* (Rodale's Successful Organic Gardening™ series). Emmaus, Pa.: Rodale Press, 1993.
McGourty, Frederick. *The Perennial Gardener.* Boston: Houghton Mifflin, 1989.
The Ortho Book of Gardening Basics. San Ramon, Calif.: Ortho Books, 1991.
The Ortho Home Gardener's Problem Solver. San Ramon, Calif.: Ortho Books, 1993.
Ottesen, Carole:
The New American Garden. New York: Macmillan, 1987.
Ornamental Grasses: The Amber Wave. New York: McGraw-Hill, 1989.
Perennials (The Best of *Fine Gardening* series). Newtown, Conn.: Taunton Press, 1993.
Perennials (Vol. 1 of *Index Hortensis,* compiled and edited by Piers Trehane). Wimborne, Dorset, U.K.: Quarterjack Publishing, 1989.
Perennials (Time-Life Gardener's Guide series). Alexandria, Va.: Time-Life Books, 1988.
Phillips, Ellen, and C. Colston Burrell. *Rodale's Illustrated Encyclopedia of Perennials.* Emmaus, Pa.: Rodale Press, 1993.
Reader's Digest Illustrated Guide to Gardening. Pleasantville, N.Y.: Reader's Digest Association, 1978.
Schneck, Marcus:
Creating a Butterfly Garden. New York: Simon and Schuster, 1993.
Creating a Hummingbird Garden. New York: Simon and Schuster, 1993.
Seddon, George, and Andrew Bicknell. *Plants Plus.* Emmaus, Pa.: Rodale Press, 1987.
Sedenko, Jerry. *The Butterfly Garden.* New York: Villard Books, 1991.
Smith, Miranda, and Anna Carr. *Rodale's Garden Insect, Disease, and Weed Identification Guide.* Emmaus, Pa.: Rodale Press, 1988.
Still, Steven M. *Manual of Herbaceous Ornamental Plants* (4th ed.). Champaign, Ill.: Stipes Publishing, 1994.
Taylor, Norman. *Taylor's Encyclopedia of Gardening.* Boston: Houghton Mifflin, 1961.
Taylor's Guide to Gardening in the South. New York: Houghton Mifflin, 1992.
Taylor's Guide to Perennials. Boston: Houghton Mifflin, 1986.
Thomas, Graham Stuart. *Perennial Garden Plants; or, the Modern Florilegium* (3d ed., rev.). Portland, Ore.: Sagapress, 1990.
Welch, William C. *Perennial Garden Color.* Dallas, Tex.: Taylor Publishing, 1989.
Wyman, Donald. *Wyman's Gardening Encyclopedia* (2d ed., expanded). New York: Macmillan, 1986.

Periodicals:
"Proper Preparation Lays the Groundwork for Success." *Neil Sperry's Gardens*, Spring 1994.

Index

Numerals in italics indicate an illustration of the subject mentioned.

A

Acanthus: 22, *26,* 69, 76, 81, 89, *chart* 111, *112; mollis,* 28, 37, *chart* 107, 112. *See also* Bear's-breech
Achillea: 14, *19, 20-21,* 22, 27, *30,* 39, 44, 64, 69, 75, 81, *chart* 111, *112; filipendulina,* 30, *64, chart* 105, 112; *millefolium,* 49, *62, 66-67,* 74, 77, *chart* 106, 112; 'Moonshine', *16-17, 21,* 30. *See also* Yarrow
Aconitum: 19, 74, *chart* 104, *chart* 109, *chart* 111, *113. See also* Monkshood
Agapanthus: chart 104, *chart* 109, *chart* 111, *113*
Air circulation: 17, 47, 92; and disease prevention, *chart* 96, *charts* 100-103
Ajuga: 17, 22, 28, 29, 37, 49, *70-71,* 81, *chart* 108, *chart* 111, *113. See also* Bugleweed
Alchemilla: 81, *chart* 105, *chart* 111, *114. See also* Lady's-mantle
Allium: 14, 29, 30, 69, 76, 81, 90, *chart* 108, *chart* 111, *114*
Alstroemeria: 16-17, 62
Alumroot: *chart* 101. *See also Heuchera*
Alyssum: saxatile. See Aurinia
Alyssum: sweet, *66-67*
Amsonia: 44, 69, 81, 87, *chart* 109, *chart* 111, *114*
Anaphalis: 30, 69, 75, *chart* 104, *chart* 111, *115*
Anchusa: 44, 74, 81, 89, *chart* 109, *chart* 111, *115. See also* Italian bugloss
Anemone: 37, 44, 81, 89, 90, *chart* 104, *chart* 107, *chart* 111, *115-116;* Japanese, 10, 30, 37, 44
Annuals: 7, 30, 45, *47,* 80, 92
Anthemis: 39, 69, 75, 77, 87, 90, *chart* 105, *chart* 106, *chart* 111, *116*
Anthracnose: chart 100
Aphids: 95, *chart* 96
Aquilegia: 24, 37, 65, 69, 90, *chart* 105, *chart* 109, *chart* 111, *116*
Arabis: 39, 81, 85, 87, *chart* 104, *chart* 111, *117*
Arenaria: 37, 69, 81, *chart* 104, *chart* 111, *117*
Armeria: 75, 81, *chart* 106, *chart* 111, *117*
Artemisia: 22, 24, *28,* 39, 44, 49, 69, 75, 81, *chart* 111, *118; lactiflora,* 30, 74, *chart* 104, 118; *ludoviciana,* 30, *64,* 118; 'Powis Castle', *66-67,* 118; *schmidtiana,* 92, *118. See also* Wormwood
Arum: italicum, 28
Aruncus: 19, 37, 39, 69, 74, 76, 81, *chart* 104, *chart* 111, *118*
Asclepias: 69, 76, 88, 89, 90, *chart* 111; *incarnata, chart* 107, 119; *tuberosa,* 19, 24, 39, 44, *chart* 106, *chart* 111, *119*
Aster: 8, 10, 47, *chart* 102, *chart* 103; Japanese, *60-61;* New York, *chart* 96
Aster: 14, 24, 69, 75, 87, 90, *119;* x *frikartii,* 77, *chart* 109, 119; *novae-angliae,* 74, *chart* 108, *119*
Asteromoea: mongolica, 65
Aster yellows: *chart* 100
Astilbe: 29, 30, 37, 44, 74, 76, *78-79,* 81, *chart* 96, *chart* 106, *chart* 111, *120;* x *arendsii,* 39, 74, 120; *chinensis, chart* 107, *120;* x *japonica, chart* 104, 120
Astrantia: 39, *chart* 107, *chart* 111, *120*

Aurinia: 39, 44, 69, *chart* 105, *chart* 111, *121*
Azalea: *10*

B

Baby's-breath: 73, *chart* 98. *See also Gypsophila*
Bachelor's-button: *chart* 111
Bacillus: thuringiensis, chart 97
Balloon flower: *chart* 103. *See also Platycodon*
Baptisia: 69, 76, 87, 88, 89, 90, 92, *chart* 109, *chart* 111, *121*. *See also* Wild indigo
Bare-root perennials: 44, *45, 46,* 47, 48-49
Base plan: 10-*11, 31*
Bear's-breech: 9, 24. *See also Acanthus*
Beds: existing, 41; preparing, *36,* 38, *40, 41, 42-43;* raised, 9, *43*. *See also* Design; Soil
Bee balm: *chart* 102. *See also Monarda*
Beetles: 95, *chart* 96
Begonia: grandis, 37, *chart* 107, *121*
Belamcanda: 32-33, 69, 76, 90, *chart* 106, *chart* 111, *122*. *See also* Blackberry lily
Bellflower: *73*, *chart* 100. *See also Campanula*
Bergenia: 37, *45,* 81, 84, 85, *chart* 101, *122*
Bishop's hat: *chart* 111
Blackberry lily: 22. *See also Belamcanda*
Black-eyed Susan: 24, *chart* 111
Blackroot: *52-53*. *See also Veronicastrum*
Blanket-flower: *chart* 100, *chart* 102. *See also Gaillardia*
Bleeding heart: *54-55,* 82, *chart* 103. *See also Dicentra*
Blight: 95, *chart* 100, *chart* 103
Bloom: *19*-20, 29, 45-46. *See also* Color
Bloom season: autumn-blooming plants, 10, 30; manipulating, 10, 29-30, 75, 77; spring-blooming plants, 10, *25*, 26, 29; summer-blooming plants, 10, *26,* 29-30; winter-blooming plants, 27-28
Bluebell: Scottish, 124
Boltonia: 30, 44, 75, 87, *chart* 102, *chart* 104, *122*
Borago: officinalis, 6-7
Borders: 29-30, *31, 33*. *See also* Design
Boxwood: 15. *See also Buxus*
Brunnera: 25, 37, 39, 44, 81, 89, *chart* 109, *chart* 111, *123*
Buddleia: 6-7, 30, *chart* 111
Bugleweed: *chart* 103. *See also Ajuga*
Bulbs: 7, *10, 25*
Butterflies: 24
Butterfly bush: *6-7,* 30, *chart* 111
Buxus: 32-33

C

Calamagrostis: 26, 28, 29, 76, *chart* 107, *chart* 111, *123*
Campanula: 6-7, 14, 25, 37, 65, 69, 74, 75, 81, 85, *chart* 104, *chart* 111, *123-124; carpatica,* 77, *chart* 109, *chart* 111, 123-*124; glomerata,* 49, *123*
Campsis: radicans, 63
Candytuft: 10, 17, 29, *chart* 98. *See also Iberis*
Cardinal flower: *chart* 101. *See also Lobelia*
Carnation: *chart* 111, 128
Caryopteris: 30, *32-33, 64*
Catananche: 89, 90
Caterpillars: *chart* 97
Catmint: 16, *17, chart* 98. *See also Nepeta*
Centaurea: 24, *28,* 75, 81, 82, 90, *chart* 105, *chart* 107, *chart* 111, 124; *montana,* 39, 74, *chart* 111, *124*
Centranthus: 69, 77, 90, *chart* 106, *chart* 111, *124*
Cerastium: tomentosum, 64, 65
Ceratostigma: 69, 87, 89, 92, 95, *chart* 109, *chart* 111, *125*
Chamomile: 47. *See also Anthemis*
Chasmanthium: latifolium, 29
Chinese silver grass: 29
Chives: 30, *114*
Chrysanthemum: 8, 14, 30, *65,* 67, 73, 74, 75, 77, 87, 93, *chart* 104, *chart* 107, *chart* 111, *125-126;* care of, 47, 80, 86, *chart* 100, *chart* 101, *chart* 102, *chart* 103
Cimicifuga: 37, 39, *chart* 104, *chart* 111, *126*
Cinquefoil: *chart* 101
Clematis: 24, *63,* 74, 87, *chart* 98, *chart* 99, *chart* 102, *chart* 103, *chart* 109, *126*
Cleome: 30
Climate zone map of United States: 8, *110*
Color: 92; in cottage gardens, 16, *32-33;* foliage and, 19-20, 22; plant selection guide to, *charts* 104-109; schemes for, 19-20, 21, 22; wheel, 20-21
Columbine: 10, 13, 25, 29, *chart* 96, *chart* 98, *chart* 100, *chart* 102, *chart* 103. *See also Aquilegia*
Compost: 37, 38, 40, 48, 82, 94
Compost pile: 70, 94
Coneflower: *chart* 102, 130; purple, *50-51,* 52, *chart* 96, *chart* 98, *chart* 99, *chart* 100, *chart* 101, *chart* 102, *chart* 103. *See also Rudbeckia; Echinacea*
Container-grown perennials: 45, *46,* 47, 48, 49
Convolvulus: cneorum, 65
Cooperative Extension Service: *chart* 96
Coral bells: *chart* 99. *See also Heuchera*
Coreopsis: 14, 17, 24, 29, 39, 44, *50-51,* 52, 90, *chart* 111, 127; care of, *chart* 98, *charts* 100-103; *grandiflora,* 74, *chart* 105, *127; lanceolata, 62, 64,* 77, 127; *rosea,* 49, *chart* 107, 127; *verticillata,* 45, 49, 77, *chart* 105, *127*
Cortaderia: selloana, 29
Cosmos: 29, 30
Cottage garden: *14,* 15-16, *31, 32-33*
Cowslip: 24
Crambe: chart 104, *chart* 111, *127*
Cranesbill: *chart* 101, *chart* 103. *See also Geranium*
Creeping Jenny: 144
Crocosmia: chart 106, *128*
Cupid's-dart: 89, 90
Curtonus: paniculatus, 128
Cutting back: 75, 77
Cutting garden: 14, 16
Cuttings: 46, 86-*87, 88-89,* 92
Cutworms: *chart* 97

D

Daisy: *14, 16, 43;* English, *chart* 100; Michaelmas, *119;* Shasta, *chart* 98; Transvaal (gerbera), *chart* 100. *See also Chrysanthemum*
Damping-off: *chart* 101
Daylily: 10, 16, 18, 22, 24, 29, 92, 93, *136-137;* care of, *45,* 48, 81, 82, 83, *84, chart* 98, *chart* 99, *chart* 103. *See also Hemerocallis*
Deadheading: 45, 58, 61, *75-76*
Delosperma: 64
Delphinium: 6-7, 10, 14, 16, 30, *34-35, 47,* 73, *74,* 75, 77, 81, 87, 90, 93, *chart* 108, *chart* 109, *chart* 111, *128;* care of, 93, 94, *chart* 96, *chart* 98, *chart* 99, *charts* 100-103
Design: base plan in, 10-*11, 31;* beds in, 16-17; borders in, 16-17; color in, 19-20, 22, 92; combining components of, 23-24; cottage garden, *14,* 15-16, *31, 32-33;* country garden, *50-51, 62;* desert garden, *56-57, 64;* English-style garden, *58-59, 65;* foliage in, 22-23; formal, *12,* 13, *14-15;* garden styles, 12-17; idea sources, 12-13; informal, *13,* 15, 31; mass, 22, 23; moon garden, *60-61, 65;* natural garden, *50-51, 62;* plant placement in, 23-24, 92; prairie garden, *52-53, 63;* property assessment, 8-11; scale, 24; scale drawing, *32-33;* seasonal changes and, 10, 25-30; shade garden, *54-55, 63;* texture in, 22-23; woodland garden, *54-55, 63*. *See also* Style
Dianthus: 25, 28, *32-33,* 44, 65, 69, 81, 85, 87, *chart* 102, *chart* 111, *128-129; barbatus, 19,* 24, 128; *deltoides, 12, chart* 106, 128-129; *gratianopolitanus,* 24, *128,* 129; *plumarius,* 20, 24, *129*. *See also* Pinks.
Dicentra: 37, 44, *63,* 81, *89, chart* 104, *chart* 107, *chart* 111, *129*
Dictamnus: 24, 74, 76, 90, *chart* 108, *chart* 111, *129*. *See also* Gas plant
Digitalis: 6-7, 14, 74, 75, *chart* 105, *chart* 111, *130*. *See also* Foxglove
Disbudding: 75, 77
Diseases: 17, 69, *70,* 94, *chart* 96, *charts* 100-103
Division: 45, 46, 80-81, *82-83, 84, 85,* 92
Doronicum: 81, 90, *chart* 105, *chart* 111, *130*

Drainage: 37; correcting poor, *42-43;* and disease control, *chart* 96, *charts* 100-103
Dropwort: 39, *chart* 111, 132

E

Echinacea: 14, 29, 44, 75, 76, 89, 90, *chart* 111, 130; *purpurea, 18,* 24, 39, *62, 63,* 74, *chart* 107, *130. See also* Coneflower, purple
Echinops: 14, 27, *28,* 30, 39, 44, 69, 75, 76, 77, 87, 89, 92, *chart* 109, *chart* 111, *131. See also* Globe thistle
Engelmannia: pinnatifida, 62
Epimedium: 22, 37, 69, 95, *chart* 106, *chart* 111, *131*
Erianthus: ravennae, 29
Erigeron: 22-23, 65, 75, 87, 90, *chart* 108, *chart* 111, *131*
Eryngium: 14, 30, 39, 63, 69, 89, *chart* 109, *chart* 111, *132*
Eschscholzia: californica, 66-67
Eulalia: *76. See also Miscanthus*
Eupatorium: 44, 49, 75, 76, 87, 90, *chart* 108, *chart* 111, *132*
Euphorbia: 22, *63*

F

Feather grass: *66-67*
Fern: *25, 70-71, 78-79*
Fertilizer: 36, 37, 38-39, 42, 72, 74, 94, 96
Fertilizing: 55, 58, 70-71
Festuca: 28, 29, *64*
Filipendula: 39, *chart* 104, *chart* 108, *chart* 111, *132*
Flag: *39,* 139-140. *See also Iris*
Fleabane: *22-23*
Fleeceflower. *See Polygonum*
Flowers: *19*-20. *See also* Color
Foliage: 19-*20,* 22-23
Fountain grass: *76. See also Pennisetum*
Fouquieria: splendens, 64
Foxglove: 25, *47,* 74, *chart* 96, *chart* 98, *chart* 99, *chart* 101. *See also Digitalis*

G

Gaillardia: 14, 22, 39, 69, 74, 75, 80, 89, 90, *chart* 105, *chart* 106, *chart* 111, *133. See also* Blanket-flower
Gas plant: 81. *See also Dictamnus*
Gay-feather: *19, chart* 102. *See also Liatris*
Geranium: 6-7, 9, 16, *17,* 20, 24, 37, 44, 69, 75, 81, 85, 108, *chart* 109, *chart* 111, *133;* propagation of, 85
Geum: 22, 81, *chart* 101, 106, *chart* 111, *134*
Gillenia: 75, *chart* 104, *chart* 111, *134*
Ginger: 23, 28
Gladiolus: *chart* 99, *chart* 103
Globe thistle: *77,* 81, *chart* 96. *See also Echinops*
Grass: ornamental, 10, 19, *26, 27,* 29, 30, *chart* 102. *See also Calamagrostis; Chasmanthium; Cortaderia; Erianthus; Festuca; Imperata; Miscanthus; Pennisetum; Stipa*
Gypsophila: 14, 29, 30, 74, 88, 89, 90, *chart* 104, *chart* 111, *135. See also* Baby's-breath

H

Helenium: 74, 87, *chart* 105, *chart* 106, *chart* 111, *135*
Helianthemum: 9
Helianthus: 39, *64,* 74, 87, *chart* 105, *chart* 111, *135*
Heliopsis: 14, 73, 74, 75, 87, *chart* 105, *chart* 111, *136*
Helleborus: 27-28, 37, *chart* 104, *chart* 111, *136*
Hemerocallis: 20-21, 24, 39, 44, *48, 62,* 69, 74, 81, *charts* 105-108, *chart* 111, *136-137. See also* Daylily
Herbs: *58-59*
Heuchera: 22, 24, 37, 44, 75, 89, *chart* 104, *chart* 107, *chart* 108, *chart* 111, *137*
Hibiscus: 45, 90, 92, *chart* 107, *chart* 108, *chart* 111, 137, *138. See also* Mallow, rose
Hollyhock: 29, *66-67, chart* 96, *chart* 98, *chart* 99, *chart* 102
Hosta: 18, 20, *22,* 23, 24, 30, *32-33,* 37, 39, *70-71,* 81, 95, *chart* 104, *chart* 111, *138;* care of, *45,* 48, *chart* 99, *chart* 101, *chart* 103
Hydrangea: macrophylla, 34-35

I

Iberis: 39, 44, 69, 87, *chart* 104, *chart* 111, *139. See also* Candytuft
Imperata: cylindrica, 29
Insects: beneficial, 95, *charts* 96-99; pests, 94, 95, *charts* 96-100
Inula: chart 105, *chart* 106, *139*
Invasive perennials: *49,* 82
Iris: 6-7, 10, 14, 16, 18, *22-23,* 24, 29, 65, 69, 81, 92, 93, *chart* 104, *chart* 107, *139-140;* bearded, *6-7,* 25, 29, 30, 84, *139*-140; care of, *45,* 81, 83, 84, *85,* 94, 95, *charts* 96-99, *charts* 101-103; *cristata,* 37, 44, *140; ensata,* 39, *chart* 108, 140; Japanese, 22, 29, 39, 140; *pseudacorus, 39, chart* 105, *140*; *sibirica,* 22, 44, 74, 76, *78-79,* 81, 92, *chart* 104, *chart* 108, *140; tectorum, 34-35,* 140. *See also* Flag
Iris borer: 85, 95, *chart* 97
Irish moss: *117*
Italian arum: 28
Italian bugloss: *chart* 98. *See also Anchusa*

J

Joe-Pye weed: 30. *See also Eupatorium*
Johnny-jump-up: 161
Juniperus: x *chinensis, 62*

K

Kniphofia: 22, 69, 81, 83, *chart* 111, *141. See also* Torch lily

L

Lady's-mantle: 22. *See also Alchemilla*
Lamb's ears: 22, *43, 60-61. See also Stachys*
Lamium: 22, 37, 81, 87, 95, *chart* 111, *141*
Larkspur: *6-7,* 16, *34-35, 43, chart* 111, *128. See also Delphinium*
Lavandula: 6-7, 14, 24, 28, 30, 69, 87, 92, *chart* 108, *chart* 111, *141. See also* Lavender
Lavender: 13, 15, *22-23,* 29. *See also Lavandula*
Layering: 85
Leafhoppers: *chart* 98
Leaf miners: *chart* 98
Leaf spot: *chart* 101
Liatris: 14, *19,* 30, 39, 44, 69, *chart* 104, *chart* 108, *chart* 111, *142. See also* Gay-feather
Light: and color, 21; as factor in plant growth, 36; full sun defined, 8, 36; as major planning factor, 8; plant requirements for, 95
Ligularia: 22, 23, 37, 39, 74, 81, 89, *chart* 105, *chart* 111, *142*
Lily: chart 96, *chart* 99, *chart* 100, *chart* 101
Lily-of-the-Nile: *chart* 111
Limonium: 30, 39, 44, 65, 69, 74, 81, 88, 89, 90, *chart* 108, *chart* 111, *143; latifolium,* 30, *chart* 108, *143; perezii, 65. See also* Sea lavender
Linum: 66-67, 74, 75, 87, 92, *chart* 105, *chart* 109, *chart* 111, *143*
Lobelia: 39, 65, *chart* 109, 143; *cardinalis,* 24, 37, 39, 75, 81, 90, *chart* 107, *chart* 111, 143. *See also* Cardinal flower
Lobularia: maritima, 66-67
London pride: 28
Lupine: *charts* 100-102. *See also Lupinus*
Lupinus: 24, 69, 90, *chart* 104, *chart* 107, *chart* 111, *144. See also* Lupine
Lychnis: 65, 81, *chart* 106, *chart* 111, *144. See also* Rose campion
Lysimachia: 39, 49, *chart* 104, *chart* 106, *chart* 111, *144*

M

Macleaya: 23, 28, 29, *32-33,* 49, *62,* 69, 74, *chart* 105, *chart* 111, *145*
Magnolia: *25, 26, 27*
Maiden grass: 28
Mallow: rose, *chart* 96, *chart* 100. *See also Hibiscus; Malva; Sidalcea*
Maltese cross: *144*
Malva: 24, *32-33,* 39, 87, *chart* 108, *chart* 111, *145*
Maple: Japanese, 9
Marguerite: 125
Marigold: 30, 45, *chart* 103; desert, *56-57*
Meadowsweet: *chart* 111, *132*
Mildew: *chart* 101, *chart* 102
Minuartia verna ssp. *caespitosa:* 117
Miscanthus: 23, 39, 62, 76, *chart* 111; *floridulus, 26, 27,*

28, 29, *62; sinensis,* 28, 29, *64,* 74, *chart* 107, *145*
Mites: *chart* 98
Monarda: 81, *chart* 111, 146; *didyma,* 24, 37, 39, 49, 87, *chart* 107, *146*
Mondo grass: *13*
Moneywort: 144
Monkshood: *chart* 98, *chart* 101, *chart* 102, *chart* 103. *See also Aconitum*
Montbretia. *See Crocosmia*
Mosaic viruses: *chart* 102
Mountain rosebay: *78-79*
Mulch: 38, 69, *70,* 71, 83
Mullein: 88. *See also Verbascum*

N

Nematodes: 95, *chart* 97, *chart* 101, *chart* 103
Nepeta: 6-7, 12, 15, 24, 44, 64, 69, 75, 77, 81, 87, *chart* 109, *chart* 111, *146. See also* Catmint
Nicotiana: 30
Nursery bed: 45-47

O

Oat grass: *12*
Obedient plant: *chart* 111
Ocotillo: *56-57*
Oenothera: 24, 39, 44, *65, 66-67,* 69, 81, *chart* 106, *chart* 111, *146. See also* Primrose, evening
Onion: 9, 30, *chart* 111. *See also Allium*

P

Pachysandra: 48
Paeonia: 14, 24, *34-35,* 76, *charts* 105-108, *chart* 111, *147. See also* Peony
Pampas grass: 29
Pansy: *10, 60-61*
Papaver: 44, 69, 76, *chart* 111; *nudicaule,* 147; *orientale, 9, 19,* 89, *chart* 106, *chart* 107, *chart* 108, *147. See also* Poppy
Pasqueflower. *See Anemone*
Pelargonium: 6-7, 133
Pennisetum: 28, 29, 39, *66-67,* 69, 76, *chart* 105, *chart* 111, *148*
Penstemon: 29, *58-59, 64, 65,* 75-76, 90, *chart* 107, *chart* 111, *148*
Peony: 15, 18, 24, 29, *32-33, 34-35,* 73, 74, *77,* 92, *147;* care of, 35, *45,* 47, 95, *charts* 99-102. *See also Paeonia*
Perennials: advantages of, 19; characteristics of, 80; sources of, 18, 19, 44
Perovskia: 29, *32-33,* 39, 69, *74,* 75, 76, 87, 92, *chart* 109, *chart* 111, *149*
pH level: 37
Phlox: 14, 18, 23, *32-33,* 62, 77, 149; care of, 42, 47, 82, 83, 85, *chart* 98, *chart* 101, *chart* 102, *chart* 103; *divaricata,* 29, *34-35,* 37, 39, 44, *63,* 87, *149; maculata, 65, chart* 105, 149; *paniculata, 62,* 75, 77, *78-79,* 81, 87, 89, *chart* 106, 149; *stolonifera,* 44, *chart* 109, 149; *subulata,* 39, 92, *chart* 111, *149;* wild blue, *10, 54-55. See also* Wild blue phlox
Phormium: chart 107, *chart* 111, *150*
Physostegia: 32-33, 39, 44, 49, *62,* 69, 74, 75, 87, *chart* 108, *chart* 111, *150*
Picea: pungens, 62
Pinching: *75,* 76, 93
Pinks: 24, *chart* 103. *See also Dianthus*
Planning: and property assessment, 8-11; and base plan, 10-*11. See also* Design; Style
Plant bugs: *chart* 99
Planting: 35, 38, 47-48; bare-root plants, *45, 46,* 49; container-grown plants, *46,* 49; spacing, 32, 45, 47, 92
Plant names: cross-reference guide to, *chart* 111
Plant selection: for autumn flowers, 10, 30; for butterflies, 24; for cutting, 14; for disease resistance, 44; for drought tolerance, 69; for drying, 30; for dry soil, 39; to extend blooming season, 10, 25-27; for fragrance, 24; guide, *charts* 104-109; of healthy stock, *44;* for hummingbirds, 24; and invasive perennials, 49; for moist soil, 39; for ornamental seed heads, 27, 76; for pest resistance, 44; for shade, 37, 95; sources for, 18, 19, 44; species vs. varieties, 92; for spring flowers, 10, *25,* 26, 29; for summer flowers, 10, *26,* 29-30; for winter flowers, 27-28; for winter interest, 10, 27-*28,* 30
Platycodon: 69, 75, 90, *chart* 108, *chart* 109, *chart* 111, *150. See also* Balloon flower
Polygonatum: 24, 37, 39, 44, 49, *63, chart* 111, *151,* 158
Polygonum: 24, 81, *chart* 108, *chart* 111, *151*
Poor Robin's plantain. *See Erigeron*
Poppy: *14,* 22; California, 29, *66-67;* care of, 47, 88, 89, *chart* 96, *chart* 101, *chart* 103; oriental, 29, 47, 88, 89, 93, 94. *See also Papaver*
Porteranthus: trifoliata. See Gillenia
Potentilla: 39, 69, 81, *chart* 106, *chart* 107, *chart* 111, *151-152*
Primrose: care of, 81, 83, *chart* 96, *chart* 98, *chart* 100; evening, *69. See also Oenothera*; *Primula*
Primula: 24, 37, 39, 81, *chart* 106, *chart* 107, *chart* 111, *152*
Propagation: 70, 92; by division, 80-85; by layering, 85; nursery bed in, 45-46; by root cuttings, 46, *88-89;* by seed, 90-91; by stem cuttings, 46, 86-*87*
Pulmonaria: 37, 81, *chart* 109, *chart* 111, *153*
Pulsatilla: vulgaris, 115-*116*

R

Raised beds: 9, 42, *43*
Ranunculus: 39, *chart* 106, *chart* 111, *153*
Rattlesnake master: *52-53*
Rhizomes: *45,* 81, 84-*85, chart* 97
Rhododendron: 34-35, 78-79
Rhus: aromatica, 63
Rodgersia: 37, 39, *chart* 105, *153*
Romneya: chart 105, *chart* 111, *154*
Root cuttings: 46, *88-89,* 92
Root rot: *chart* 102
Roots: *46, 69;* fibrous, *45,* 81, *82-83;* fleshy, *45,* 81, 83-*84. See also* Rhizomes
Rosa: 6-7, 58-59, 65
Rose campion: *60-61. See also Lychnis*
Rosemary: 15
Rose of Sharon: 30
Rosmarinus: officinalis, 65
Rudbeckia: 14, 16, 24, 27, 29, 39, 44, 45, 69, *76,* 77, 80, 81, 90, *chart* 106, *chart* 111, *154. See also* Coneflower
Rust: *chart* 102

S

Sage: *6-7,* 30, 47, *58-59, 66-67,* 74, *chart* 100, *154-155;* Russian, 10, white, 30, 118. *See also Artemisia; Perovskia; Pulmonaria; Salvia*
Salvia: 6-7, 12, 30, *32-33,* 65, *66-67,* 69, 74, 75, 87, *chart* 109, *chart* 111, *154-155. See also* Sage
Sanitation: and disease control, *chart* 100, *chart* 101, *chart* 102, *chart* 103; and insect control, *chart* 97, *chart* 98, *chart* 99; in propagation, 84, 86, 89, *chart* 101
Santolina: 22, 39, 64, *chart* 111, *155*
Saponaria: 24, 39, *chart* 108, *chart* 111, *155*
Saxifraga: 22, 28
Scabiosa: 75, 90, *chart* 109, *chart* 111, *156*
Sea holly: 88. *See also Eryngium*
Sea lavender: 30, *chart* 101, *chart* 102. *See also Limonium*
Sedum: 10, *24,* 27, 28, 30, 39, 44, 69, *70-71, 76,* 80, 81, 87, *charts* 106-108, *chart* 111, *156-157; aizoon, chart* 106, *156;* propagation of, 80
Seedlings: *91, chart* 101
Seeds: 90-*91*
Senecio: 65
Shade: 8, *10, 13,* 37, *54-55,* 95
Shrubs: in perennial garden, 29-30
Sibbaldiopsis: tridentata, 152
Siberian bellflower: 37
Sidalcea: 75, *chart* 108, *chart* 111, *157*
Silene: chart 105, *chart* 111, *157*
Slugs: *chart* 99
Smilacina: 37, 39, 81, *chart* 105, *chart* 111, *158*
Snails: *chart* 99

Snapdragon: *14,* 45
Sneezewort: 30
Snow-in-summer: *60-61*
Soil: amendments to, 8-9, 36, 37, 38, 40, 41, 42, 82, 94; appraisal of, 36-37; clay, 8, 37, 38, 40, 94; composition of, 36-37; cultivation of, 39-42, *41,* ***chart*** 97, ***chart*** 99; fertility of, 37; loam, 37, 38, 40; moisture of, 37, 39-40; preparation of, 36, 38, 39-42, *40,* 94; sandy, 8, 37, 38; structure of, 37, 38; texture of, 8, 36-37, 94. *See also* Fertilizer; Fertilizing
Solanum: 6-7
Solidago: 14, 16, 69, 74, 76, 81, ***chart*** 106, ***chart*** 111, *158*
Solomon's-seal: *13,* 22, 24, 49, ***chart*** 101
Southernwood: 118
Speedwell: ***chart*** 101. *See also Veronica*
Spittlebugs: ***chart*** 99
Stachys: 20, 28, *30, 39, 64,* 65, *66-67,* 81, 90, 92, ***chart*** 109, ***chart*** 111, *158. See also* Lamb's ears
Staking: 71, *72-73,* 74, 75, 77, 93
Star flower. *See Amsonia*
Stars-of-Persia: 114. *See also Allium*
Stem cuttings: 46, 86-87, 92
Stipa: tenacissima, 66-67
Stokesia: 75, 77, 81, 88, 89, 90, ***chart*** 109, ***chart*** 111, *159*
Strawberries: woodland, 95
Strawberry geranium: 28
Style: cottage garden, *14,* 15-16, *32-33;* cutting garden, 14, 16; knot garden, 15. *See also* Design
Sunflower: 77, ***chart*** 96. *See also Helianthus*
Sweet William: *19,* 24, 128. *See also Dianthus*

T

Thalictrum: 14, 37, *62,* 74, 81, ***chart*** 106, ***chart*** 109, ***chart*** 111, *159*
Thinning: 61, 75, 76-77
Thrips: 95, ***chart*** 99
Thyme: *22-23, 32-33*
Tools: 82, 84, 86, 89
Torch lily: ***chart*** 103. *See also Kniphofia*
Tradescantia: ohiensis, 62
Tricyrtis: 81, ***chart*** 105, ***chart*** 111, *159*
Trollius: 39, 44, 81, ***chart*** 106, ***chart*** 111, *160*
Tulip: *10, 25*

V

Verbascum: 39, 49, 69, 89, ***chart*** 105, ***chart*** 106, ***chart*** 111, *160*
Verbena: 6-7, 16-17, 29, 44, *56-57, 58-59, 64, 65, 66-67,* 75, 87, 90, ***chart*** 107, ***chart*** 109, ***chart*** 111, *160*
Veronica: 14, *20, 32-33,* 44, 65, 75, 77, 81, 87, ***chart*** 105, ***chart*** 107, ***chart*** 109, ***chart*** 111, *161. See also* Speedwell
Veronicastrum: 30, 63, ***chart*** 108, ***chart*** 111, *161. See also* Blackroot
Viburnum: prunifolium, 63
Viette: André, 74
Viola: 24, 37, *65,* 81, 95, ***chart*** 109, ***chart*** 111, *161*
Violet: ***chart*** 103. *See also Viola*

W

Watering: 68; devices, *68;* diseases and, 94; effect of proper, *69;* time of day and, 94
Weeds: 29, 40-41, 69-70, 71, 94; and disease prevention, ***chart*** 100, ***chart*** 102; and insect control, ***chart*** 97, ***chart*** 98, ***chart*** 100
Whiteflies: ***chart*** 100
Wild blue phlox: *10, 54-55. See also Phlox divaricata*
Wild indigo: 47, ***chart*** 101. *See also Baptisia*
Wilt: vascular, ***chart*** 103
Windflower: ***chart*** 101. *See also Anemone*
Wolfsbane: ***chart*** 111
Wormwood: 49, ***chart*** 101. *See also Artemisia*

Y

Yarrow: *43, 73. See also Achillea*
Yucca: elata, 64

Z

Zexmenia: 50-51, 52, *62*
Zone map of United States: 8, *110*